Coastal Zone Management in India and Australia

Coastal Zone Management in India and Australia

ANAND MALIK

RESEARCH INDIA PRESS
New Delhi (INDIA)

ISBN : 978-93-5171-021-9

Price 1395/-

First Edition: 2015

Published by :
RESEARCH INDIA PRESS
E-6/34, Sangam Vihar
New Delhi-110062
Phone: 011-26047013, (M) 9818085794
E-mail: researchindiapress@gmail.com

Typesetting by
G. R. Sharma

CONTENTS

PREFACE

Due to the uniqueness of coastal zone such as daily tides, mangrove forests, coral reefs, tidal flats, sea beaches, storm waves and barrier islands are found only at the coast. Due to this distinctive features and dynamism where huge amount of natural energy is released and great abundance of life is nurtured; it is place of high priority interest to people, to commerce, to the military and to a variety of industries; most countries have recognize the coastal zone as a distinct region with resources that require special attention.

With Global climate change has made the coastal zone the most challenging frontier in environmental planning and management. Climate change has threatened the world's coastal population as large portion of world's population lives near coasts (nearly 40%). Coastal ecosystem will also be impacted in many ways. Sea level raise will be an obvious impact, and the inundation will led to damage of infrastructure, habitats that will have to migrate inland or drown. Coasts are a vital geographical region in terms of transportation, commerce, and trade. Coasts are dynamic and complex as the quality of our coastal marine ecosystems is largely a result of human activity on land. Point and nonpoint pollution, sedimentation and changes in fresh water flow all have profound impacts on marine ecosystems.

The present book is divided into five chapters and conclusion. The first two chapters are devoted to the basics of coastal zone problems and management issues at various levels i.e. from local to regional and International level. Chapter three and four critically analyses the coastal geomorphology, coastal problems & environment and spatial analysis of policies related to coastal zone of both the countries and Goa (India) and Queensland (Australia) states in particular.

July, 2015

Dr. Anand Malik
Associate Professor, Geography
University of Delhi, Delhi

Chapter 1

INTRODUCTION

THE PROBLEM

Coastal areas contain some of the world's most diverse and productive resource. They are unique and valuable not only from ecological point of view but also from socio-economic view, which include extensive areas of complex and specialized ecosystems, such as mangroves, coral reefs and sea-grasses. Many coastal problem being encountered in the world wide have been accentuated because of lack of integrated and holistic approach towards coastal management keeping sustainability at bay and senseless exploitation of coastal resources for short term economic gains.[1] Besides the attitudinal problems towards environment, population growth and associated economic developments place additional demand on coastal resources. These problems pose another threat to the sustainability of the areas. Also coastal zone is also likely to be affected significantly by climate change and accelerated sea level rise in future.

All these are resulting in certain grave consequence like accumulation of contaminants in coastal areas, erosion and rapidly increasing decline of habitats and natural resources. Recent decades have witnessed a new well-documented expansion and intensification in the world seas. The movement has been paralleled or perhaps more accurately exceeded by an expansion and intensification in the use of coastal land and near-shore water. Beside unsustainable coastal developments, coastal zone can also be significantly affected by the climate change and sea level raise due to some human induced or some other physical forces (Table 1).

Table 1
Percent of Coastlines under Potential Threat

Region	*Low* [(a)]	*Moderate* [(b)]	*High* [(c)]
Africa	49	14	38
Asia	31	17	52
North and Central America	71	12	17
South America	50	24	26
Europe	14	16	70
Former USSR	64	24	12
Oceania	56	20	24
World	49	17	34

Notes:

(a) Threat ranking depicts potential risk to coastal ecosystems from development – related activities in 1995.

(b) Low potential threat: coastal areas with population density of less than 75 people/km^2. A road network density of less than 100 km of road/km^2 or on pipelines known to be present.

(c) Moderate potential threat: coastal areas with a population density of between 0 and 10 km of pipeline/km^2. Between 100 and 150 km of road/km^2 or a pipeline density of between 0 and 10 km of pipeline/km^2.

Source: World Resources Institute, 1996. Byrant et. al., 1995 http:/www.wri.org/wr-96-97.

One of the many anticipated effects of climate change is accelerated rise in global mean sea level. Increasing concentrations of Carbon dioxide, methane, chlorofluorocarbons and other gases released by human activities can heat the earth to temperature warmer than at any time in the last two million years and thereby raise sea level. Since the industrial revolution, the combustion of fossil fuels, deforestation and cement manufacturing have released enough CO_2 into the atmosphere to raise the atmospheric concentration of CO_2 and concentration has increased 8% since 1958.[2,3] Recently the concentrations of chlorofluorocarbon and some other trace gases that also absorb infrared radiations have also been increasing.[4] Physicists and climatologists generally accept the estimate that a doubling would directly raise the earth's average temperature by 1.2 C^0 if nothing else changed (Figure 1).[5] The inter-governmental panel on climate change (IPCC)[6] [7] estimate that over the next century the sea level will raise by 31-110 cm by the year 2100 and that this could have severe impacts on coastal areas and their resources (Figure 2). Wetlands are likely to be threatened, coastal erosion will increase, and coastal resources, population and economies will be adversely affected. Already in short term, other aspects of climate change may have serious effects; these include change in the frequency, intensity and pattern of extreme weather events such as tropical cyclones, intense precipitation, associated storm surges and flooding. Some low laying coastal areas particularly those that are frequently hit by tropical cyclones and monsoons are already now facing significant threats posed by climate variability, independent of climate change.

The world's coastal zone thus faces a multifaceted challenge, which will become apparent over various time scales. Decision making on the use of natural resources needs making trade-offs. Many uses of natural resources are mutually exclusive. For instance, a forest cannot be cleared for logging, while at the same time being used as a nature reserve for an endangered species of birds. The opportunity of using natural resources in one way necessarily, involves giving up the opportunity to use them in another way. Most nations of Asia and the Pacific were involved in United Nations conference on the environment and development (UNCED), 1992 in Rio de Janiero and have given support to provisions and proposals which are contained in chapter 17 of Agenda 21.[8] These call for programs to achieve integrated coastal zone management and sustainable use and management

Figure 1: Global Monthly Temperature Anomalies (*Jones, P.D. and Moberg, A., 2003)*

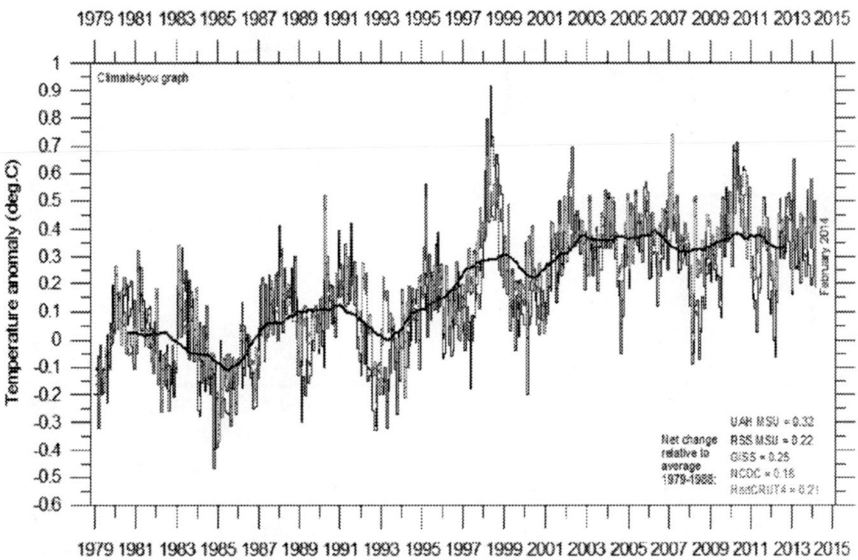

Figure 2: Greenhouse Effect and Sea Level Rise in Last Century

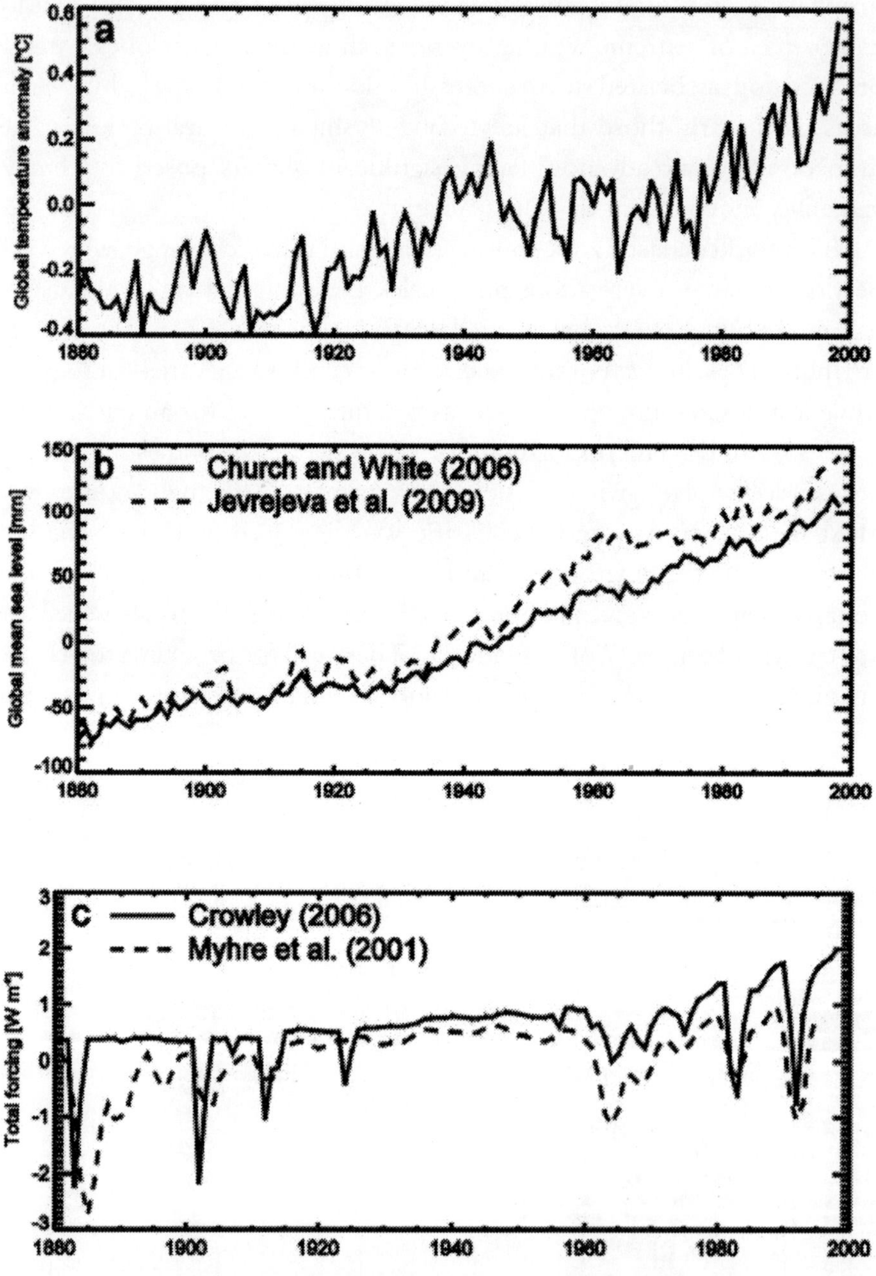

Source: (a) Temperature curve from Hansen J. E. *et al.* 1981. Climate impact of increasing atmosphere Carbondioxide, science 213: 957-66. (b) Gornitz V.S. 1982, "Global Sea Level Trend in the Past Century" Science 215: 1611-14.

of marine and coastal environments and natural resources. Such calls are not new. In 1992 one of the four fundamental principles of United Nations Stockholom Declaration State: 'In order to achieve more national management of resources and thus improve the environment state should adopt on integrated and coordinated approach to their development planning so as to ensure that development is compatible with the need to protect and improve the human environment.[9] Similar conclusions were reached in 1980 in World Conservation Strategy.

An environmental impact assessment[10] can be useful to identify areas where possible trade off or compromise may be needed. For example, consider the case of aqua farming in West Bengal coastal areas, where land was previously either a paddy field or natural mangrove forest. Nowadays it is common practice to convert a paddy field or mangrove forest in coastal area to economically lucrative aqua farming. However this conversion may be effect the basic primary food production or the reduction of mangrove forest land which is the habitats of many endangered animals. Therefore, a trade off must be made between the short term benefits of aqua farming, versus the long term benefits of primary food production land or natural forest land. In coastal areas where tourism is an important source of income, the continued making of tourist resort could lead the reduction of beach area, which in term affect the ecology and bio-diversity of the area.[11]

According to Saw (2000), if the laws are introduced to present uncoordinated use of the coastal land, they need to be supported by widespread education program to explain the reasons behind them. Careful consideration will also be needed for the individuals will suffers the economic consequence of such a change in practice. Existing laws are not sufficient to meet the challenge of the present day. That is why laws should be made to ensure maximum benefits of the habitats.

Integrated Coastal Zone Management (ICZM) has been identified as the most appropriate process to address current and long term coastal management issues, including habitats loss, degradation of water quality, and changes in hydrological cycle, depletion of coastal resources and adoption to seal level rise and other imparts of global climate change. It is also a means to identify and anticipate future opportunities. Thus ICZM is a major tool for achieving sustainable development in coastal areas.

Coastal Zone Management effectively started in Australian during 1879 when the state of Victoria pout a blanket prohibition of further sales of coastal lands down to high water mark. Other state followed this lead and in most parts of Australia, a strip of coastal land, often only 100 meter wide,[12] is in public ownership. This means that coastal zone management in Australia includes both the management of these public coastal reserves as well as the planning control on private lands in the coastal zone. The coastal reserves have traditionally been managed either by local governments of by specifically elected Committees of management in some state.

The Port Phillip Authority, Australia's first coastal management agency, was established in 1966.[13] Since then Australian states have developed some form of coastal zone management program. Now the Australian coastal management council coordinates and supervises the coastal planning and management issues in the country. Australian states have taken 400 meters land from high tide line.

The Queensland Green Paper suggests that "only coastal related industrial and commercial facilities such as ports, harbors, mariculture, marinas, tourist facilities, and appropriate service industries should be located on the coast. On the other hand town land, local government town planning schemes could be used to prevent further development in key areas[14].

Traditional concepts for accommodating this tension between public and private interest in Australian Planning Law include the statutory protection of existing use and compensation requirement for injurious affection. Implementation of coastal management through local town planning schemes that incorporate relevant regional and state coastal plan and policies may require a greater variety of accommodation techniques than existing use and injurious affection.

While in India, the laws pertaining towards the coastal zone management are different from Australia. In India, the Ministry of Environment and Forest, Government of India, New Delhi, came out with Coastal Regulation zone Notification (CRZ) in 1991, that says that there are certain activities which are not permissible at all and some other activities which needs permission from Ministry of Environment and Forest Government of India, But it did not work as people of coastal states say that the laws in CRZ are negative and anti development. An amendment made in 1994 made it even less effective, but in 1996, the Supreme Court has struck down 1994 amendment and only CRZ notification of 1991 is valid and now CRZ of 2011 is final, which is thus creating lot of confusion.

One of the major drawbacks in CRZ is that it does not include local people, as in case of Australia. In Australia govt. have emphasized on local people participation in each and every stage of regulation, so that their interests are not overlooked and coastal areas can be maintained at the same time.

LITERATURE SURVEY

The following literature may throw light on the varied issues and problems of our research.

Crawford (1992)[15] assessed that in April 1991 the House of Representatives Standing Committee on Environment, Recreation and the Arts presented a report to the Australian Parliament on the protection of the coastal environment. The report follows an extensive public inquiry by the parliamentary committee during which it visited various parts of Australian coastline and held discussion with approximately 500 people from all section of the community. Some of the major current issues of the coastal zone identified by the committee are: the fragmentation of the public decision-making, sewage disposal into the ocean, and endemic conflict among competing interest groups. The committee recommended that the Australian government develop a national coastal zone management strategy in cooperation with state and local governments.

Goldin and Sann (1993)[16] described the coastal zone as where various activities are conflicting, mainly due to absence of management policies, state control or incidentally, lack of essential scientific knowledge. Urbanization and industrialization growth versus other activities that need good water quality, e.g., aquaculture or leisure and tourism. The coastal environment is very sensitive to all these misuses. The coastal zone concept shall not restricted to the marine water, but should also includes all littoral zones, fresh water flowing into the coastal zone , and watersheds, since the quality of fresh water influence the marine water quality.

Haward (1993)[17] observed that the governments of Australia and New Zealand are attending more closely to issues related to coastal zone management in the regions surrounding their countries. Several initiatives and other government responses to the problems involving coastal zone management in the region are described. The Ocean Rescue 2000 program, being conducted under the aegis of the Australian government, will fund a 10 – year marine conservation effort. A number of state government initiatives being enacted in Australia are also examined. Features of the New Zealand Resource Management Act are reviewed.

Haward and Bergin (1991)[18] conducted a survey of state and federal coastal management regulations in Australia. Which indicates that degradation of the coastal environment has been recognized as a critical issue. Queensland, in particular, has initiated new regulations in response to development and attendant pressure on coastal resources. These state-level initiatives are recommended for future coastal management strategies, with in the frame work of federal legislation and financial support. These initiatives are compared with coastal management policies in North America.

Haward and Davis (1994)[19] in this edited volume observed that Australia's lengthy coastline transcends numerous of biogeographic regions, each containing a diversity of marine habitats. Management of the Australian coast reflects a similar diversity in legislative and administrative arrangements. Management and policy making concerning the coastal zone is shaped by the political, legislative and administrative overlap between different spheres of government in Australia. As a result of this overlap in the responsibilities it is probably inevitable that the coastal zone has been a perennial focus for government inquiries in Australia.

In the paper, Hildreth (1992)[20] conducted a survey of state and federal coastal management regulations in Australia and identified that degradation of the coastal environment has been recognized as a critical issue by the government. Queensland, in particular, has initiated new regulations in response to development and attendant pressure on coastal resources. These state-level initiatives are recommended for future coastal management strategies, within the framework of federal legislation and financial support. These initiatives are compared with coastal management policies in North America.

Hildreth, (1991) compared the legal regimes for ocean resources management of New Zealand, Australia, Canada and the United States. Australia, Canada, New Zealand and the United States were active participants and major players in the international negotiations which resulted in the 1982 United Nations convention on the law of the sea.

The United States (over 2.2 million square nautical miles), Australia (1.9 million square nautical miles), Canada (1.4 million square nautical miles) and New Zealand (1.2 million square nautical miles) have the world's first, second, fourth and seventh largest EEZs respectively. Canada (2.5 millions square, the world's second largest), the United States (1.12 million square miles) and Australia (1 million square miles) have expensive continental shelves as well. All four nations are the process of making modernizing their legal regimes for their offshore resource management.

Hunt (1993)[21] investigated the importance of the coastal zone and about the natural resources as four out of five Australians lives in the coastal zone. Their quality of life and that of their children will be affected by how the natural assets of the zone are managed. The consequences of rapid population growth and unsympathetic development have been compounded by fragmented decision making by government at the state and local levels. the Commonwealth is now moving to take up the problem, but if the inquiry currently being conducted is to produce more than just another report, it needs to be realistic about the limitations on jurisdiction and innovative in its strategies. The author reviews the progress of efforts to improve coastal management.

Miller and Mumford (1990) have suggested the use of environment assessment as a planning tool for coastal development in Australia is presented as a model for UK coastal management. Basic theory of environmental protection and its application in developed and developing nations is outlined. The Australian procedure for project assessment and its inherent weakness are evaluated. The goals of preservation, improvement, and social management are applicable to UK coastal management.

Smith and Jackson (1990)[23] have explained that the Gold Coast of Australia is a major resort coastal area in need of environmentally sound coastal management policies. Intensive tourist development has jeopardized the very attractions it has sought to exploit. Coastal management by the local authorities has been opportunistic and variable. Some measures addressed have included artificial nourishment, hazard value zoning, development of demountable buildings and revetments, emergency protection, wind resistance, wave erosion, and transfer relocation.

Brahtz, (1972)[24] have explained the specialized matters on conservation of biological and mineral resources, the needs of systems planning to control coastal zone development, marine waste disposal and marine transport system. These studies are framed for policy derivation in general and status assessment in particular. Each physical Character has been assumed as either extractive or non-extractive and non-appropriate primary resources. This activity has been identified for the multiple use of coastal environment. The major conflicts involved in the use of Marine and coastal resources and anticipated technology Measures are discussed with reference to proper policy guidelines and decision making.

Ketchum (1972)[25] has clearly outlined, why and how coastal zone management. He has identified the critical problem of the US coastal zone. Coastal zone management is a process designed to achieve set or stated objectives. The stated objectives would be to maintain and to improve coastal zone's usefulness for man by ensuring the quality and extent of the natural system upon which depends. It puts forward some guidelines for policy and decision makers.

Honikawa (1978)[26] has approached planning and management issue in coastal zone from stand points of either controlling or avoiding unwanted impacts of physical coastal process on assets and communities by engineering solutions and installations.

Coastal Management Journal (1973-93)[27]; in its various volumes, consists of articles focusing on all aspects of coastal planning and management in different parts of the world. This is land mark publication in this field in inquiry. Most of the articles focus on the status of coastal management in development and developing countries. They also comprise articles on the methodological aspects of the coastal planning and management.

The Quarterly Journal named Indian Journal of Marine Sciences (1980-93)[28] comprises of articles focusing on scientific and technological aspects of Indian coasts and oceans. They deal mainly with geological, physical and chemical biological aspects of oceanography. They also have articles on marine instrumentation and technology. These articles give US an insight on coastal processes, pollution, deep sea mining and exploration, availability of oceanic resources; coastal and marine water quality etc. both of micro and macro level.

James (1986) analyzes the factors which led to management of coast. It examines the implications of future seal-level rise and identifies anticipatory measures that may be appropriate today in spite of current uncertainties. The article deals with scientific data to show the increasing concentrations of carbon dioxide and other gases that are expected to warm the earth by several degrees in the next century by a mechanism known as the green house effect. Such a warming could cause sea level to rise two to five feet by expanding ocean water, melting mountain glaciers, and perhaps eventually causing polar glaciers to melt. Thus raising an alarm and providing suggestions so that many of adverse consequences can be avoided by taking timely measure.

Richard (1992)[30] discussed the recent Australian state and federal coastal management initiatives are reviewed form a North American perspective. Queensland's 1991 coastal protection strategy is emphasized. Declining coastal water quality is identified as a critical problem. Sub state multiple-use regional planning encompassing coastal catchment (watershed in recommended for emphasis in Australian Coastal Management).

Hence (1991)[31] discussed a specific two part approach for integration of human activities in the Management of sea. In which he focuses on use of applied geography in sea-use management and major tasks of marine geographers, in which he stressed upon to identify the major applied research opportunities in technical management fields, general management aspects and education. Jolliffe and Patman (1986)[32] in their article highlighted the problems regarding the coastal zone. And there are certain basic needs which have to be understood to solve the problem of coastal zone management, namely, the need to integrate natural and man-made systems; the need for a sound environmental knowledge base, need for public awareness etc.

Maritime Policy Issues Workshop (1994)[33] discussed national and international legal regimes covering coastal and maritime zone planning and Management and how these might be improved. The workshop demonstrated the scope for more work on the relevant legal frameworks and importance of appropriate training and education programs. The advantages and disadvantages of model coastal zone legislation were discussed and there were aspects of Australia legislation which could serve as a useful example for regional countries.

Ramachandran and Rajagopal (1991)[34] discussed about the "Coastal Pollution" in Coastal areas and how to manage major coastal activities responsible for marine pollution. It has been discussed by taking Tamil Nadu as a case study.

REVIEW OF THE COURT CASES RELATED WITH COASTAL REGULATION ZONE

The case of Indian Council for Enviro-Legal Action v. Union of India (1996(3) SCALE 579)[35] involves examination of the processes of rule-making concerning the coast. Judicial intervention in this case brought into sharp focus and critically reviewed the factors responsible for issuance of the original notification and the rationale for subsequent amendments to the same. Some of the observations made by the apex court in the case are worth noting and should act as a beacon light for the rule making and its implementation by the state. strongly criticizing frequent changes effected in the law concerning the coastal environment, the Supreme Court impressed upon the government the need for proper preparation and abundant precaution in fashioning rules and regulations and to implement the same with all seriousness. Cautioning the government, the court observed that enactment of a law without bothering to enforce the same or becoming oblivious to its infringement would shake the confidence of people in both the law and institutions of its enforcement.

Ambiguity in the demarcation of the High Tide Line was the done of contention in the cases of *Jacob Vadakan Cherry v. State of Kerala* (1998 AIHC 1688)[36] and *Institute of Social Welfare v. state* (1996(1) KLT 718).

In both the cases, the government took advantage of the discrepancy and successfully reclaimed land on the coast for construction of bridges. The court advised the government to explore the possibility of going ahead with the proposed activity without taking recourse to reclamation.

The right to relevant environmental information received a boost through judicial pronouncements made in *Goa Foundation v. Goa State committee on coastal Environment* (W.P. 115/1192)[37] and *Kaloor Joseph v. State of Kerala and Ors.* (OP No. 20278) (1999) decided on 2nd June 1998-unreported). In both the cases the court ordered the appropriate governmental authorities to make available the coastal zone Management Plan in all public places, for the information and scrutiny of the people.

Prof. Sergio Carvalho v. the Staff of goa and Others (1989 (1) GLT 276)[38] *and Goa Foundation and Ors. V. North Goa Planning and Development authority and ors.* (1) GLT 181) (1995)[39] are cases concerning eco-tourism decided by the Bombay High Court. The activist stance taken by tempered by the economic considerations for facilitating construction of hotels and beach resorts on the coast in these two cases. The judicial mind appears to have been convinced by the kind of guidelines evolved for promoting Eco-Tourism in the area.

Upon an examination of these cases, it can be concluded that the environmental justice would have been served better if expert opinion on such highly sensitive and technical subjects was sought before the court arrived at its judgment. In contrast to these decisions is the stand upheld by the Orissa High court in *Dinabhandu Sahoo and anr. v. Ministry of Tourism and Ors.* (Writ Petition (Civil) 899/93)[40] that kept the Petitioners' option open to approach the High Court if and when the government violated any of the stipulations under the Coastal Regulation zone Notifications to promote development of beach resorts in the area.

The approach of the courts of law in encouraging developmental activities on the coast appears un-uniform. In the *Konkan Railway Case (Goa Foundation and anr. v. Konkan Railway Corporation and ors.* Mh. L.J.21) (1994)[41] the court those the path of supporting as a developmental activity notwithstanding the damage it cased to the fragile environment. The reasons given were that the court chose not to interfere in a policy decision of the government in which heavy investments were already made. The legal basis of drawing conclusions is debatable as provisions of Railways Act were interpreted to prevail over the stipulations under the Environment Protection Act.

Meeting the demands of energy by the government weighed heavily on the judicial mind when the Supreme court in the *Dahanu Taluka Environment Protection groups and anr.v. Bombay Suburban Electricity Supply Company Ltd. and Ors and Bombay Environment Action Grup and Anr. v. The state of Maharashtra and Ors.* (AIR sc 910) (1991)[42] gave the go ahead to the proposed Thermal Power Projects. Flouting of government guidelines and adverse impact on the coastal environment did not cut ice with the court as it felt power generation and making the same available as most essential for overall economic progress. All the same, there was a praise worthy element in the judgment that required the involvement of well informed groups in the decision- making processes of the government concerning such developmental activities.

In a few cases the apex court and High courts have taken pains in the protection of traditional rights over resources that are environment friendly. In the Aqua Culture cases (*S. Jagannath v. Union of India* (1997) 2 SCC 87 *and Gopi Aqua Farms v. Union on India* (1997) 6 SCC 577) the Supreme Court issued a number of directions that warned against the practice of intense aqua farming that violated a number of principles of good environmental management and encouraged promotion of traditional aqua farming methods. *Chilika Lake Case (Kholamuhana Primary fisherman Co-operative Society and Ors. V. State of Orissa* AIR 1994 *Orissa* 191)[43] is an interesting case in which the Orissa High Court upheld the fishing rights of both the fishermen and non-fishermen.

OBJECTIVES OF THE STUDY

Recognizing the importance of coastal ecosystem and urgent need for Integrated Coastal Zone Management (ICZM), the main objectives of the study have been taken as follows:

(i) To prepare a complete inventory of uses and activities that take place in the Indian, and Australian Coastal Zone.

(ii) To identify ecologically harmful development in coastal zone.

(iii) To examine and critically appraise the current role and Jurisdiction of central, state and local agencies in managing the coastal zones of the two study areas.

(iv) Spatial analysis of administrative actions related to integrated coastal zone management enforcement of Coastal Zone Regulations.

(v) Comparative analysis of two states one from India and one from Australia to help evolve a functionally applicable model for Integrated Coastal Zone Management.

HYPOTHESIS

1. Integrating coastal and ocean space for sustainable Management is the Major challenge before Integrated Coastal Zone Management.
2. The two countries have different prospective with regard to whether Integrated Coasted Zone Management, is an extension of Ocean Management towards Coastal Areas.

3. Community participation in decision–making and enforcement of relevant regularities are the most important issues before any successful Integrated Coastal Zone Management.

DATA BASE

Coastal Management programs are information drivers and can be divided into four basic components: Social, economic, spatial, and environmental, each of which can further elaborated.

The data and information for this study have been derived from - published and unpublished secondary sources. However, to understand the ground realities with respect to the environment factors, a reconnaissance survey was conducted. This survey gave a feel of the environmental realities in both countries.

The major secondary sources of data are:

(i) Census data and plan reports

(ii) Data collected by Town and Country planning organizations of maritime states/UTs.

(iii) Statistical Abstracts published by directorate of Economics and Statistics of Maritime States/UTs.

(iv) Government of India/UNEP reports and documents.

(v) Data and information regarding environmental degradation and pollution from various sources such as books, Journals, reports, scientists at NIO, Goa etc.

METHODOLOGY

Methodology adopted to pursue this study are: the first may be termed as descriptive/analytical. This involves the collection of facts and figures and organizing them as a descriptions/analysis of the distribution of some phenomena in an area.

The second type may be called problem solving. This involved keen observation of some phenomenon and requires adequate scientific explanation in terms of their occurrence though space and/or time. Also interviews with Indian and Australian scholars will help plug gaps wherever they may exist.

OVERALL CONTEXT OF INTEGRATED COASTAL ZONE MANAGEMENT IN INDIA

- Collected the environmental and social baseline information on the coastline of India. Reports and other published information were perused to identify the management and conservation issues persist in the coastal region. The documents related to various policy initiatives and regulations, were collected and analyzed to see the compliance of project activities.
- The strength and weakness of the current coastal zone management policies, practices and programs were critically assessed and major issues leading to environmental degradation and other impacts were identified through a consultation process with experts and decision makers.
- The need to adopt ICZM approaches and details of the process of ICZM approaches was prepared by taking clue from the various national level studies and by the three pilot ICZM project states and consulting the state level ICZM project authorities.
- An analysis of various stakeholder consultations with respect to ICZM approaches was done, covering national level consultations by CEE, state level project consultations by participating states of ICZMP, MoEF consultations, consultations by the project's Communication Consultants and others held within the states specifically for this project.
- The possible alternatives considered at the policy and project levels by the ICZM project states to assess the environmental and social impacts of the programs and the institutional arrangements for conflict resolution were analyzed by going through the project documents, stakeholder consultations and discussions with various officials.
- Considering the major beneficiary of the ICZM project as the coastal communities including traditional dwellers and the marginalized communities especially tribal's, the project team consulted with experts and various stakeholders in the three ICZM project states and assessed the process of benefit sharing from the ICZM project within the marginalized local coastal community
- Critical assessment of the process of benefit sharing suggested in the ICZM project reports of the three states was undertaken. Procedures

for involvement of stakeholders in relevant decision making process were discussed during the consultation with experts and decision makers.

NOTES

1. UNEP, (1990), The Marine Environment. UNEP Regional Seas Report No. 115, U.N. Environmental Program, Nairobi.
2. Hansen, J. E. *et al.* (1981): "Climate Impact of Increasing Atmospheric Carbondioxide," Science 213: 957-66.
3. Keeling, C.D., R.B. Bacostown, and T.P. Whort (1982), "Measurements of the Concentration of Carbon Dioxide at Mauna Loa Observatory, Hawaii", In Co2 Review; 1982, ed. W. Clark pp. 377-82, New York, Oxford University Press.
4. Ramanathan, V., H. B. Singh (1985): "Trace Gases Trends and their Potential Role in Climate Change," Journal of Geophysical Research 92 (03); 5547-66.
5. Green house gases, "In General House effect and Sea level rise, ed. Barth and Titus (1984).
6. IPCC (Inter Governmental Panal on climate change (1990). "Strategies for adaptation to seal level rise: Ministry of Transport and Public Works, the Hague, The Netherlands, 122 pp.
7. IPCC (Inter Governmental Program (1992). "Global Climate Change and Rising Challenge of the Sea" Ministry of Transport and Public Works, the Hague., The Netherlands.
8. UNEP (1992). "Agenda 21", in: The Outcomes of the United Nations Conference on Environment and Development, Rio de Janerio, Brazil, 3-14 June, 192.
9. *Ibid*, 8.
10. Hopkins J. N. (1973). Environmental Impact Statements. A Hand book for writers and reviewers, University of Illinois; Urban Campaign, Illinois 1973.
11. Tortlage, C. A. (1990). Environmental Assessment. A practical guide, Gower Publishing Company, Aldershot, U.K..
12. Cullen, P. (1982). "Coastal Zone Management in Australia." *Coastal Zone Management Journal* 10: 183-212.
13. *Ibid.*, 12.
14. Lobry de Bruyn; L. A. (1992). Draft Coastal Management Plan: Shire of Coorwo. Department of Construction and Environment, Bulletin 237, Perth.
15. Crawford, D. (1992). The injured coastline-a parliamentary report on coastal protection in Australia. Coastal Management. 20 (2), pp. 189-198.

16. Goldin, P. and Sann, A. (1993). South East Tasmania case study, Australia. Coastal zone Management: Selected Case studies. Organization for Economic Cooperation and Development, Paris, France, pp. 199-236.

17. Haward, M. (1993). Ocean and Coastal Zone Management in Australia and New Zealand: Current Initiatives, Ocean and Coastal Management. 19(3), pp. 292-300.

18. Haward, M. and Bergin, A. (1991).Australian Intergovernmental relations and Coastal Zone Policy. Coastal Zone 91', Proceedings of the Seventh Symposium on Ocean and Coastal Management Long Beach California, USA July 8-12, 1991. America Society of Civil Engineers, New York. Pp.737-751.

19. Haward, M. Davis, B.W. (1994). Current Developments in Australia Coastal Zone management. Coastal Zone Canada'94, Cooperation in the Coastal Zone, Halifax, NS, Canada, 1994(eds. Wells, P.G.Ricketts, P.J.) pp. 19-29.

20. Hidertth, R. C. (1992). Australian Coastal Zone Management: Some North American Perspectives on Recent Queensland and Other Initiatives. Coastal Management. 20(3), pp. 255-269.

21. Hunt Colin. (1993). The management of coastal resources: A job for the Commonwealth?. Current Affairs Bulletin. 69 (10).

23. Smith, w. and Jackson, L.A. (1990). An application of Coastal Management Tactics: Gold Coast, Queensland, Australia. Shore&Beach. 58 (3), pp. 3-9.

24. Blahtz, J.F.R. (1972) ed.: Coastal Zone Management: Multiple uses with Conservation, John Wiley K. Sons, New York.

25. *Ibid.*, 14, M. ketchums, Blt.

26. Honikawa, K. (1978) Coastal Engineering: An Introduction to Ocean Engineering, University of Tokyo Press, Tokyo.

27. Coastal Management Journal (1973-93).

28. Indian Journal of Marine Science (1980-93).

30. Hildreth Richard (1992). Australian Coastal Management: Some North American Respective on Recent Queensland and other initiatives:, Coastal Management, London.

31. Smith Hence D. (1991) "The Application of Maritime Geography: A Technical and General Management," ed. Book by Hance D. smith and Adalberto village. The Development of Integrated Sea use Management, Routledge, London.

32. Jolliffee I.P. and C.R. Patman (1986): The Coastal Zone: The Challenge. In *Journal of Shoreline Management*, N. Ireland, 1986.

33. Outcomes of the workshop on "Maritime Policy Issues Workshops" (September 1994), Coastal and Maritime Zone Planning and Management, University of Wollongong, Australia.
34. Ramachanderns and S. Rajagopal (1991) coastal Pollution ed. Book, Coastal Zone Management in Tamil Naidu State?: India.
35. Indian Council for Environ Legal Action Vs. Union of India: 1996 (B) Supreme Court Almahac.
36. Jacob Vadakancherry V. State of Kerala, 1998, High Court – 1688.
37. Institute of Social Welfare V. State 1996(1) Kerala Law Times 718.
38. Goa State Committee on Coastal Environment (Writ petition 115/1192) Goa High Court, Bombay.
39. Prof. Sergio Carvalhi V. the Staff of Goa another (1989(1) Goa Law times 276).
40. Dinabhandhu Sahoo and Aur. V. Ministry of Tourism and others Orissa High Court (Writ Petition (Civil 899/93).
41. Goa Foundation and others Vs. Konkon Railway Corporation and others (1994) Maharahstra Law Journal, 21.
42. S. Tagnnath V. Union of India 1997 (2) Supreme Court Cases, 87.
43. Gopi Aqua Farms V. Senior of India 1997 (6) Supreme Cases 577.

CHAPTER 2

INTEGRATED COASTAL ZONE MANAGEMENT: Conceptual Context and Perspective

The place where the waters of the seas meet the land – the coasts – are indeed unique places in our global geography. They are unique in a very real economic sense as sites for ports and harbor facilities that capture the large monetary benefits associated with waterborne commerce and as locations for industrial processes which require water cooling for example, power generation plants. The coasts are highly valued and greatly attractive as sites for resorts and as vacation destinations. The combination of fresh water creates some of the most productive and richest habitats on earth, resulting bounty in fishes and other marine life can be of great valve to coastal rations[1]. Therefore, for most coastal rations, the coasts are an asset of incalculable valve, an important part of the national patrimony. Population growth in the coastal zone is major concern. The world population is expected to grow at an exponential rate from 5.8 billion in 1995 billion by the year 2025.

At present, one quarter of world's population of some 5.9 billion live in the coastal areas; most of the largest urban concentrations are on the coast. The current coastal urban population of 220 million is projected to almost double in next 20 to 30 years[2]. There would be 11 megacities of more than 20 billion population and 14 megacities with more than 10 million people. By the year 2015, there will be some 7 megacities of more than 20 million people and every one of them, except Tokyo, would be in the third world namely, Mexico City, Greater Bombay, Shanghai, Jakarta, Sao Paulo and Karachi[3].

Thus, the coastal zone is an area of a agriculture, are concentrated in these cities. This is an area of convergence of activities in urban centers, such as shipping in major parts and wastes generates from domestic sources and by major industrial facilities.[4] Thus, traditional resource based activities, such as coastal fisheries agriculture, forestry and agriculture, are found side by side with activities such as industry, shipping and tourism. The potential, for economic opportunities in coastal cities is a strong alternative force, fuelling immigration, often from economically depressed rural areas. As a result, in future much larger, younger populations can be expertise in the coastal areas of developing countries. These future coastal residents will demand employment, housing, energy, food, water and other goods and services, thus imposing a substantial development challenge[5].

Apart from demographic backdrop, coastal areas are extremely important for the social and economic welfare of current and future generations, as coastal resources support by economic and subsistence activities. The economies of most developing countries are currently very dependent on natural resources, for agriculture, fisheries and forestry subsectors (e.g., in Vietnam, 50 per cent of national rice production comes from the Mekong delta in the South and 20 per cent is produced in the Red River delta near Hanoi).[6]

COASTAL ISSUES OF GOA

Over one third of the world's population lives either at the coasts or in adjacent coastal low land areas. Coastal lands and coastal waters comprise substantial quantities of the nation's agricultural, mineral and living resources. The coastal zone is characterized by a large variety of forms sandy beaches, rocky shores, river mouths, estuaries, lagoons, inter-tidal flats, wetlands and barrier islands, which have been shaped in the course of geological history. In and around these landforms, a number of specific biological communities have developed, including inter-tidal and marsh communities, mangroves, sea grass and coral reefs. Man has settled in the coastal zone for reasons such as easy accessibility, availability of basic facilities and abundance of food. The coastal zone is a scarce, vulnerable and dynamic territory, where natural, economic, demographic, social and environmental aspects come together. With the increase in population, its pressures on coastal zone in general, coastal resources in particular are rising. This can cause rapid decline in the quality of the coastal zone if no initiation is taken to conserve and manage. India has about 7500 km long coastline. The coastline of India has been undergoing morphological changes throughout the geological past. The present coastal geomorphology of India has evolved largely in the background of the post – glacial transgression over the pre-existing topography of the coast and offshore. Goa a small state along west coast of India has about 100 km long coast and is characterized by pocket beaches flanked by rocky cliffs, estuaries, bays, and at some places mangroves. Beaches in southern Goa are long and linear in nature with sand dunes. The Mandovi and Zuari estuarine system in Goa is the largest in this part of the coast. Mud flats, swampy marshes and wetlands are found mainly along estuaries and creeks. The beaches of Goa are stable beaches with seasonal morphological changes and annual cyclicity. The coastal zone in Goa is exposed to environmental and anthropogenic pressures. Some of the factors attributing to these pressures can be due to demographic settings and population growth, rapid urbanization, mining, migration, recreation and tourism activities, fishery activities, transportation problems, socio-economic shift and transformation in occupation like, fishing, tourism, trade, salt industry; wetlands conversion, degradation of agriculture land and fallow lands. In addition, social, financial issues and anti social activities are also the factors. The environmental issues are erosion at Anjuna and Kerim beaches, seasonal erosion during monsoon in several parts of the coastal stretch including headlands, garbage and sewerage disposal, mining waste, indiscriminate tapping of ground water resources, violations of the CRZ notification, establishment of unplanned aquaculture ponds, salt inundation in Khazan lands, eutrophication and encroachments in wetlands and agriculture land rendered fallow. The coastal zone in Goa contains habitats and ecosystems, such as, estuaries, mangroves and is entailed with a galaxy of resources, which have definite role in the maintenance of the ecological balance and economic vitality of the coastal region. Climate change and associated sea level rise can be disastrous to small state like Goa. The understanding of coastal system in macro as a whole would therefore need to address these issues coupled with the social and economic fabric of the zone under question. It is now realized that uncontrolled activities either on the waterfront or beyond or on the land-based side could cause irreversible damage to the ecosystem. Moreover the developmental activities that ignore the dynamics of the coastal system can be catastrophic as evidenced by the increasing loss of lives, property and investment due to coastal flooding and erosion. It is evident that the multitude of increasing pressures on the coastal systems, coastal wetland transformation and ecological stress on the estuaries is posing a threat to the human population and the coastal resources. In this context, it has to ensured that these ecosystems maintain their ecological, productive and natural functions, a detailed coastal zone resource information system is a prerequisite. In order to achieve sustainable development, it is important to have strategies such as, conserving and enhancing the coastal environment, managing risks and coastal vulnerability and merging coastal environmental considerations with economic decision through the mechanism of a comprehensive Coastal Zone Management Plan.

COASTAL POLLUTION

Most marine pollution is from land-based sources: domestic and industrial effluents, drainage from agricultural run-off, strong water runoff in urban areas, or from solid waste disposal, airborne source of pollution and sediments from erosion or land reclamation.[7] Marine sources of pollution are operational discharges (water and ballast) from marine transport and auidental discharges, including spills. The severity of reflects on coastal resources will depends upon the composition of pollution (nutrients, toxic substances)[8], their quality and level of concentration, and on hydrological

Figure 1: Demands on Coastal Waters

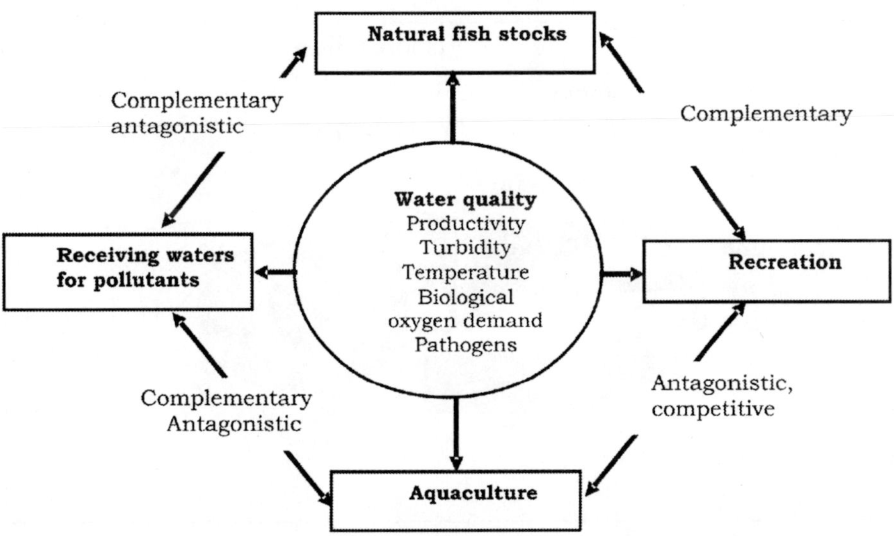

conditions in the recipient waters, their quantity and level of concentration, and on hydrological conditions in recipient waters.

Major Constituents

Sea water is composed of a number of different components that can be divided into four different phases: solids, gases, colloids and dissolved solutes. Major constituents are those which occur in concentrations greater than about 1 ppm by weight and include Na^{+}, Mg^{2+}, Ca^{2+}, K^{+}, SO_4^{2-}, HCO^{-}_3, Br^{-}, C_3^{2-} $B(OH)^{-}_4$, F^{-} and $B(OH)_3$. They account for over 99.9% of the salinity of sea water which is simple terms is the sum of all the dissolved salts in water[9]. In surface water of open oceans, salinity requires from 33 to 37 ppt but when self shelf and local conditions are taken into account the range can be as wide as 28-40 ppt or more.

The major dissolved gases in seawater are N_2, O_2, CO_2 and Ar. The solubility of CO_2 in seawater is many times greater than that of nitrogen and oxygen since dissolved CO_2 reacts with water forming carbonic acid and its association products[10]. The main concern of waste disposal at sea arises from possible effects on man through accumulation of substances by marine animals, tainting of seafood and reduction of amenities by discoloration or floating debris.

By far, domestic sewage is the most widespread continuant in coastal waters. The organic matter in sewage is aerobically oxidized and where

Figure 2a: Major Sources of Marine Pollution

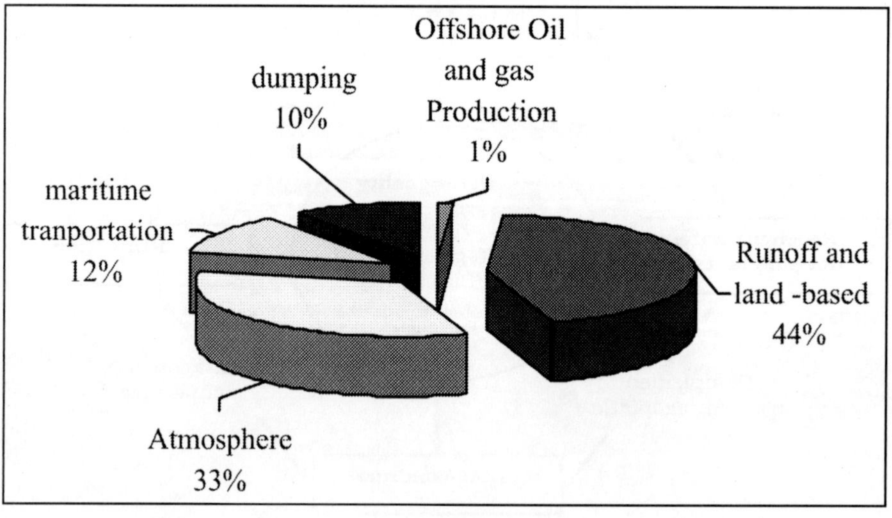

disposal conditions are poor, an excessive depletion of oxygen and deposition of organic matter may occur leading to anaerobic sediments. Sewage also contains pathogens and viruses, which may in fact the swimmers or may contaminate the fish and shell fish (Figure 2).

As, India is one of the growing industrialized countries in the world, and out of total industries located in both sides the coast of which 52 per cent is in west coast and remaining 48 per cent in east[11]. It has been observed that there is a good concentration of large and medium industries in narrow coastal belt. State wise coastal length, area and number of large and medium industries as also aquaculture firms (may be regarded as industries) located in coastal area within 25 km-landward along with in number of industries with high pollution potential. There are about 308 large and medium industries are located within the coastal belt of the country which discharge/ dispose their liquid and solid wastes directly or indirectly into the coastal water. Out of these, 233 industries are located in west coast and 75 on the east coast and there are 138 aquaculture forms predominantly for shrimp facing.[12] In generation of liquid waste out of total quantity of 1.35 million cubic meters per day about 6.85 million cubic meters per day is from west coast industries.

The east coast industries generate the total quantity of about 0.5 million cubic meters per day. The liquid waste/effluent generation from aquaculture forms from east coast is to 2.37 million cubic meters per day.[13]

COAST, COASTAL AREA AND COASTAL ZONE

The terms "coastal" is, in the majority of cases, defined as a "sea-land interface" or "a place where land, water and air meet"[14]. Consequently, a "land affected by its proximity to the sea and that part of the sea affected by it proximity to the land "or", in other words, the area[15] where the processes which depends on the sea-land interaction are the most intensive. This interface is taking place along two axes: the axis running along the coast and the axis perpendicular to the coast line. In terms of the basic definition of the coastal zone, there is little controversy related to the coast-wise axis, since it enables an easy definition of the boundaries of the coastal ecosystems[16]. Quite the contrary, there is much dispute with regard to the cross-share axis. Those definitions of the coastal zone vary from those covering the entire watershed areas in the hinterland part of the coast to

Table 2
Pollution Potentials of Coastal Industries

State	*Number of industries*	*ETP provided*	N^0 *ETP*	*Effluent qty. (10^6 m^3/ day)*	*Discharge Type*	*Solid waste*	*Discharge type*
Gujarat	35	34	1	0.566	ID (32) D (3)	9506	LF/D&I
Maharashtra	167	150	17	0.08	ID (130) D (37)	2628	LF/DI
Goa	2	2	—	0.151	ID (19) D (1)	76	D/I
Karnataka	3	3	—	0.043	ID (2) D (1)	76	D/I
Kerala	26	26	1	0.151	ID (19) D (7)	2431	LF/D/I
Tamilnadu	30	29	—	0.125	ID (12) D (18)	9112	D/I/S
Aquafarms	20	(Uncr-eated 90%)	0.253	D (20)	—	D	
Pondicherry	4	4	—	0.006	D (4)	1.25	LF/S
Andhra Pradesh	30	29	1	0.35	ID (26) D (4)		LF/D/I
Aquafarms	88	(Untr-eated 100%)		2.116	ID (46) D (42)	—	D
Orissa	4	4	—	0.001	ID (4) D	3505	N.A.
Aquafarms	20	(Untr-eated 100%)	—	—	D	—	D
Best Bengal	7	7	—	0.022	ID (7)	25	LF
Aquafarms	10	(Untr-eated 100%)			D	—	D

Note: ID – Indirect, D – Direct, LF – Land Falling, D- Dumping, I – Incarnation, S – Stored, n.a. – not available, FTP – Effluent Treatment Plant.

Source: Ministry of Environment and Forests, 1994, New Delhi.

those including a narrow coastal strip only. In any case, the definition of the boundaries of a coastal zone depends on criteria stemming from the goals of ICAM processes.

"Coastal area" is a notion which is geographically broader than the coastal zone[17], the borders of which require a less strict definition. This notion indicates that there is a national or sub-national recognition that a distinct transitional environment exist between the ocean and terrestrial domains. This notion is of extreme importance for ICAM, many processes, they terrestrial domains. This notion is of extreme importance for ICAN. Many processes are environmental, demographic, economic or social, which take place within the boundaries of the environmental, demographic, economic or social regions and actually take place within the boundaries of the coastal area, with their extreme manifestations being most visible in the area of the coastal zone[18]. In other words, 'coastal area' refers to the geographic area along the coast that has not yet been defined as a zone for management purposes (Figure 3)[19].

Figure 3: Relationship between Coastal Zone and coastal Resource System

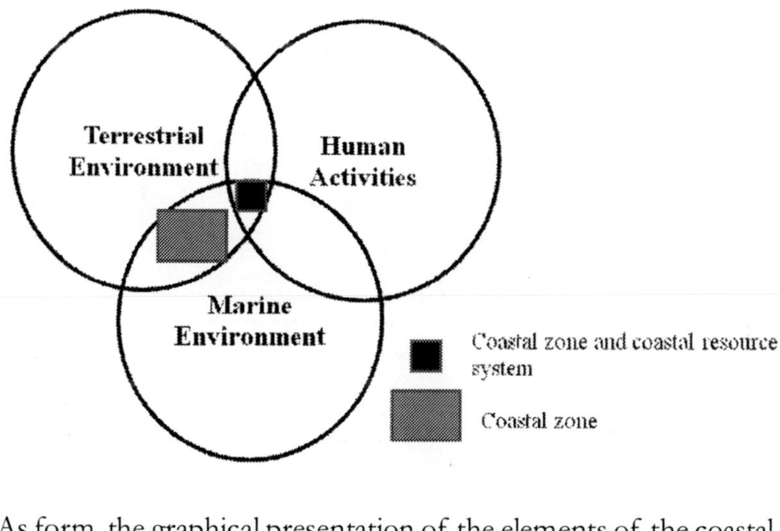

As form, the graphical presentation of the elements of the coastal zone and the coastal area is given in figure. "Ocean water" covers the largest part of the sea belt, up to 200 national miles off shore (exclusive Economic Zone). "Coastal waters" cover a narrow near-share sea belt, its width varying from one country to another."

"Inertial area" is the area between the lowest tide line and the shoreline" (The landward extent of the tidal influence). "Coastline" is the contact line dividing the land from the water bodies.

"Ocean front or shore lands area" is the part of the land up to heights line of tidal influence.

This is a relatively narrow belt, with its inner borders which rarely wider than 1,000m.

"Coastal uplands" are defined as an area of the interview between the shore lands and most frequently, the heights peak of the closest maintain range.

"Inland" may be any area outside the aforementioned belts. Thus, the coastal waters, inter tidal area, coastline, shore lands area and coastal uplands are the elements of the coastal zone.

Figure 4: Pacts of the Coastal Area. Maritime Zones

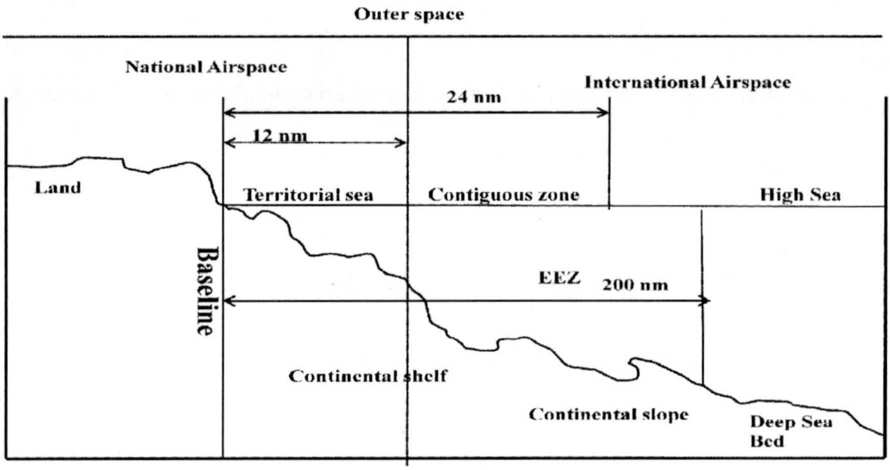

Note: In some areas, the continental shelf, slope or rise may extend beyond the 200-miles EEZ.

Source : California coastal some Conservations Commissions 1975. California coastal plan. California coastal zone conservation Commissions San Francisco, U.S.A

There can fine main zones be identified in the coastal marine spectrum;

Inland Areas: those affect the oceans mainly via rivers and non-point sources of pollution.

Coastal Lands: Wet lands, marshes, and the like-where human activity is concentrated and directly affects adjacent water;

Coastal Water: Generally estuaries, lagoons and shallow waters – where the affects of land based activities are dominant;

Offshore Waters: Mainly out to the edge of national jurisdiction (2000 nautical – miles offshore);

High Seas: Beyond the limit of national jurisdiction

Thus, the coast is best viewed as zone of mixing or adjustment. A more formal definition can be:

> "The coastal zone is that space in which terrestrial environments influence marine environments and vice-versa. The coastal zone is of available width may also change in time. Delimitation of coastal boundaries is not normally possible, more often such limits are marked by environment gradient or transition. At any one locality the coastal zone may be characterized according to physical, biological or cultural criteria. These need not, and in fact rarely do coincide."[20]

Coastal zones are unique. Such things are daily tides, mangrove forests, coral reefs, tidal flats, sea beaches, storm waves and barrier islands are found only at the coast[21]. Because of these features and because coastal enterprise is also distinctive, most countries recognize the coastal zone as a distinct region with resources that require special attention.

The coastal area or coastal zone is defined by Sreson and McCreary[22] as the interface or transitional zone, specifically "that part of the land affected by its proximity to the sea and that part of the ocean affected by its proximity to the land … an area in which processes depending on the air pollution from industries, energy production, traffic and adour. Under certain conditions, photochemical smog develops. The severity of the effects on air quality will depends on the composition of emissions, their quantity, their concentrations, the height at which they are emitted and topographical and meteorological conditions for dispersal. Several coastal areas suffer particularly from heavy concentrations of air pollutions sources and others from smog where dispersal conditions are inadequate. Damage from all pollution is predominantly to the health of local inhabitants, but it may also degrade the quality of the environment for tourism and result in damage to historic buildings and movements. Air pollution is also indirect cause of marine pollution.

The interaction between land and sea are most intensive. But it must be noted that the border between land and sea is not fixed – it changes daily with tides, with moon stages, seasonally with astronomic forces, and sporadically with sea storms and great river floods. The coastal zone may be drawn wide or narrow in order to meet program goals.

The coastal zone management is a hybrid concept[23], combining elements of regional analysis and environmental management. The coastal zone is a band of varying width which includes a land component and sea word component. Within in the national context, it is a region which contains a certain proportions of a national capital, income and employment. The question of how to allocate these aggregates among the various national capital, income and employment. The question of how to allocate these aggregates among the various national regions is one of the traditional problems of development planning. Coastal zone manager has been described by Doray (1986)[24] as a "wicked problem". Wicked problems are not necessarily wicked in perverse sense of being evil. Rather they are wicked like the head of hydro. They are ensured with tentacles. The more you attempt to time them, the more complicated they become.

Pitts (1993)[25] noted that the recurring themes in the Australian inquiries relevant to the coastal zone bear a strong resemblance of the six characteristics of complex wicked problems identified by Manson and Mitroft (1981)[26]:

(a) ***Interconnectedness:*** strong connections link one problems with another;

(b) ***Complicatedness:*** numerous elements including feedback loops;

(c) ***Uncertainty:*** wicked problems exist in an uncertain environment which creates a heed to accept risk, perhaps incalculable risk.

(d) ***Ambiguity:*** the problems can be seen in quite different ways depending upon a person's characteristics and experience. There is no single "correct" view.

(e) ***Conflict:*** Competing claims, conflicts of interests and complex interactions among powerful interests that are unlikely enter cooperative arrangements.

(f) ***Societal Constraints:*** Social, political and technological been.

Thus, it becomes very much clear that the paramount objective of coastal management is to devise a framework with in which man may live harmoniously with nature or, to provide "sustainable utilization" of coastal resources. Thus, effective manages should aim at balancing cause and effect, but remain alert to change and have the skill to adjust.

Coastal zone management can be divided, into three broad areas[27], policy, planning and practice. Policy relates to the political and administrative frame work through which coastal management is regulated, be it legislation, education or a combination of both. Planning is the process or resource allocation be it by environments ecological, social, or economic yardsticks. Practice covers the techniques needed for implementation of planning decisions, or for understanding restorative or remedial work. Practice range from building seawalls to planting beach grass and to disposing nuclear waste.

According to Sorehson and McCreary, "The coastal zone is defined as the interface or transition zone, specially that part of the land affected by its proximity to the sea and that part of the ocean affected by its proximity to the land ... an area in which processes depending on the interaction not fixed – at changes daily with tides, with the moon stages, seasonally with astronomic forces, and sporadically with sea storms and great river floods".[28]

The limits of the coastal zone are after arbitrarily defined, differing widely among nations, and are often based on jurisdictional limits or demarked by reasons of administrative cease.[29] Coastal zone should include the land area from the watershed to the sea, which theoretically would make sense as this is the zone where biophysical interactions are strongest. For planning purposes this definition is after quite impractical. For practical planning purposes, the coastal zone is a special area, endowed with special characteristics, whose boundaries are often determined by the specific problems to be talked. Its characteristics are (Figure 5)[30]:

- It is dynamic area with frequently changing biological, chemical and geological attributes.
- It includes highly productive and biologically diverse ecosystems that offers nursery habitats for many marine species.
- Coastal zone features such as coral reefs, mangrove forests, and health and done systems serve as critical natural defenses against storms, flooding and erosion.
- Coastal ecosystems may art to moderate the imparts of pollution originating from land (example, wetlands absorbing excess nutrients, sediments, human waste).

- The coast attracts vast human settlements due to its proximity to ocean's living and non-living resources, as well as marine transportation and recreation.

Figure 5: Coastal Zone Functions, Uses and Values

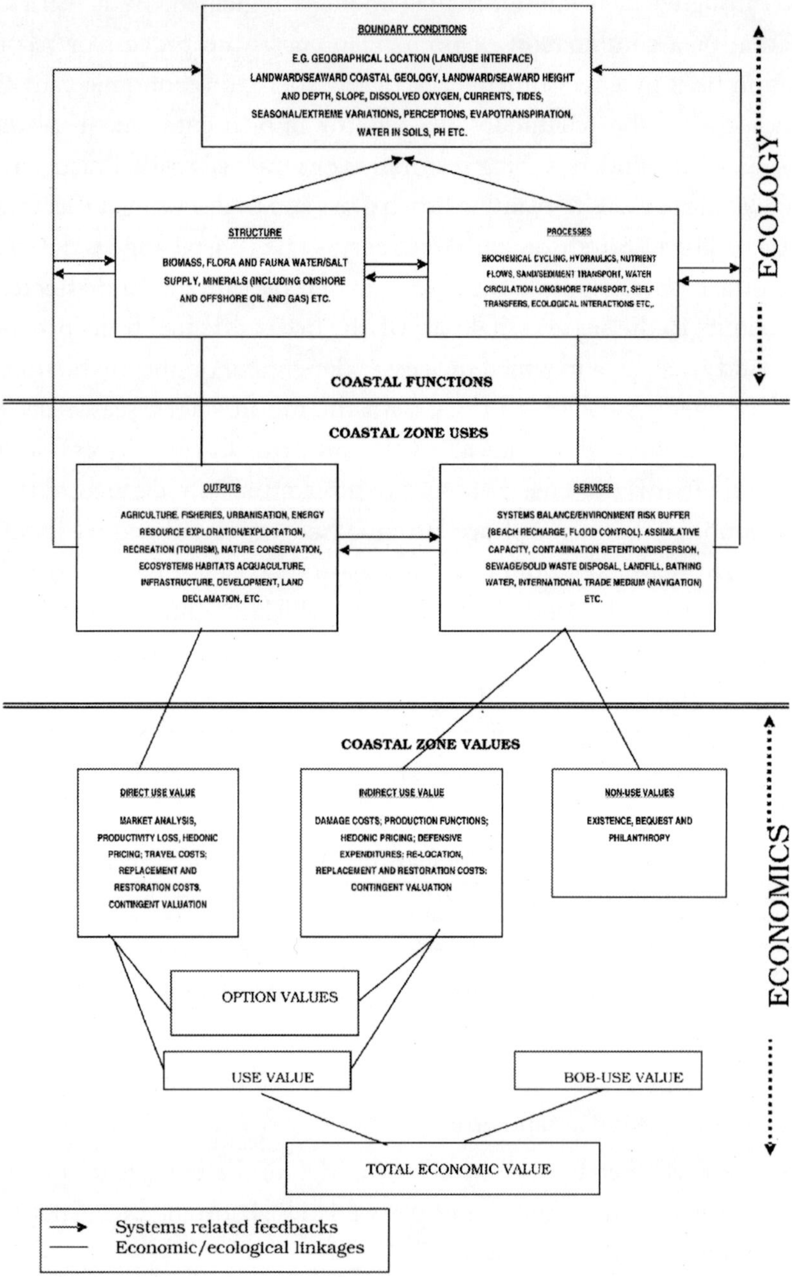

Geographical Characteristics of Coastal Zone

(a) *Narrow and Prone to Flooding:* Where land meets sea, is generally at its shallowest and the land it's lowest. Flooding is common. Both by daily flooding of sand and mud flats and storm tides that others from time to time.

(b) Beaches: Beaches are mainly unconsolidated sediments (mainly sand and gravel) that most parts of the share. Erosion of beaches, both national and caused by people, has attracted much attention in recent days. Man can affect coastal some by degrading and filling to create extra land, damming rivers, construction of jetties and coastal structures and destruction of coastal done area.

(c) Coastal changes and Placer Deposits: The shallowness of the sea near the sea shore has an effect on the concentration of sea energy at the coast. Much of the coined emergency on the sea surface is carried in the form of waves. Where it is quickly dissipated in the breaking up of waves against the share. The position of bars may be changed, channels may get filled in and braces may be moved up and down and may even disappear completely. Some of there one produced by the share processes themselves while others are placer deposits which are subsequently placed in the coastal zone by rising sea level.

(d) Estuaries, Lagoons and Marshes: There is another common feature of many coastal areas. An estuary is a body of water partially enclosed by land that has a connection to the ocean as well as to a river. The area where salt water and fresh water mix. Lagoons are somewhat similar to estuaries; Chilka Lake on the southern side of the Mahanadi River delta in the Bay of Bengal is a good example of a lagoon. Where marshes are generally located inter tidal areas along the banks of tidal rivers, or behind barrier beaches.

(e) *Delta:* Deltas are large accumulation of sediments that are deposited at the month of a river. All rivers transport sediments to the ocean. Usually some or all of the sediments is deposits when the river enters slower flowing or standing body of water. Delta are generally flat areas that are extremely fertile because of sediments deposited by river; rich in nutrients.

INTEGRATED COASTAL ZONE MANAGEMENT (ICZM)

ICZM can be defined as a continuous and dynamic process by which decisions are made for the sustainable use, development and protection of coastal and marine areas and resources[31]. First and foremost, the process is designed to overcome the fragmentation inherent in both the sectoral management approach and the splits in jurisdiction among levels of government at the land-water interface. A key part of ICZM is the design of institutional processes to accomplish this harmonization is a politically acceptable manner. It is a process that recognizes the distinctive character of coastal zone-itself a valuable resource – and the importance of conserving it for current and future generations (Figure 6).

The goals of integrated coastal zone management are to achieve sustainable development of coastal and marine areas, to reduce vulnerability of coastal areas and their inhabitants to natural hazards and to maintain essential ecological processes, life support systems, and biological diversity

Figure 6: Simple Schematic of the Elements of ICZM

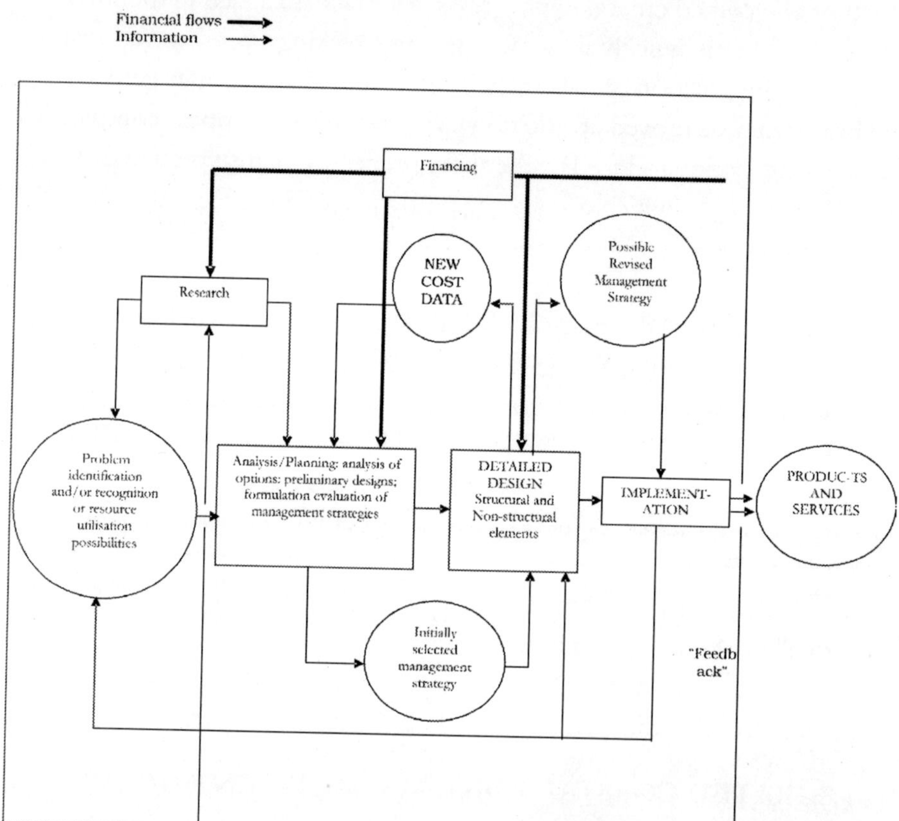

Source: Bower, B.F. (1992). Producing Information for Integrated Coastal Management Decision: An Annotated Seminar Outline, NOAA, Washington, D.C.

in coastal and marine areas[32]. it is a multipurpose oriented concept: it analyzes implications of development, conflicting uses, and interrelationships among physical processes and human activities, and it promotes linkages and harmonization between coastal and ocean activities.

Here, are questions arises, what does 'integrated' mean in ICZM? It means 'holistic'[33] which us to think about the entire spectrum of area encompassing both the land, and water, sides through its call for "integrated management and sustainable development of coastal and marine areas, including exclusive economic zones" this means, concept has broadness in land and in sea. It emphasis as well the need for proper management of marine fishery resources under national control and importance of the connection between land and sea, particularly regarding land based sources of marine pollution (Figure 7 and 8).

Figure 7: Components of a Management Strategy

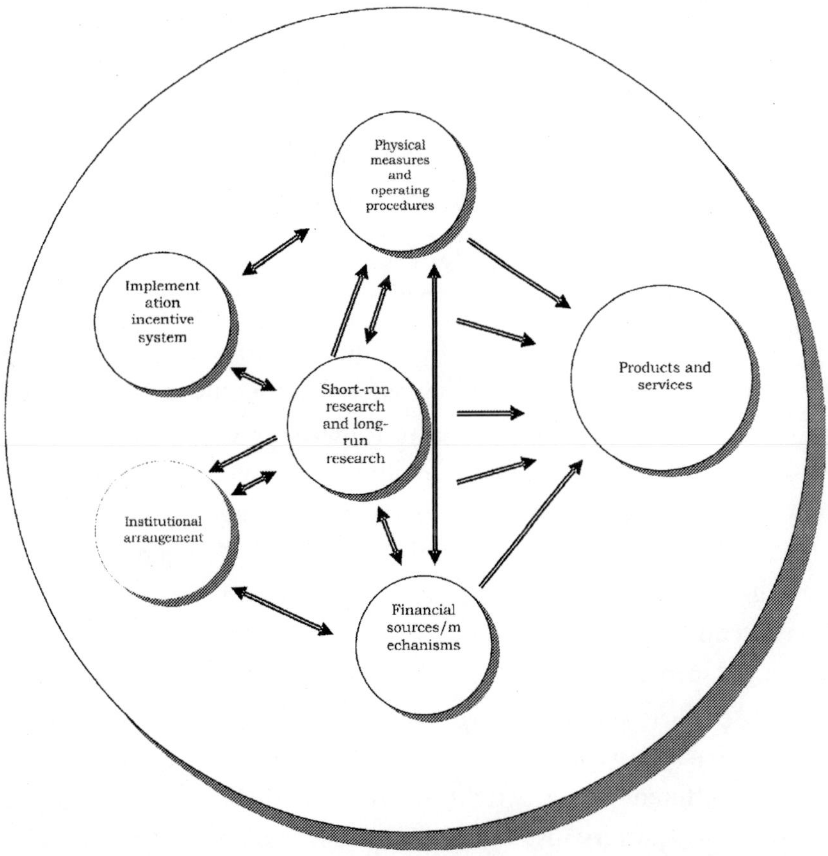

Figure 8: Coastal Problems Requiring an ICAM Approach

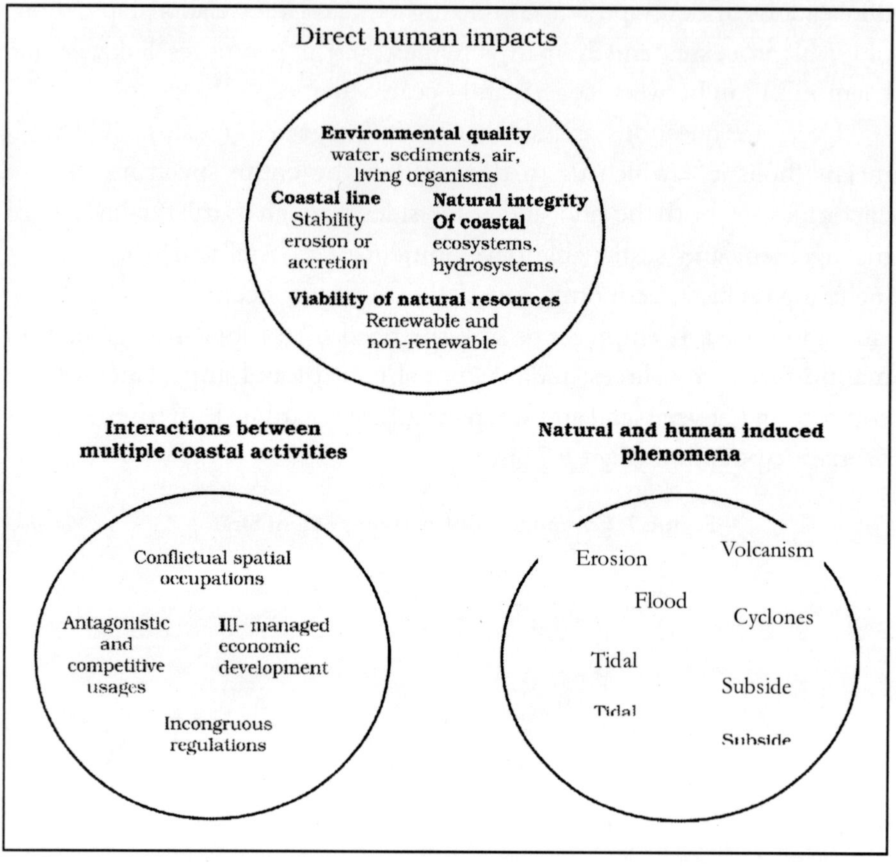

The natural processes in these five zones tend to be highly interviewed; it is difficult to integrate management regimes across the zones because the nature of property, the nature of government interests, and the nature of government institutions tend to differ in these zones.[34] In the upland areas, private property and in coastal and offshore waters, public property concerns are predominant. This generalization, though, varies from country to country. With regard to the nature of government interests, local or provincial interests tends to predominate in inland areas, whereas there tends to be mix of local, provincial, and national interests on coastal lands and coastal waters. In offshore waters and high seas, national and international interest becomes most important.

Due to different property right and interests, the nature of government institutions also differs in various zones. On land, there are often well-established "multipurpose" government institutions at the local and provincial levels to address such questions as control of land use and conflicts among uses. On the water side, there tends to be only "single purpose" provincial or national agencies operating, each concerned primarily with a single use of the ocean; such as fisheries operations or oil and gas extraction.[35] Thus, given these differences, management of coastal zone become a management of integration of complex problems may require common and complementary, yet somewhat differentiated approaches and institutions.

Table 3
Nature of Property and Government Interests and Institutions in Coastal and Ocean Areas

	Inland areas	*Coastal land*	*Coastal water*	*Offshore water*	*High sea*
Nature of property	Private	Private or public	Predominantly public		
Nature of Govt. interest	Local or provincial	Mix of local, provincial and national	—	Mainly national	Mainly
Nature of Govt. Institutions	Multipurpose agencies	—	— Single purpose agencies		

There are several dimensions of integration which can be identified:

(a) ***Intersectoral Integration:*** Integration among different sectors involves both "horizontal" integration among different coastal and marine sectors e.g. oil and gas development, fisheries, coastal tourism, marine mammal protection port development. Also addresses conflicts among government agencies in different sectors.

(b) ***Intergovernmental Integration:*** Integration among different levels of government e.g. National, provincial, local. They tend to play different roles, address different public needs and thee differences often pose problems in achieving harmonized policy development between national and sub-national levels.

(c) ***Spatial Integration:*** Integration between the land and ocean sides of the coastal zone.

(d) *Science- Management Integration:* Integration among the different disciplines important in coastal and ocean management (the natural sciences, the social sciences and engineering) and the management entities.

(e) *International Integration:* Integration among nations is needed when nations border enclosed or semi-enclosed seas or there are international disputes over fishing activities, transboundary pollution, establishment of marine boundaries, passage of ships and other issues.

Major Functions and Typical Activities of ICZM

1. **Area Planning**

   Plan for present and future uses of coastal and marine areas; provide a long term vision.

   - Studies of coastal environments and their uses
   - Zoning of uses
   - Public education about valve of coast
   - Regulation of public access to coastal areas

2. **Promotion of Economic Development**

Promote appropriate uses of coastal and marine area.

- Industrial fisheries
- Mass-tourism
- Ecotourism
- Marine aquaculture
- Marine transportation
- Post development
- Marine recreation
- Ocean research

3. **Stewardship of Resources**

   Protest the ecological base of coastal and marine areas, pressure biological diversity.

   - Conduct of environmental assessments

- Establishments and enforcement of environmental standards
- Protection and improvement of coastal water quality
- Protection of marine bio-diversity

4. Conflict Resolution

Harmonize and balance existing and potential uses; address conflicts among coastal and marine uses.

- Studies of multiple uses and their interactions
- Applications of conflict resolution methods.

5. Protection of Public Safety

Protect public safety in coastal and marine areas typically prove to significant hazards.

- Reduction of vulnerability to natural disasters and global changes
- Regulation of development in high risk areas
- Construction of coastal defense measures

6. Proprietorship of Public submerged lands and waters

As governments are often outright owners of specific coastal and marine areas and resources wisely and with good economic returns to public.

- Establishment of bases and fees for use of publicly held coastal and marine resources and space.
- Establishment of joint ventures to exploit non-renewable resources.

Thus, ICZM is a very systematic process which involves

(a) A set of both substantiate and procedural principles

(b) A management strategy that emphasizes adoption and feedback.

(c) The use of particular approaches, methods and techniques.

EVOLUTION OF THE CONCEPT OF COASTAL ZONE MANAGEMENT IN INTERNATIONAL CONTEXT

There have been two major stages in the process of worldwide recognition of the importance of marine affairs in national economics[36] (Figure 9).

One: During the decade of the 1970s there was general recognition of the importance of marine resources for economic growth of states, an increase in scientific research activities and a sustained negotiation effort at

Figure 9: The Coastal Zone Ties, Showing the Principal Distinguishing Functions and those Involved in their Implementation

Level	Functions	Players
Hemispheric	Modalities Instruments Forum Resources Technologies Methodologies	International organization International institutions
Regional	Advice Instruments Information Technologies Methodologies Training/Education	Regional Government Regional Institutions
National	Polices plan Infrastructure Regulations Capacity building	Central Government Regional institutions
Local	Valves/Priorities Infrastructure Implementation Public awareness	Non-governmental organization Local governmental organizations Public media

Source: Hay J.E. and Kay R.C. (1993): Possible Future Directions for Integrated Coastal Zone Management in the Eastern Hemisphere: A Discussion Paper. IPCC 1993, The Hague, The Netherlands, 10 pp.

the international level that culminated in the adoption of the UN convention on the Law of The Sea, 1982. Concern of the part of the developed countries over the quality of their coastal and marine environment promoted enactments such as the US coastal zone Management Act 1972 and specific measures in various supreme countries. Their experiences, although not formally replicated in the developing world. International organization started research and training programs in this field.[37]

Two: During the decade of the 1980s there has been an incipient response of governments of the opportunities available, as well as a further recognition of the responsibilities involved, in the newly acquired rights over exclusive economic zones (EEZS).

Countries are taking concrete measures relative to legal, economic and technological aspects of ocean development especially in the area of coastal zone management.[38]

These two decades have witnessed profound legal and technological changes as well as the emergence of how management practices that are intended to replace ad hoc crisis responses to marine resource problems with planned, anticipatory and integrated strategies. The evolution of the conceptually emerged as having two distinctive geographical components: coastal zone and the ocean area. The first significant modern state legislative action directed at an explicit coastal management problem was undertaken in 1959. In that Texas based an open beaches low designed to confirm public ownership of, and unimpeded access to, beaches[39]. But it was the passing of the coastal some Management Act (CZMA) in 1972 that created the greatest interest. The CZMA was designed as a finite life bill, authorizing and funding the establishment of coastal zone management programs in all coastal states.

The act had four objectives:

(i) To protect fragile coasts creeps, wetlands, lagoons sets,

(ii) To minimize life and property loss from coastal hazards,

(iii) To create better conditions for coastal resource use, especially in terms of access for recreation,

(iv) To promote inter-governmental co-operation though policy and procedural standardization, leading, hopefully, to a reduction in bureaucracy. In addition, the CZMA contains recommendations on public participation urban water front renewal and other issues. But it did not long survive in that form and changed in many new forms. If we compare the United States model, the British coastal zone management equivalent is cumbersome, middle and unlikely to be effective. Much the best coastal zone management in Britain is provided by non-statory organizations like the Nahoval Trust. Both Sheie (1976) and Steers (1978)[40] have explained how the overhaul of view United Kingdom coastal planning procedures. Coastal management in Britain has two distinct faces. A large and

> increasing portion of coastline in privately owned by the National Trust – This is strictly maintained, perceptivity, for open space, for open space amenity purposes. And other most of remaining coastline come under the direct control of planning of local planning authorities who may not make special provisions for its unique character and problems. In Holland, due to marine flooding during storm surges has led to one of the most rigorous coastal zone management programs in the world. The Dutch are highly conscious of the need to preserve the shoreline, and they have created a successful industry importing their expertise other countries, including South Korea, Bangladesh, Guyana and Egypt.

After the U.S., Britain, France and the Netherlands successful attempt towards CZM, many other developed nations also pursue active coastal management programs like Sweden, Denmark, Japan etc. Coastal Management in Denmark is integrated in a general nation wise urban and environmental planning system.[41] New Sea-land legislation and town planning practices one modeled on those of England, some recent innovations in coastal management have been borrowed from US experience[42].

While looking into the matter of coastal zone management in developed nations, the historical circumstances had played an important role. Every nation tends to face its own distinctive assemblage of contemporary problems.[43]

Hence, on a priori grounds one would not expect close similarity between different nation coastal zone management politics. It is pedagogically useful to characterize certain CZM programs in developed western nations as alternative, "deal" types or models, but it is misleading to think that these represent the full large of possible approaches the "best" programs . As those CZM policies in developing countries fall under different problems, which include corals, mangroves and beach rock.[44] One of the another aspect of CZM in developing nations is the characteristics or overuse or conflict among competing coastal resource uses. The example can be of the South Asian countries India Bangladesh and Sri Lanka. Another case can be taken of South East Asian countries, where conflicts may occur between recreational uses and off shore mining, sewage disposal or industrial dumping. Expansion of part and coastal metropolitan districts bring more serious problems.

ROLE OF UNITED NATIONS IN CZM

In bringing the management and planning the coastal zone, at International level, United Nations has played a vital role. The United Nations, through the Ocean Economics and Technology Branch (OETB) has played a fundamental role in promoting coastal zone management and enhancing the capacity of countries to deal with the variety of technical problems and policy issues involved in the design and implementation of a national program.

There can be fivefold specific goals underlie the effort at the international levels (UNEO, 1980).

- Creating awareness and familiarizing government with concept (CZM)
- Training specialists in the scientific disciplines (CZM)
- Preparing region-wide or country diagnoses of environmental conditions/economic activities taking place along the coastal areas.
- Training trainers.

Beginning in 1958, three Law of the Sea (LOS) conferences were held under the auspices of the United Nations to sort out the right and duties of nations regarding the ocean. It was, finally, after the United States, the Soviet Union and other maritime nation lauded to the demands of developing nations to include consideration of an international regime for the resources of the deep seabed, agreement was reached to hold a third United Nations conference on the Law of the Sea (UNECOS III) in 1973. After nine years of negotiation, in 1982, that world's oceans, giving legitimacy to concept of 200 nautical-mile exclusive economic zones. The convention comes into force (after ratification by sixty nations) twelve years after conclusion of the conference in 1982, on November 16, 1994.

Section 17.6 – 'Management Related Activities" states: each coastal should consider establishing, or where necessary strengthening coordinating mechanisms (such as a high level planning policy body) for integrated management and sustainable development of coastal marine areas and their resources, at both local and national levels such national coordinating mechanisms could provide, inter alia, and implementation of integrated coastal and marine management and sustainable plans and programs at appropriate levels.

AGENDA 21

The World Meteorological Organization (WMO) and the United Nations Environment Program (UNEP) with assistance of the International Council of Scientific Unions (ICSU), in 1988, created Inter Governmental Panel on Climate Change (IPCC). The IPEC (largely a scientific body) was charged with assessing the magnitude of the climate change problem and responses. In first formal assessment in June 1990, the IPCC predicted that global temperature could be expected to rise by about 2-3^{0}C over the next 100 years. As a part of the work of this group, an IPCC subgroup on Coastal Zone Management developed a program for assessing the vulnerability of low laying coastal nations to seal-level rise.

The United Nations Conference on Environment and Development (UNCED) conversed in Rio de Janeiro on June 3-14, 1992. Fire major outputs emerged from UNCED.

- The Rio Declaration on environment and development
- The framework convention on climate change
- The convention on biological diversity
- Agenda 21
- A set of forest principles

The Rio Declaration is a set of twenty-seven principles to guide national and international actions on environment, development and social issues, was approved by all nations attending the conference.

While, Agenda 21, a forty chapter action plan, was intended to serve as a kind of road map pointing the direction towards sustainable development. In the areas of natural resources and the environment, Agenda 21 deals with the atmosphere, land resources, deforestation, desertification and drought, mountain ecosystems, agriculture and rural development, biological diversity, biotechnology, ocean and coastal areas, fresh water resources, toxic chemicals, hazardous wastes, solid wastes, and radioactive waste. It has chapters devoted to the roles of major groups, including women, children and youth, indigenous peoples, non-governmental organizations, local authorities, workers and trade unions, business and industry the scientific and technological community, and farmers. Finally, the concerning means of implementation. It discusses financial resources, transfer of technology, the roles of science, education, public awareness and training, capacity building, institutional arrangements, legal institutions, and information for decision making.

OCEAN AND COASTAL ISSUES IN CHAPTER 17 OF AGENDA 21

Chapter 17 of Agenda 21 deals with the major prescriptions for ocean and coastal management under titled, "Protection of the Oceans, All Kinds of Seas, including enclosed and semi-enclosed seas and coastal areas and the protection, rational use and development of their living resources."[45] This is the longest chapter of Agenda 21 (forty – two pages). The introduction to the chapter (Page 17.1) stresses both the importance of oceans and coasts in the global life support system and the positive opportunity for sustainable development that ocean and coastal areas represent. The introduction stresses upon new approaches to marine and coastal area management will be needed and also scores that the United Nations conversion on the Law of the Sea" provides the International basis upon which to pursue the protection and sustainable development.

Search major program areas are included in Chapter 17,[46]

(1) Integrated management and sustainable development of coastal areas, including exclusive economic zone

(2) Marine environmental protection

(3) Sustainable use and conservation of living marine resources of the high seas;

(4) Sustainable use and conservation of living marine resources under national jurisdiction;

(5) The addressing of critical uncertainties in management of the marine environment and climate change.

(6) The strengthening of international, including regional, cooperation and coordination and;

(7) Sustainable development of small islands.

While every section of program area contains a text of relevance to coastal managers and decision makers. Sections 17.5 and 17.6 are perhaps the most important in the context of this study. Section 17.5[1] "objectives", states: coastal states commit themselves to integrated management and sustainable management of coastal areas under this national jurisdiction.[47]

Section 17.5 contains a number of sub-sections which elaborate specific coastal management objectives, including inter – sectoral planning, adopting a precautionary approach, and monitoring needs.

THE COASTAL REGULATION ZONE OF GOA

Current developmental trends along the coast of Goa offer an opportunity to evaluate the effectiveness of the Coastal Regulation Zone (CRZ) legislation. The mandatory 'No Development Zones' in proximity to, and as buffers for, ecosystems have sufficient oceanographic and environmental validity to be upheld. However, this instrument is being opposed and misinterpreted. Sectoral practices, partisan policies, unbalanced tourism, and absence of political will have all contributed to the CRZ being breached. A national authority that can interact authoritatively with multiple agencies appears to be the only way to attenuate impacts on and restore resilience of coastal ecosystems. Until the 1970s, the coastal zone of Goa was largely pristine. Subsequently, this zone witnessed a rapid increase in population and a dramatic growth in developmental activities after tourism was avidly promoted. Since unplanned development had started along other coastal strips of the country as well, a national legislation, known as Coastal Regulation Zone (CRZ) notification, was formulated in 1991. Goa became a focus of the legislation because coastal tourism is a major economic activity in the state.

Socio-economic pressures drive changes in coastal ecosystems. The international program on Land–Ocean Interaction in the Coastal Zone (LOICZ) has identified four areas of investigations. One of these addresses changes to coastal systems due to social and economic activities. Since coastal tourism and related anthropogenic activities (figure 6) have intensified during the last two decades, and considering various adverse impacts of tourism on coasts worldwide, the Goa coast offers an opportunity to test the use and effectiveness of coastal legislations with respect to human activity and eco-sensitive coastal systems. This study attempts to analyze issues related to the CRZ of Goa from oceanographic, environmental and societal viewpoints. The coastal zone of Goa is characterized by sandy stretches and an intricate network of water bodies across lowlands. The sea front is marked by a combination of beaches, rocky shores and headlands. Of the 105 km long coast, more than 70 km comprise linear and wide sandy beaches, all backed by 1 to 10 m high dunes; sandy pockets and secluded coves backed by rocky cliffs are also found. The coastal plain, 20 to 35 km in width, consists of lowlands traversed by seven major and four minor river systems that experience tides. Small islands, shoals and mangrove swamps are observed within water bodies.

NOTES

1. Label, G.H. and H.Kane (1987). Sustainable Development. A guide to our Common future. The report of the world commission on environment and Development. Oxford University Press Oxford.
2. The world's largest coastal urban agglomerations (i.e.) Tokyo, New York, Mexico City, Sao Paolo, shanghai, Bombay, Los Angeles, Calcutta, Buenos, Aires, Seoul, Osaka, Rio De Jamero, Jakarta, Metro Manila, Karachi, Logos, Istanbul, Bangkok and Dacca) are expected to increase from a total population of 216.9 million in 1990 to 353.5 million in year 2015 (UN, 1994).
3. Sinha P. C. (1998). Impact of globalization of coastal Megacities in the Indian Ocean Rim Countries, Conference on Coastal Magazines, June 21-24.
4. Carter, R.W. Civil (1988). Coastal Environment. An introduction to Physical, Ecological and Cultural Systems of Coastlines, Academic Press, London.
5. Chua, T.E L.F. Secura, eds. (1992). Integrated Framework and Methods for coastal Area Management. ICLARM conference proceding 12, Manila.
6. Edwards, S.F (1987). An introduction to coastal zone Economics: Concepts Methods, and case Studies, New York: Taylor and Francis.
7. The world's largest coastal Urban agglomerations (i.e.) Tokyo, New York, Mexico city, Sao Pasolo, Shughai, Bombay, Los Angeles, Calcutta, Burno airs, Aeoul, Osaka, Riode Jamero, Jakarta, Metro Manila, Karachi, Lagos, Ustanbul;k, Bangkok and Dacca). Are exported to increase for a total population of 216.9 million in 1990 to 353.5 million in year 2015 (UN 1994).
8. Sen Gupta. R. (1986). Marine Pollution, Proc. Haudian Acada, Sci. (Anim-sei) vol. 95. No. 3Kime 86 pp 325-339.
9. Krishna Moorthy. R. *et al.* (1994) study of suspended sediment concentration in coastal water in Tamil Nadu. Proceedings ISRS silver jubilee symposium (Published by ISRO H.Q. Bangalore ISRO Dehradun, India) pp 222-229.
10. Naidu B.R and A. Manmohan (1990) import of distillery effluent through sub marine out fall on Pondicherry coast, All India seminar on Sea out falls, Bombay.
11. *Op. Cit.* No. 10.
12. Pollution potential of industries in coastal Area of India, COPOCS 1995-1996.

13. National Inventory of large and Medium industry and state of effluent treatment and mission control system (vol I & II), control pollution control Board, PROB & S/68/1997-98.

14. Clark, J.R (1996). coastal zone Management Hand book. New York: CRC Lewis Publications.

15. Clark J. R. (1992). Integrated Management of Coastal Zone: FAO Fisheries Technological Paper No. 327. Rome.

16. Hinrichsen D (1994). "Coast under pressure". People and Planet 3(1) 6-9.

17. *Ibid*, 16.

18. Broadey, James M and Gaines, A.G (1987). Coastal and Marine are management in Gatapagos Islands' coastal Management 15: 78-88.

19. Shipiro, Harvey A. (1980). "Two Approaches to coastal area planning in Japan", in coastal Zone 80 New York: American Society of Civil Engineers.

20. Harou Akoi, (1989). A comprehensive utilization, Method for Coastal Areas River Bureau, Ministry of Construction, Tokyo, Japan. Pp. 265-67.

21. UPEP (1991). Strategies for Protection and Development of ocean and coastal Areas, 1991.

22. Srenson, J and S.T. McCreary (1990). Institutional Arrangements for Managing Coastal Resources and Environments, coastal management Publication No.1 (rev.) NPS/US AID series. National Park Services, Washington D.C. 194.

23. Resource Assessment Commission (1993) Coastal Zone Inquiry final report, common wealth of Australia, Australian Government Publishing service.

24. Dorcuy, A.J.H. (1986) Bergaining in the governance of Pacific coastal Resources: Research and Reform. West water Research centre, Faculty of Graduate studies, University of British Columbia Vancouver.

25. Pitts D (1993). Analysis of Strategic Planning Processes of ==== for Coastal Zone Management Resource Assessment Commission Consultancy Report, Commonwealth of Australia, 53.

26. Mason, R.O. and Mitroft I.T. (1981). Challenging strategic Planning Assumptions: theory, cases and Techniques, John Willy and Sons, New York

27. *Ibid*, 4, pp. 9.

28. Sorensen, J.C. and S.T. McCreary (1980): Institutional Arrangements for Managing Coastal Resources and Environment, Coastal Management Publication No.1 (Rev.) NPS/US AID series. National Park Service, Washington D.C. 194.

29. Chua, T.E. (1993). "Essential Elements of Integrated Coastal Management," ocean and Coastal Management 21 (1-3): 81–108.

30. Lundin, C.G. and O.Linden (1993) coastal Ecosystems: Attempts to Manage a Threatened Resource". AMBIO XXII (7): 468-73.

31. *Ibid*; 16.

32. *Ibid*; 15.

33. Chua, T.E, and L.F Suvra edc, (1992). Integrative framework and methods for coastal area management. ICLARM conference proceeding 12, Manila.

34. Prescott, J.R.V. (1985). The Maritime Political Boundaries of the world, London; Methuen.

35. *Ibid*, 42.

36. Vallego, Stella Maris A. (1986). 'Coastal Areas and the Exclusive Economic Zone: Basic Consideration for Planning and Management', integrated Ocean Management 5: 9.30.

37. Vallego, S. (1987), Existing Coastal Zone Management Training Programs and Resources at the International Level, report prepared for the Coastal Resources Culture, Kingston R. I. University of Rhode Island.

38. Ascher, A.N. (1987): Coastal Management in United States: A Selective Review and Summary, report prepared for the Coastal Resource Centre, Kingston, R.I.: University of Rhode Island.

39. Earl H. Bradley, Jr. and John M. Armstrong (1972). A Description and Analysis of Coastal Zone and Shoreland Management Programs in U.S., Seagrant Technical Report No. 20 (Ann. Arbor: University of Michigan, Sea Grant Program Coastal Zone Management Project, 1972) pp. 385-87.

40. Sheie John (1976). "Coasts and Planning in Great Britain," Geographical Journal 142 (July 1976): 411-37.

41. Richard G. Hildreth (1976), "Coastal land use control in Sweden and Denmark", *Coastal Zone Management Journal* (2): 1-30.

42. Mcban R.F., "Coastal Research in New Zealand; Geoscience and Man, Vol. VI Coastal Research (Baton Rouge): Louisiana State University school of Geoscience.

43. Valtego Stella Maris A. (1987). "Existing Coastal Zone Management Training Programs and Resources at International Level," Report prepared for the Resource Centre, Kingston, R. I., University of Rhode Island.

44. (UNEP 1980). Ecosystem in Danger in Nairobi UNEP Report – No.4.

45. United Nation (1992): "Agenda 21" in : The Outcome of the United Nations Conference on Environment and Development Rio de Janerio, Brazil, 3-14 June, 1992.
46. *Ibid*, 47.
47. *Ibid*, 47.

CHAPTER 3

SPATIAL ANALYSIS OF ADMINISTRATIVE ACTIONS AND PROBLEMS OF INTEGRATED COASTAL ZONE MANAGEMENT: GOA (INDIA)

GEOGRAPHY OF GOA

Goa has been described as a tropical paradise ensconced in the Western Ghats with a coastline dotted with palm groves. The name Goa derives from the pastoral and cattle herding communities (go-) of Gopa. They gave such names as Goparashtra, Gaurashtra, Gomantak and Goa, and the lent their name to the river Gomati. They are probably the ancestors of present day Gauda of the Western Ghats. The name Gouba is mentioned by Ptolemy in second century A.D. but probably the first explicit reference to Goa occurs in the 12th century. The Portuguese attempt to link Goa to Lisbon. Etymologically and phonetically, was a little too farfetched.

Goa remained a Portuguese colony for 451 years (1510 to 1961). In this period, a large number of people were converted to Christianity. There was a dark phase that witnessed ruthless oppressor. However, there was also a great deal of interaction between the indigenous and alien cultures, which is reflected in art.[1]

On the 30th of May 1987, Goa became a State within the Indian Union, thus becoming the twenty-fifth State India, the youngest state in the country. Goa, however, had been integrated into the Indian Union on 19th December 1961 after 451 years of Portuguese colonial rule. Goa is considered 'a pearl of the Orient' and is well known for its scenic beauty, long stretches of golden beaches, beautiful temples, architecturally rich churches and the green countryside situated on the one side of the Arabian Sea.

Regional division Goa forms part of Western Coastal Region Goa coast micro region is comprised of Goa district only. It spreads between 14°-54' and 15° – 48' north latitudes and 73°-41' and 74°-20' east longitudes. It is flanked by district Ratnagiri (Maharashtra state) in the north, district Belgaum and Uttar Kannad (Karnataka State) in the east and south respectively. The Arabian sea makes its western boundary.

Goa, the smallest state in India with an area of 3702 km^2, lies in the west coast. Goa is the prime tourist destination of India, and the tourism industry is growing rapidly. Associated with this growth, changes could be detected in the land-use, especially along the coastal belt such as construction of buildings, environment-friendly industries, resorts, breakwaters, minor harbors, expansion of a major port, etc. Goa has been experiencing a lot of changes in its land-use patterns. It has become necessary to detect the changes happening around this region as this may help determine the level of stress that the coastal zone of Goa is facing. Increasing tourism appears to drive land-use/land-cover changes in Goa. Coastal geomorphic features, sediment transport and coastal vegetation (mangroves) have been studied using remote sensing data. As Goa is one of the global tourist destinations of the world, more development is expected along the coastal zone, and subsequently there will be changes in the land-use/land-cover pattern in the coming years.

Location and Climate

The Goa State lies between 14° and 16° North latitude and 73° and 75°East longitude. It is situated on the West Coast of India and is surrounded by the Arabian Sea on the west, Sindhudurg district of Maharashtra on the north, Sahyadri Mountains on the east and Uttara Kannada district of Karnataka on the south. For administrative purpose, the State is divided into two districts viz. North Goa District and South Goa District with 6 and 5 Talukas respectively. The climate is warm and humid. It receives heavy precipitation varying from 1500 to 3400 mm during the period from June to September from South-West monsoons. The maximum and minimum temperature ranges from 17.4°C to 36°C with relative humidity variation from 76 per cent to 86 per cent.

Geology of Goa

The geology of Goa is varied ranging from Recent to Archaean ages. Large area of the district had grey wackeargillite covering most part of Goa plateau

Figure 1: Rainfall Record in Goa, 2005

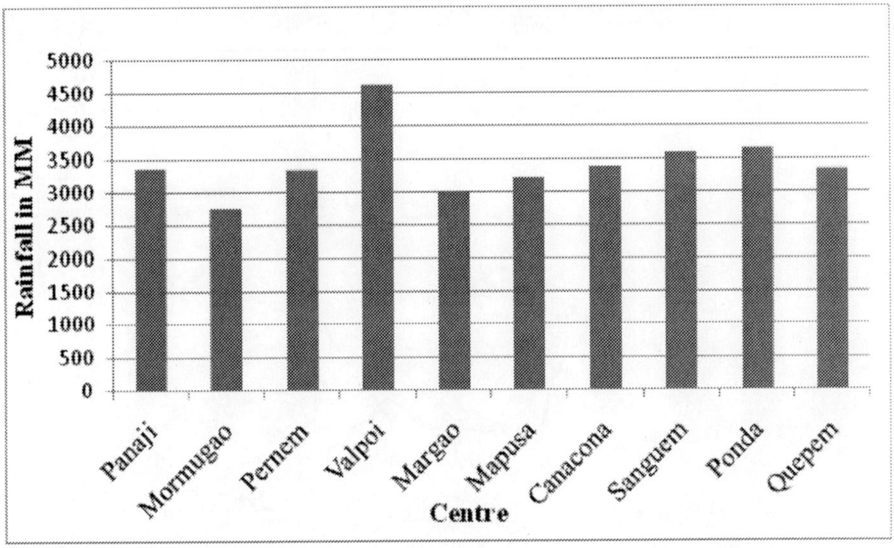

Source: Statistical Handbook of the Government of Goa for the relevant years.

and northern half of coastal Goa.[2] There is a long strip of Ultramafic magic complex in the plateau region in north west to south east direction with many bends. The rocks of the Goa Group exhibit evidences, essentially of three cycles of folding . The first fold movement resulted in a general E-W trending, round hinged upright normal fold. The second cycle of folding, which was the most powerful movement, was responsible for the development of NW-SE trending folds overturned towards southwest, and plunging towards NW and SE. The third fold movement has resulted in a NW plunging broad open synclinal fold with its axis running in N30~ direction. Along the coast, west of Margao and river Sal there is an elongated stretch of the recent alluvium. The south western part of Goa mostly covered under dense forests, has metabasalt and polymict conglomerate of Chitradurga group and migmatites and granodioritic to tonalitic Gneisses of Archaean age. In the western part, the extension of metabasalt and Gneisses is found along the coast and even implateau area and the southern part of goa Sahyadri hills. The geology of Sahyadri hill area is relatively complex. Besides large patches of granites (Sensu Lato) and greywacke-argillite there are rocks of limestone and dolmite, quartzite and conglomerate in the area falling west of Valpoi town in Satari Taluk. In the northwestern portion of Satari Taluk deposits of Deccan Trap are also observed. The

Figure 2: Location of Study Area

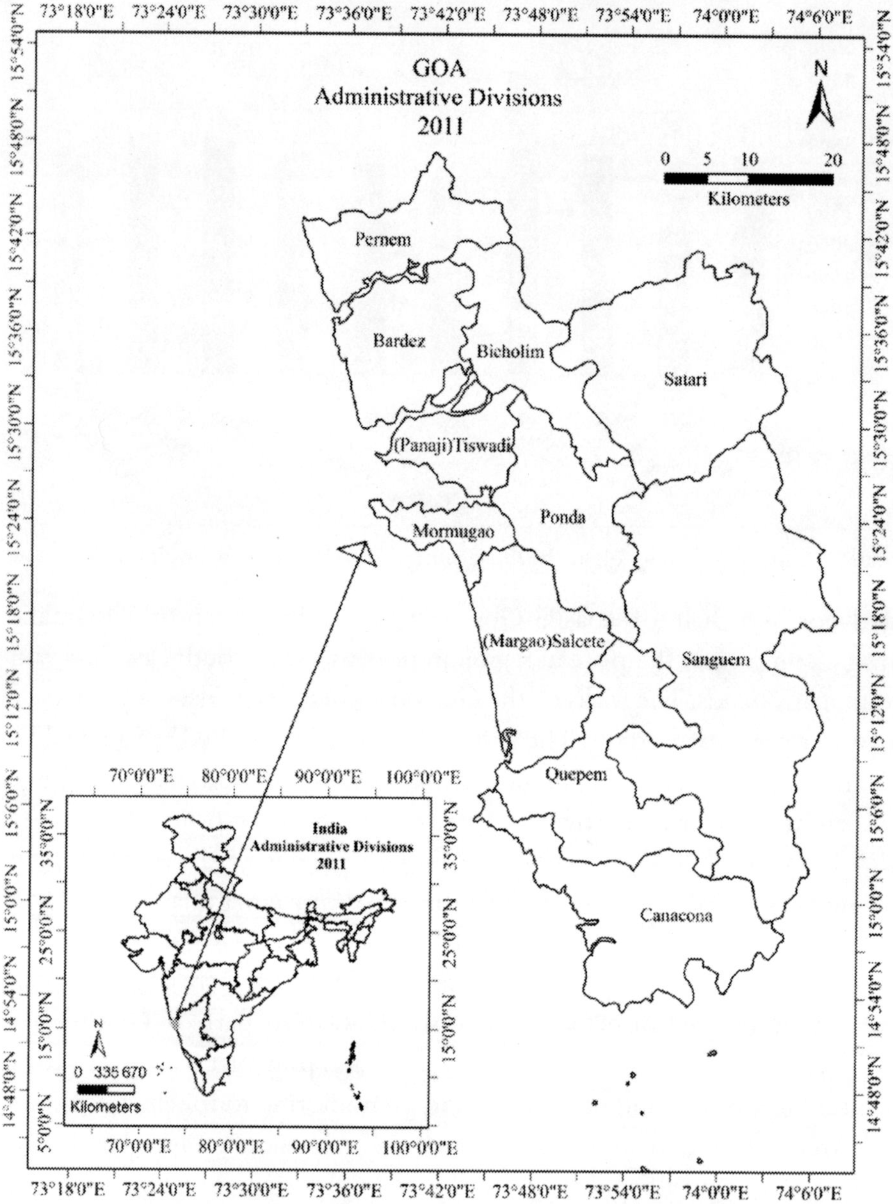

hilly region from where river Dudhasagar emergence has some lateritic formation of Paleocene to Recent ages. The dykes are frequently seen all over the district.

The Soils of Goa

The soil, in general, is laterite. The agricultural lowlands especially in the coastal tract, are alluvial flats formed through sedimentation along the principal rivers. Nearly one fourth area in the district is under forest.

The region has undulating hilly terrain with diverse soil conditions especially on its eastern side, where lies the southern end of the Sahyadri ranges. The terrain is intersected by a number of rivers flowing westwards, which provides a network of internal waterways. Three types of soils viz. i) Laterite or lateritic, ii) Alluvial and iii) Sandy are found in the region. About 2,75,900 ha. (81 per cent of the total area) are of the first category and are highly acidic in nature, sandy loam to silt loam in texture and well drained. They are poor in lime, Phosphorus and Potash, but fairly good in organic matter and Nitrogen. About 24,950 ha. (7.4 per cent of the total area) is alluvials, 17,600 ha. of which are subject to inundation of saline water and have to be protected by bunds to grow crops successfully. The nine kilometers coastal inland comprises of a stretch of 38,000 ha. (11.2 percent of the total area) half of which has a high water table and could be exploited for irrigation. These soils are also acidic, sandy to sandy loams, fairly rich in organic matter but very deficient in Phosphate and Potash.

Regional Division

Based on physiogeographic details, Goa district permitted itself to be sub-divided into four sub-micro regions i.e. 4th order regions. These are:[4]

1. Goa Coast
2. Goa Plateau
3. Sahyadri Hills
4. Chauri forested coast

Goa Coast

This region is largest and is situated in western part of the district comprising whole of Bardez, Tiswadi, Mormugao and Salcete talukas and parts of quepem, Pernem, Bicholim and Ponda talukas. The region extends between river Terekol in the north and estuary of Sal river in the south. With the exception of few local hills, the elevation does not exceed 100 metres and the land slopes towards the west i.e. the Arabian Sea.

Terekol, Chapora, Mandovi, Zuari and Sal are the main rivers flowing in this region. These coastal plains are the infilled stretches of these rivers which have deposited the eroded material from the Sahyadris. River Terekol rises from the Sahyadries in Maharashtra and flows along the northern boundary of this region, more so the district, and merges-into the Arabian Sea. Chapora and Mandovi rivers have their source in Karnataka. The Zuari and Sal rivers originate within the Goa district and merge into the Sea.

Goa Plateau

This plateau region broadly curves round the region Goa coast. Goa plateau includes parts of Quepem, Pernem, Bicholim, Ponda, Satari and Sanguem talukas. In general the elevation varies between 100 metres and 200 metres. There are, however, some local spots where the height crosses even more than 400 metres and these are the offshoots of Sahyadri hills. Further, at places these offshoots extend even upto the coast where they form headlands. Al the main rivers after rising from the Sahyadris, flow through this region.

Sahyadri Hills

This region lies in the extreme east of the district and includes parts of Satari, Sanguem and Canacona talukas. A small part of Quepem Taluka also fall in this region. The Sahyadri hills serve as a water- divide between the rivers flowing towards the Arabian sea in the west and those flowing towards Bay of Bengal in the east. These hills are characterized by steep slopes. The transition from the Goa Plateau (which in general, is at an elevation of 200 meters) to the Sahyadri hills is abrupt. At some places the Sahyadrihills have an elevation of more than 800 meters. The terrain is intersected by a number of rivers. With the exception of river Sal, all the rivers flowing through the district originate from the Sahyadri hills.

Nearly three-fifths of the area in this region is under forests. Broadly speaking there are two types of forests wet evergreen and moist deciduous. The wet evergreen are typical rainforests. These are found all along the hills with heavy rainfall. The moist deciduous forests or the monsoon forests from the natural cover over the Sahyadri hills. These forests are less resistant to fire and other man induced interference.

Chauri Forested Coast

This is the smallest region in the district. It lies to the south of Sal estuary in the south-western part of the district. It includes parts of Queepem and Canacona talukas. Anjadip islands of Canacona which is situated off karwar coasts also forms part of the region.

In general, the region has an elevation of below 200 meters and the land slopes towards the sea. However, some local hills in this region have a much higher elevation. There is no major river which flows through this region. The small streams flowing through this region originate from the Sahyadri hills.

Demography

The population of Goa constitutes around 0.12 per cent of the country's population as against 0.13% during the 2001 Census. Hence, there is a slight decrease of 0.01 per cent in Goa's share in the total population of the country as compared to the previous Census. The population of Goa as per 2011 Census is 14, 58,545 as against the country's total population of 1,210,569,573. As per the last population census held during 2001, the population of Goa was 13, 47,668 which has now increased to 14, 58,545 recording an increase of 1, 10,877 persons during the last Decade, thereby registering a decadal growth of 8.23 per cent. The population of Goa and its decadal growth rate during 1900 – 2011 are given in Table 1 & Figure 3.

Figure 3: District wise Distribution of Population in Goa (1900-2011)

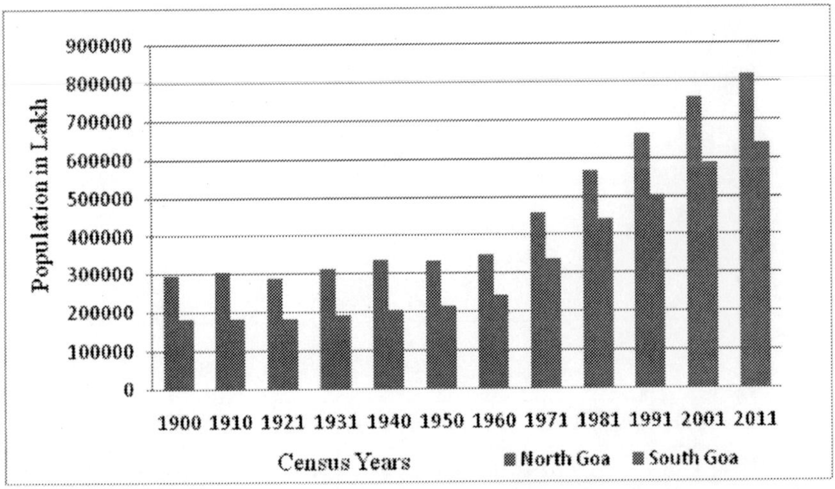

Table 1
Year wise Population and Decadal Growth of Goa1900 – 2011

Sr.No.	*Year*	*Total Population*	*Decadal variation*	*Decadal growth (%)*
1	1900	475513		
2	1910	486752	11239	2.36
3	1921	469494	-17258	-3.55
4	1931	505281	35787	7.62
5	1940	540925	35644	7.05
6	1950	547448	6523	1.21
7	1960	589997	42549	7.77
8	1971	795120	205123	34.77
9	1981	1007749	212629	26.74
10	1991	1169793	162044	16.08
11	2001	1347668	177875	15.21
12	2011	1458545	110877	8.23

Source: Directorate of Census Operations, Panaji Goa.

The decadal growth rates observed during the first two decades after liberation were very high i.e. 34.77 per cent and 26.74 per cent respectively. The rate of growth observed during the decade of 1981 - 1991(16.08%) and 1991- 2001 (15.21 per cent) were quite low as compared to the earlier two decades. The rate of growth further reduced to 8.23% during the last decade (Figure 4).

Figure 4: Decadal Growth Rate of Population in Goa (1910-2011)

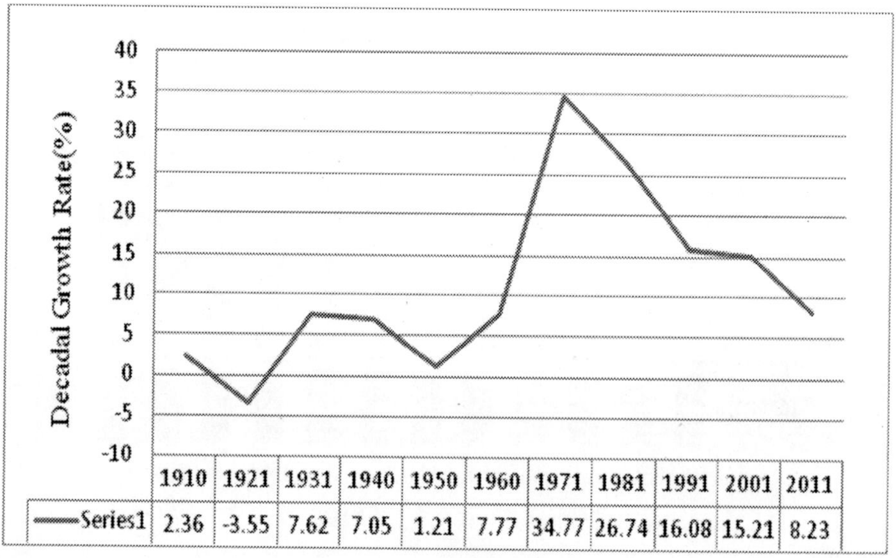

It can be seen from Table 2, out of the total population of 14,58,545, there are 8,18,008 persons in North Goa district which constitute 56.08 percent of the total population, whereas 6, 40,537 persons who comprise the remaining 43.92 percent are in South Goa district. This proportion of population a decade ago in North Goa and South Goa districts was 56.29 per cent and 43.71 per cent respectively. An analysis of the table shows the population of North Goa District was higher than that of South Goa District Throughout all the censuses from 1900 to 2011. Accounts for 8, 18,008 (56.08 per cent) of the total population while South Goa District accounted for 6, 40,537 (43.92 per cent) of the total population. The percentage variation in the composition of population in the two districts from 1900 to 1940 was around 24 per cent. Thereafter the gap started narrowing down. In 1950 the gap was 21 per cent, which went on steadily decreasing to 13 per cent in 1981, and thereafter the gap has almost stabilized around 13 per cent and in 2011 the percentage variation in the composition of population between the two districts of the State stood at 12 per cent.

Table 2

District wise Composition of Population1900 – 2011

Year	*North Goa*	*South Goa*	*North Goa (% to total Population)*	*South Goa (% to total Population)*
1900	294074	181439	61.84	38.16
1910	306323	180429	62.93	37.07
1921	288039	181455	61.35	38.65
1931	313614	191667	62.07	37.93
1940	336628	204297	62.23	37.77
1950	330874	216574	60.44	39.56
1960	349667	240330	59.27	40.73
1971	458312	336808	57.64	42.36
1981	568021	439728	56.37	43.63
1991	664804	504989	56.83	43.17
2001	758573	589095	56.29	43.71
2011	818008	640537	56.08	43.92

Source: Directorate of Census Operations, Panaji Goa.

Goa has a total population of 14, 58,545 persons of which 739140 (50.68%) are males and the remaining 719405 (49.32 per cent) are females indicating a sex ratio of 973 females per thousand males. This ratio is much above the national average of 940. Goa ranks at 10th position in the country in respect of sex ratio. The District wise sex ratio in the State as per the census from 1900 to 2011 is given in table and Figure 2, 5.

Figure 5: District wise Sex Ratio of Goa (1900-2011)

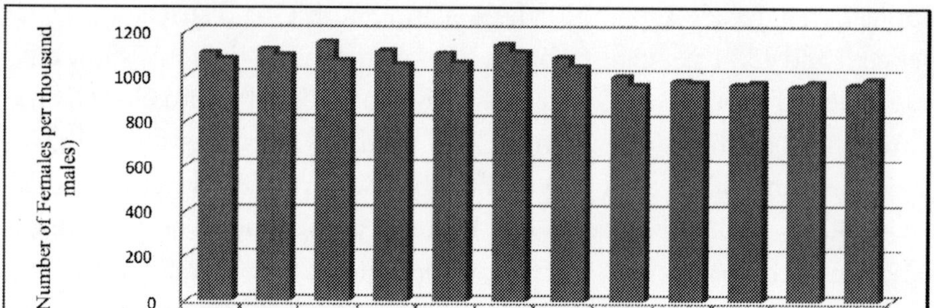

	1900	1910	1921	1931	1940	1950	1960	1971	1981	1991	2001	2011
North Goa	1102	1118	1154	1111	1100	1142	1083	998	979	963	953	963
South Goa	1074	1091	1069	1052	1058	1107	1041	959	971	971	972	986

Land Use

Out of 11 taluks in the state 7 are coastal Orchard including pasture is the dominant user of land in the region, whereas natural cover and forest is dominant in the inland talukas. Around 19 percent of the reporting area is under cultivation in the coastal talukas while it is only 8.67 percentages in land talukas.

The Goa coast has long, linear and wide beaches on the northern side and rocky cliffs mainly along the southern part (Figure). Beaches are observed at north of Cape Rama to Vasco Da Gamma, near Kalanghut, Near Ubhadanda and NW of Mapuca. Mudflats occur along the Mandovi estuary and Marmgoa Bay. Coastal dunes are found with Casurina plantation near Madgaon and Kalanghut. Table shows Coastal landuse classes of Goa. Mudflat 20.52 sq km, Forest plantation occupies 1669.96 sq km, Habitation with vegetation occupies 262.15 sq km and wasteland occupies 204.38 sq km (Table 3).

Agriculture

Agriculture is one important activity in the Goa coastal zone and paddy is the main cultivation in the coastal zone. It has the share of 40.51 percent in the total net cropped area of the state 70.40 percent of the total paddy cultivation of Goa is done in the coastal talukas (1986-87). Salcete taluka

Table 3
Coastal Land use area of Goa (2006)

Land-use class	*Area in sq km*
Agricultural-land	395.63
Forest (non-tidal) / plantation	1669.96
Beach-patch	5.5
Bar-barrier-island	1.34
Rocky-coast	0.39
Creek	15.19
Pond-lake	8.1
Rock-outcrops/gullied	116.22
Mining areas/dumps	0.84
Wasteland	204.38
Habitation	17.49
Open/vacant-land	14.41
Industrial-area	2.13
Aquaculture-ponds	1.75
Inter-tidal-mudflat	13.12
High-tidal-mudflat	7.4
Mangroves-very-dense	4.53
Mangroves-dense	17.77
Mangroves-sparse	3.69
Mangroves-degraded	5.48
River-stream	135.15
Waterlogged	5.39
Reservoir/tank	17.83
Habitation(veg)	262.15
Port/harbour/jetty	5.03
Mud-with-vegetation	3.39
Scrub-dense	96.31
Scrub-sparse	191.06
Scrub-degraded	51.67
Total Area	3274.00

Source: Space Applications Centre, ISRO, Ahmadabad

alone has the share of more than 20 percent. Paddy is followed by coconut and cashew nut cultivation in coastal zone. Other crops such as oil seeds, pulses, sugarcanes etc. are also grown. In 1989-90, the yield of rice was (Kharit) 2135 kg per hectare and rice (Rabbi) was 2500 kg per hectare in coastal talukas. Another thing which is alarming is that 95 per cent of the coastal zone paddy cultivation and others are covered by heavy dose of chemical fertilizers.

Figure 6: Coastal land use Distribution of Goa (2006)

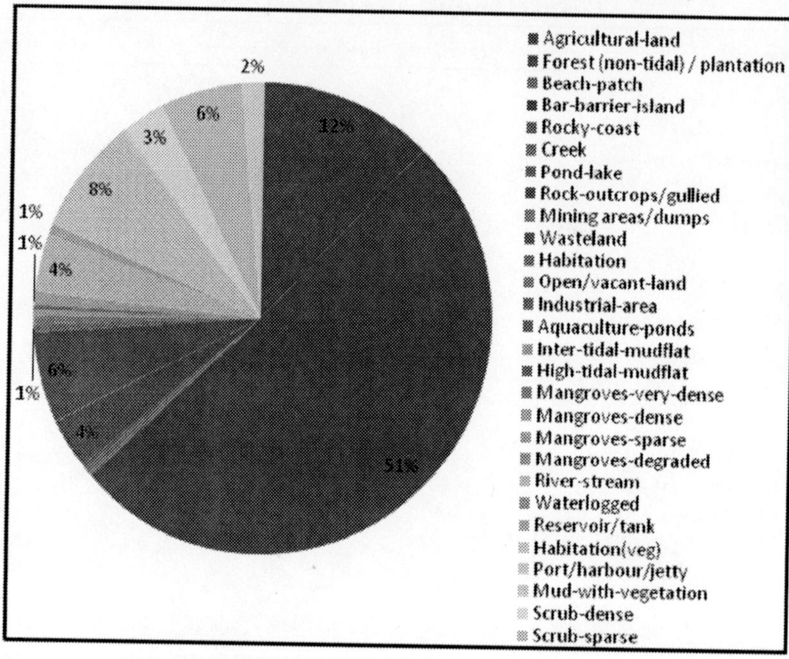

Source: Space Applications Centre, ISRO, Ahmadabad

Table 4
Agriculture Land and Production (1960-2010)

Name of the Crop	*1960-61 Area (Ha)*	*Total Production (Ton)*	*2009-10 Area (Ha)*	*Total Production (Ton)*
Paddy	50302	79948	47104	150919
Pulses	6998	3500	7890	8535
Groundnut	50	49	2828	8055
Sugarcane	70	2822	893	52343
Cashewnut	32517	3000	55732	17556
Coconut	18497	70 (million nuts)	25686	128.76 (millionnuts)
Arecanut	1721	1735	1713	2795
Banana	1100	6600	2219	24662
Pineapple	40	400	273	4520
Vegetables	78	634	5671	58130
Black Pepper	-	-	717	230

Source: Directorate of Agriculture, Government of Goa

The State has been blessed with such soils and climatic conditions that it favors growth of a variety of tropical crops. Rice is the principal crop, which covers 52,177 ha. accounting for about 30.66% of the total cropped area. It is grown both in Kharif and Rabi seasons. Ragi is another cereal which occupies nearly 441 ha. or about 0.27%. The area under Ragi is found to be declining over the years. Area under pulses is 10,978 ha. or 6.45 percent which are grown mainly in Rabi season – on residual moisture after Kharif paddy. Sugarcane covers 1,110 ha (Table 4). This is also about 1%. Cashew nut and coconut are another two important cash crops which occupy nearly 55,021 ha. and 25,312 ha. or 32 and 15 % respectively and water requirement and Demand also increase showing Table 5.

Table 5
Estimated Sectoral Water Requirement (BCM)

	Year 2010		*Year 2025*		*Year 2050*	
	Goa	*India*	*Goa*	*India*	*Goa*	*India*
Irrigation	2.56	557	3.08	561	3.2	807
Domestic	0.16	43	0.21	55	0.25	111
Industries	0.41	37	0.54	67	0.78	81
Energy				19	31	70
Inland navigation				7	10	15
Ecology				5	10	20
Evaporation				42	50	76
Total	3.13	710	3.83	796	4.23	1180

Source: Statistical Handbook of the Government of Goa for the relevant years.

Table 6
Agriculture Scenario & Land utilization in Goa Pattern of land area in Ha-2009

Total Areafor Land Utilization	3,61 ,113
Forest Cover	1.25,473 - 34.74%
Land Not Availabel For Cultivation	37 ,137
Permanent Pastures & Other Grazing Land	1,305
Cultivable Waste Land	52,533
Net Areas Own	1,31,387
Area Sown Moret Han Once	28,733
Food Grain Crops	55,148 Ha. - 37.65%
Horticulture Crops	1, 01,481 Ha. - 59 .54 %
Sugarcane, Oil Seeds	3,721 Ha. - 2.81%
Irrigated Area	38,563 Ha. - 22 %
Rainfed Area	1,21 ,757 - 78%
Population Supported By Agriculture	16%
Holding Upto 2 HA.	92%
Total Cropped Area	1,60,320 - 46 .94%

Source: Directorate of Agriculture, Government of Goa

Aqua Culture

The three different kinds of aquaculture practiced in Goa are: a) The permanent fish farm b) The use of ponds for salt and fish production c) Prown culture in "Khazan Land" paddy cum fish farming. The first one involves round the year operation and mostly found Sclute taluka, but other two types essentially include season activities. The annual yield varies from 350 kg per hectare in a salt-cum-fish farming to 1060 kg or even 2000 kg per hectare in a permanent fish firm.

Table 7
Distribution of Mangroves along the Indian Coast
(Measured through Remote Sensing)

	State/ Union Territory	*Area (Km²) (1994)*
1.	Andaman and Nicobar Groups	966
2.	Best Bengal (Sundar bans)	2119
3.	Orissa	195
4.	Andhra Pradesh	378
6.	Karnataka	n.a.
7.	Goa	3
8.	Maharashtra	115
9.	Gujarat	419
	Total	**4256**

Forestry

The heavy precipitation and hilly terrain have developed luxurious growth of vegetation but forest cover decreases towards the coastal low lands. Economically valuable species are Eculyptus, Bamboo, Cashew, Coconut, Teak etc. the deltas of Mandori and Zuari estuaries have mangroves forest.

Table 8
District wise Extent of Forest cover in Goa, 2003 and 2007

Districts	*Geographic Area*	*Moderately / Dense Forest*	*Open Forest*	*Total*	*Percent*
North	1,736	432	456	888	51.15
South	1,966	823	445	1268	64.5
Total (2003)	3702	1255	901	2156	58.24
Total (2007)	3702	1135	1016	2151	58.13

Source: State of Forest Report 2003 and 2007, Forest Survey of India, Ministry of Environment

Minerals

Coastal talukas don't have iron ore mines except some deposits in Quepem and Canacona talukas. Bauxite is exclusively found in the coastal talukas of Quepem and Canacona. These bauxites have the fireness of about 45 to 70 percent.[5] The other minerals like lime stone, clay, silica sands etc. are found both in inland and wastal zone of Goa. The iron-ore is directly exported to Japan, China and other south-eastern countries. Most of the mineral are transported by barges in 1964 and now has increased to 22 as per Goa mineral ores exporters association (Table 9).

Table 9
Mineral Resources of Goa (in '000 tones)

Mineral	*Proved*	*Probable*	*Possible*	*Total*
Bauxite	37872	16187	10223	64282
China clay		16		16
Iron (Hematite)	461013.9	149372.41	119460.8	729847.1
Iron ore (Magnetite)	67358	5416	115218	187992
Manganese ore	6253.64	23875.77	17037.04	47166.45
Quartz/Silica sand	20	1736	18248	20004

Source: Indian Mineral Year Book-2003.

Industry

A study of industrial development in Goa reveals two very distinct patterns, are as the industrial Goa comprising the coastal talukas where about 90 per cent large and medium and small scale industries are located, and other comprising the inland talukas (western ghat foothills) which almost devoid of industrial development except the midland taluka of Ponda. There are about 196 factories (as on 31-3-92) registered in operation under the factory act in the coastal talukas. 47 large and medium industries of these 23 are located in coastal talukas employing 6065 persons. And there are about 4987 small scale industries out of which 3775 are registered in the coastal zone.

The growth in the number of MSMEs since 1970. It is seen from the table that in 1970 there were 305 units, which more than doubled in the next five years and stood at 756 in 1975 registering a growth of 148 per cent during the five year period, however, thereafter the growth rate in each subsequent five years went on decreasing. As on 31st December 2013 the

Table 10
Industrial Water Demand (MLD)

North Goa	*2001 (Actual)*	*Additional (2011)*	*Total (2011)*
Ponda	9	1.935	10.935
Tiswadi	3.5	0.225	3.725
Bardez	5.64	7.754	13.394
Pernem	0.87	46.607	47.477
Bicholim	1.14	19.175	20.315
Satari	0.72	10.229	10.949
South Goa			
Canacona	0.76	13.95	14.71
Sanguem	0.51	3.6	4.11
Quepem	0.95	0.567	1.517
Salcete	15	35.109	50.109
Mormugao	20	2.813	22.813
Total	58.09	141.962	200.052

Source: Regional Plan, 2011.

Figure 7: Water Demand in South Goa

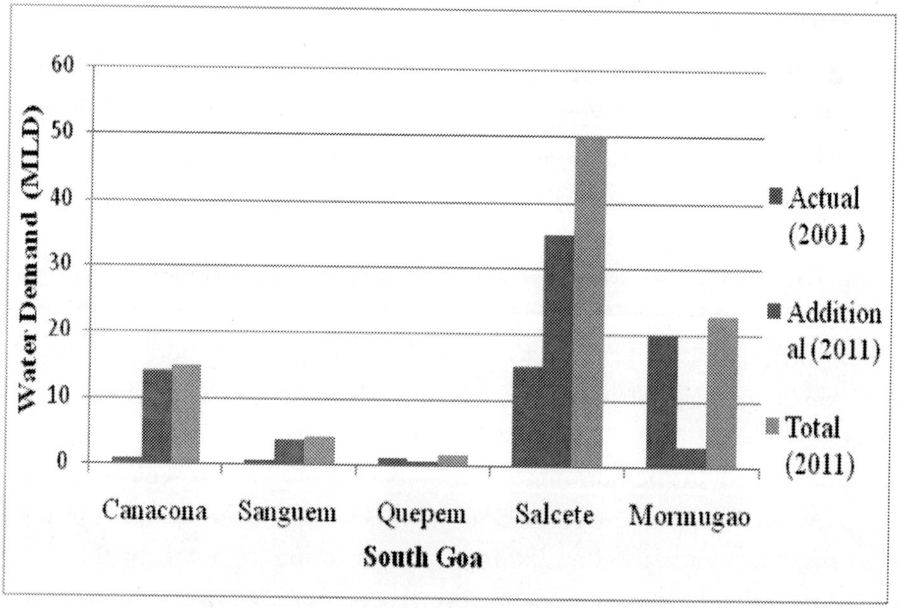

Source: Regional Plan, 2011.

Figure 8: Water Demand in North Goa

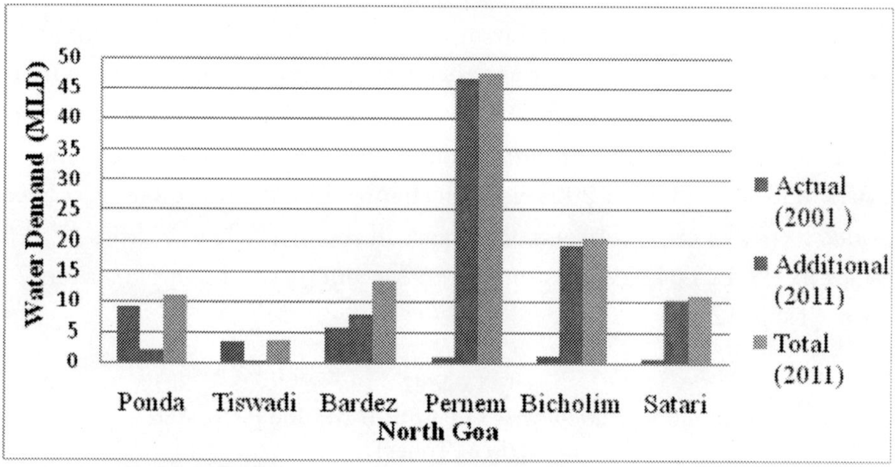

Source: Regional Plan, 2011.

number of MSMEs stood at 7793. Taluka-wise break-up of micro, small and medium enterprises is given in Table 11 below. It is seen that in North Goa District, Bardez taluka has the highest number of units followed by Ponda and Tiswadi. In the case of South Goa District, Salcete taluka had the highest number of units, followed by Mormugao taluka.

Table 11
Taluka-wise Number of Small Scale Industries (as on Dec'2013)

North Goa	*Taluka*	*Number of SSI units*
1	Pernem	204
2	Bardez	1428
3	Tiswadi	1112
4	Bicholim	459
5	Sattari	193
6	Ponda	1356
Total	(A)	4752
South Goa		
1	Salcete	1687
2	Quepem	351
3	Mormugao	704
4	Sanguem	95
5	Dharbandora	42
6	Canacona	162
Total	(B)	3041
Total	(A+B)	7793

Sources: Economic Survey 2013-14

Fishery

Fish firms an integral part of Goan life, with a coastline 105 km long and around 50,000 people being dependent on fish harvesting for a living. It would be difficult to overstate the importance of this commodity in either roan economy or diet. There are 61 marine fishing villages, 900 mechanized boats, 850 travelers and 2000 non-mechanized boats in the Goan coastal zone (1997). There is substantial increase in the fish yields, i.e. from 17,186 tones in 1965 to 64,929 tons on 1991-92 an increase of 278 percent in 26 years (Table 12)[6]

Table 12
Important Variety wise Quantity of Marine Fish catch
(in M Tones)

Mackrals (Bangdo)	*19980*	*16597*	*15169*	*23831*	*22128*	*17860*	*12994*
Sardines (Tarlo)	28574	34062	23496	23732	23120	34329	31629
CatFish (Sangot)	1821	1480	2279	1402	1545	364	383
Shark Fish (Mori)	1007	1019	1329	3159	375	234	281
Seer Fish (wiswan)	4407	3777	2285	1229	1844	1616	2751
Prawns (sungtam)	8642	7458	9795	9970	8008	8968	8380
Promprets (paplet)	559	534	284	185	376	174	1342
Cuttle Fish (Manki)	330	2201	—	—	1012	1180	4422
Tuna	1916	2095	1044	2524	3801	2621	3520
Ribbon Fish (Balle)	1368	2551	558	839	49	644	1107
Reef Cod (Gobro)	0	276	—	—	5	495	1409
Kowalkawal (Velli)	226	455	395	279	438	562	1046
Golden Anchovy (Kapsali)	3	57	0	2		50	29
SilverBelly (Karli)	1664	1688	1976	1584	1012	1146	3328
Soles (lepo)	1950	1795	1532	1606	3995	3683	2579
Silver Bar (Karli)	251	336	637	219	62	98	54
Crabs (Kurlo)	819	1021	1349	763	1236	1160	830
Sciaenoides (Dodiaro)	1938	2780	2207	1376	1448	1629	1425
Butter Fish (Soundale)	615	655	1353	1116	978	656	594
Others	15115	7934	14999	13246	14753	9159	9881
Total	91185	88771	80687	87062	86185	86628	879

Source: Directorate of Fisheries, Goa

Table 13
Anticipated State-wise Yields in India Marine and Inland Fish Catches in 1994-95

(In '000 tonnes)

state		*1994-1995*	
	marine	*Inland*	*Total*
Andhra Pradesh	197	192	389
Gujarat	392	43	435
Karnataka	195	66	261
Kerala	417	48	465
Maharashtra	434	62	496
Orissa	84	109	193
Tamil Nadu	328	232	560
Best Bengal	78	744	822
Andaman	14	—	14
Goa	56	3.2	59.2
Lakshadweep	9	—	9
Pondicherry	28	3.2	3.2
Total	2, 232	2,218.4	4,450.4

Source: Status of Fisheries in India, special publication no. 29 CMFRI, Cochin, 1996.

Tourism and the Environment Issues of Concern in the Coastal Zone of Goa

Tourism Was Adopted As A Key Sector For Goa's Development, not only For The Well-Established Reasons of Increasing Income And Employment But Also For Its Potential to Generate non·manual Employment In A State With An Increasingly Educated Work Force and Limited Industrial Growth. Tourist Arrivals In Goa Have Increased Over The Last 25years With A Higher Rate of Growth of International Tourists Than Domestic Tourists. Goa's Growing Importance on The Indian Tourist Map for International Tourists Can Be Seen From Figure. While In the Early 1980s, The Share of International Tourist that Came to Goa Was Less than 3 Percent, By the Mid-1990, The Share has increased to Over 10 Per cent.

Figure 9: Tourist Arrivals in Goa (1985-2012)

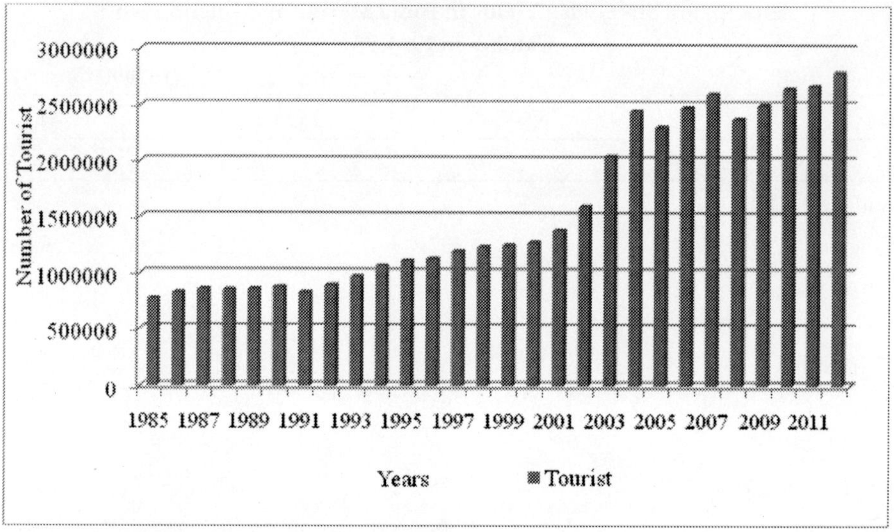

Source: Government of Goa, Department Of Tourism

Table 14
Share of Domestic and International Tourists of Goa

Year	*Total tourists*	*Share of domestic (%)*	*Share of international (%)*	*Year*	*Total tourists*	*Share of domestic (%)*	*Share of international (%)*
1981	439,015	93.33	6.67	1989	862,443	89.40	10.60
1982	477,165	94.13	5.87	1990	881,443	88.16	11.84
1983	530,015	93.67	6.33	1991	835,067	90.63	9.37
1984	669,992	90.71	9.29	1992	896,010	86.45	13.55
1985	775,212	88.05	11.95	1993	969,234	82.39	17.61
1986	834,081	88.31	11.69	1994	1.059,595	80.16	19.84
1987	861,448	89.02	10.98	1995	1,107,705	79.31	20.69
1988	854,935	89.11	10.89	1996	1,150,000	78.26	21.74

Source: Government of Goa, Department of Tourism.Personal Communications.

The various factors that have contributed to this rise in domestic tourism are:

- increased disposable income of the middle class,
- increased urbanization and stress of living in cities and towns,
- increased ownership of cars, which is making domestic tourism more attractive, especially among the upper-middle and middle classes[7]

- improved employment benefits, such as the leave travel concession,
- development of inexpensive mass transport and improved connections to various places of tourist interest,[8]
- increased number of cheap accommodations and resorts,
- greater advertising targeted at domestic tourists both by the central and the state governments, as well as the tourist industry, and
- development of time sharing of holiday accommodations, that is being targeted at the middle class.

Figure 10: Tourist Arrivals Change in Goa (1985-2011)

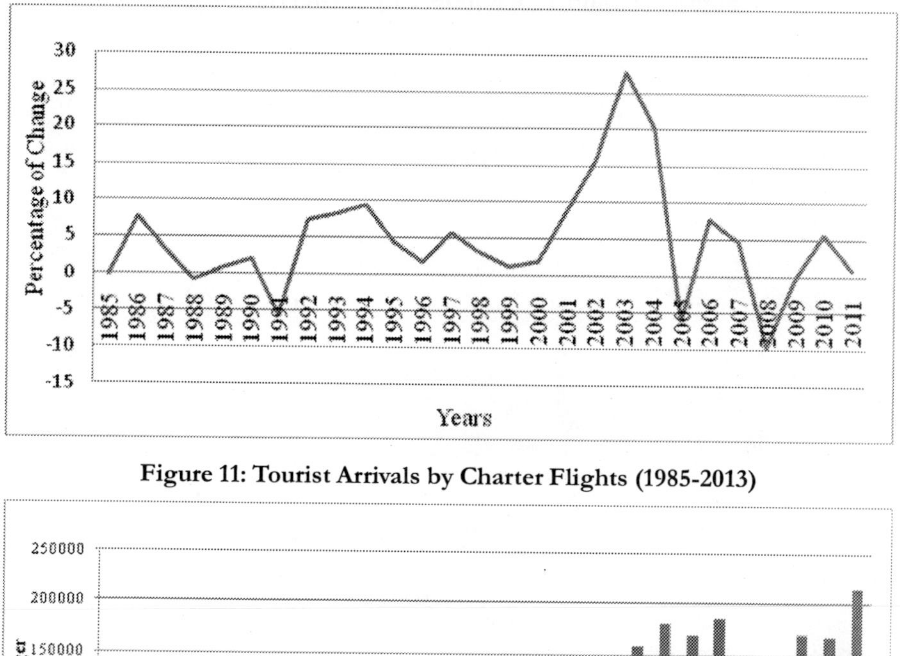

Figure 11: Tourist Arrivals by Charter Flights (1985-2013)

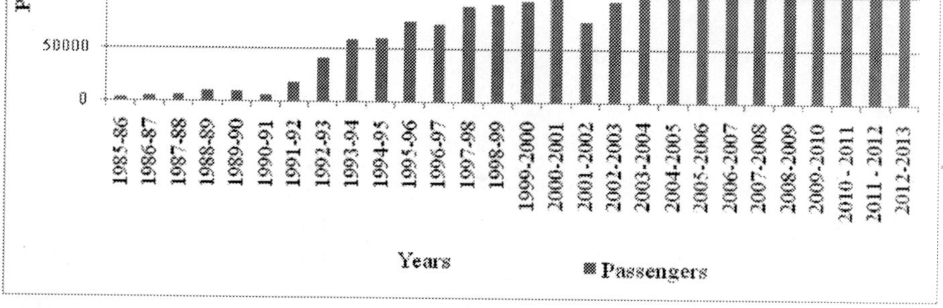

Source: Government of Goa, Department of Tourism

Table 15
Growth of Tourism in India

	Average annual growth rates (%)	
Period	*Domestic*	*International*
1981/82-86/87	7.98	27.20
1986/87-1991/92	2.75	-1.34
1991/92-95/96	3.90	31.00

Source: Government of Goa, Department of Tourism. Personal Communications

Figure 12: Tourist Arrivals by Cruise ship (1996-2012)

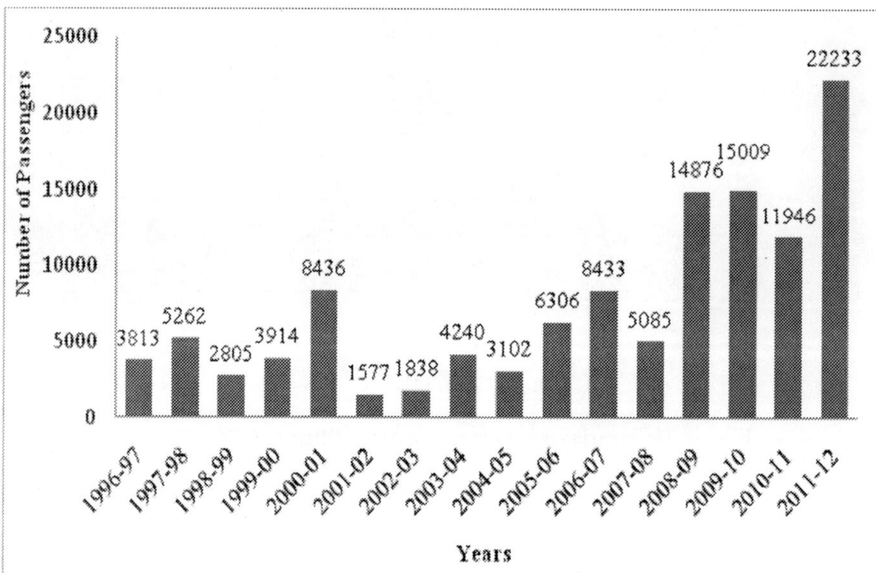

Source: Government of Goa, Department of Tourism

Tourism plays an important role in the economies of Goa. Goa, tourism generates 13.7 percent of the state's net domestic product, 7 percent of employment and 7 per cent of tax revenues. In Goa, the growth of coastal tourism has been rapid and uncontrolled. Tourism development has resulted in, the loss of biodiversity, erosion of sand dunes, declining fish catches, accretion and siltation and depletion of groundwater.

Figure 13: Domestic Tourist Arrivals in Goa (1985-2012)

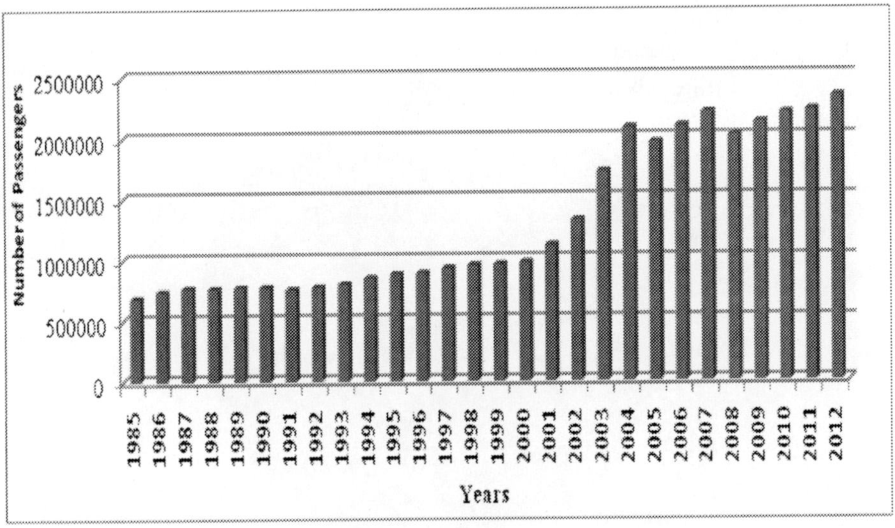

Source: Government of Goa, Department of Tourism

Figure 14 : Foreign Tiurist Arrivals in Goa during the Year 2012

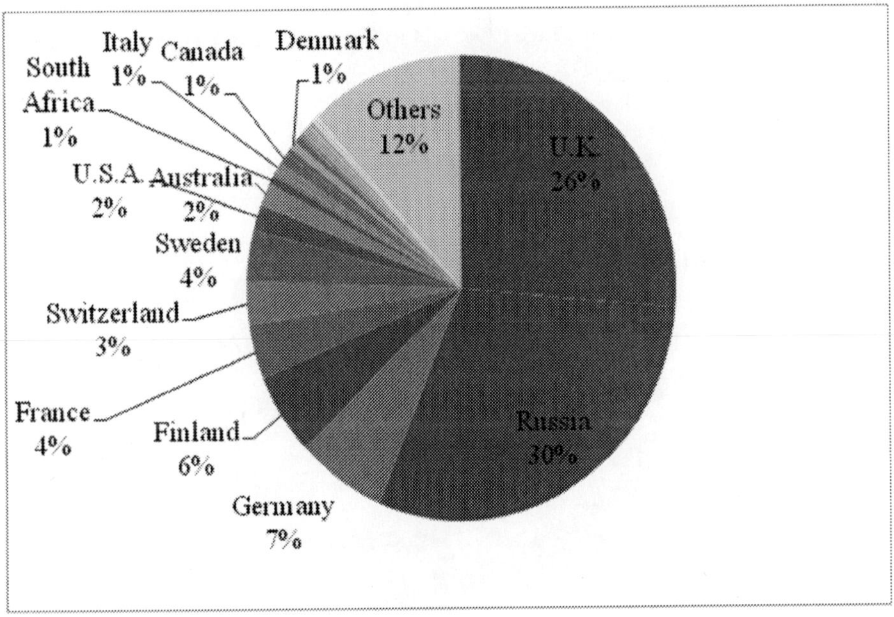

Figure 15 : Foreign Tiurist Arrivals in Goa during the Year 2013

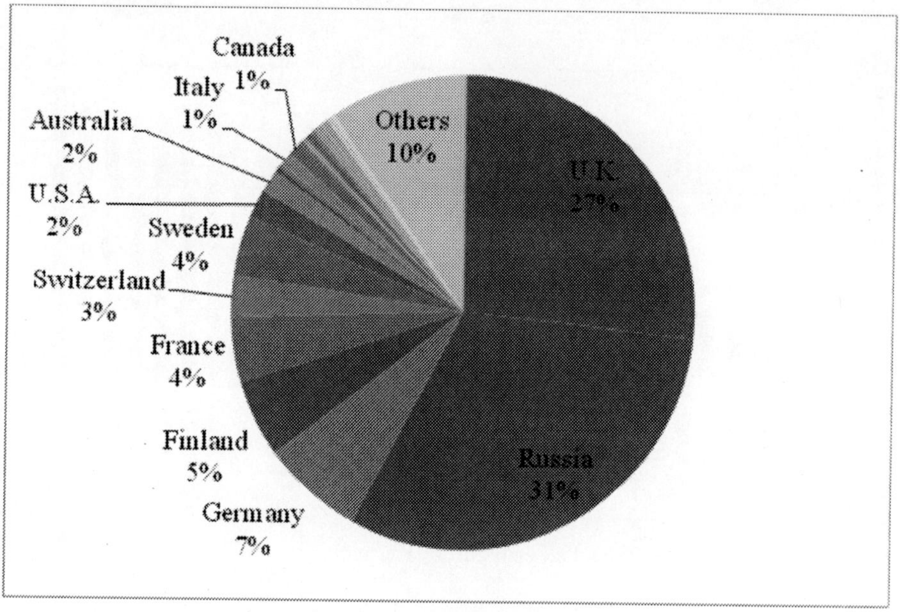

Source: Government of Goa, Department of Tourism

Figure 16 : Foreign Tiurist Arrivals in Goa during the Year 2013

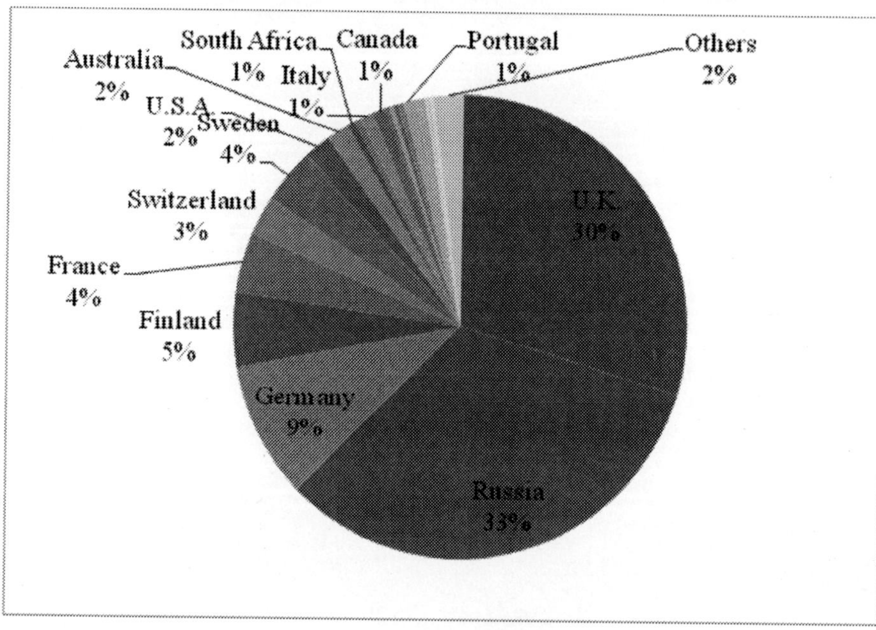

Source: Government of Goa, Department of Tourism

Table 16
International tourist Arrivals in India

Year	*Tourists arrivals in India (Millions)*	*Share of Goa in total tourists arrivals in India (%)*	*Year*	*Tourists arrivals in India (Millions)*	*Share of Goa in total tourists arrivals in India (%)*
1981	1.26	2.4	1989	1.74	5.2
1982	1.29	2.3	1990	1.71	5.9
1983	1.30	2.3	1991	1.68	7.8
1984	1.21	4.9	1992	1.87	6.4
1985	1.26	7.1	1993	1.82	9.3
1986	1.45	6.2	1994	1.87	11.2
1987	1.48	6.4	1995	2.10	10.9
1988	1.59	5.9			

Source: Center for Monitoring the Indian Economy, 1995. Basic Statistics of the Indian Economy; and India, Government of Goa, Department of Tourism. Personal Communications.

Regional Imbalances

As previously mentioned, most of the tourism development in Goa is concentrated in the four coastal stretches of Bardez, Salcete, Tiswadi and Marmagao. These areas are, similarly, the most developed regions of Goa, accounting for approximately 66 percent of Goa's Gross State Domestic Product (GSDP). They have dense settlements and are more developed in terms of infrastructural support services. About 70 percent of small-scale units, 78.5 percent of the capital investment in small industry and over 68 percent of the employment in this sector are found here. Historically, the region developed relatively faster than the rest of the state due to its coastal location, which provided easy access for sea trade and was attractive for settlement. There are a number of interesting locations with tourism potential exist in the hinterland; however, very little has been done to develop them. Hence, there is a considerable imbalance between the coastal and the hinterland regions in infrastructural and other indicators of economic development.

Figure 17: Map Showing some Anthropogenic Activities along the Coasts of Goa

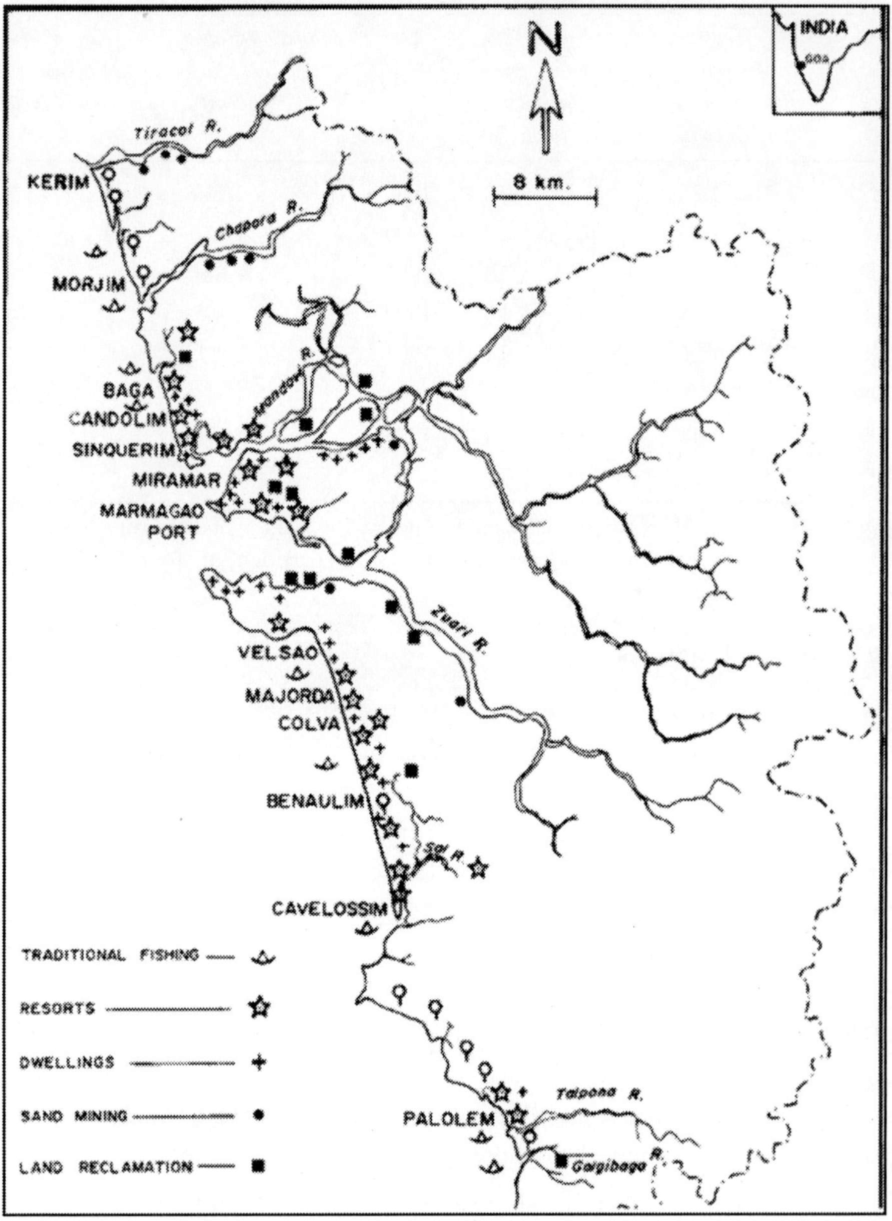

Shifts in Population and Traditional Occupations

In the tourist belts of Calangute-Candolim in Bardez, a shift in the composition of the resident population has occurred to include a large number of migrants from the states of Karnataka, Rajasthan and Kashmir due to potential employment in the tourism industry. Most of these people are engaged in selling artisanal pieces, handicrafts and garments. It cannot be denied that tourism has also given a boost to local art and handicrafts; however, the commercialization of such arts and crafts has resulted in certain deterioration in their quality as they are being manufactured for bulk sale. Much of the spontaneity of these practices has been lost. Moreover, some of the villages along the coasts have become very tourist-oriented and thus, shifted away from their traditional occupations. On the other hand, social forces are at work in the sense that tourism provides locals with an opportunity To keep their women at home rather than have them till the soil or sell fish in the market. This is perceived as a movement upwards for the locals, and a factor that cannot be ignored in the dynamics of the intersectoral movement of land and labor. Often large tourism development projects require the displacement of some of the original inhabitants of the area. Some of those displaced by present projects, chose to invest their compensations in capital assets, e.g., taxis, and have become to a degree upwardly mobile in an economic sense. However, there are others who due to their initial circumstances are unable to move along the same path, and instead become marginalized, having to replace self-employment for menial jobs in the very resorts that have displaced them. The issue of income distribution needs to be examined.

Tourism is a major industry in the state and as it is mainly concentrated along the coastal stretches of Goa, poses a severe threat to the fragile and dynamic coastal ecosystems. Although increasing tourism and other related activities have enhanced the employment related opportunities, coastal developmental activities have induced noticeable and adverse environmental and social problems. The impact gets worse because of related anthropogenic activities that follow coastal tourism, and as a result Goa's coastal scenario is prone to fast changes. Construction of resorts, residential dwellings, commercial establishments, beach side entertainment centers / eat outs have changed the coastal localities drastically in villages such as Calangute, Colva, Anjuna, etc. Today a few coastal areas are overcrowded due to haphazard growth of structures, resulting in undesirable over urbanization. Other threats faced by the coastal ecosystem of Goa are: loss of biodiversity, adverse effects on beaches, dunes, mangroves, water bodies and khazan lands and overexploitation of groundwater. In recent years after realizing the adverse environmental consequences several planning & statutory measures have been taken up by both, Central and State Government, to control coastal urbanization and divert tourism activities towards the hinter lands by encouraging eco-tourism.

Table 17
Distribution of Expenditures for International and Domestic tourists

Category	*International Tourists (%)*	*Domestic Tourists (%)*
Accommodation and food	53.95	58.20
Shopping	28.84	26.70
Internal transport	13.63	10.40
Entertainment	2.61	1.80
Miscellaneous expenses	4.97	2.90
Average length of stay	9 days	5 days
Total amount spend per visit	US$590	US$110

Source: Kirloskar Consultants Ltd., 1994. Report on Study of Tourism Industry in Goa.

Table 18
Expenditures of the State on Tourism per Plan

Annual plan	*Actual expenditure (Rs. Millions)*
1992-93	22.96
1993-94	25.93
1994-95	27.01
1996-97	30.00
Eight Plan (1992-97	135.15

Source: India, Government of Goa, Department of town and Country Planning and Department of Statistics and Evaluation Department. Personal Communications.

ENVIRONMENTAL ASPECTS

Coastal zone environment is particularly fragile and can be divided into two areas: the marine part and the land part. For the purpose of this discussion, coastal waters, bays backwaters, creeks, tidal inlets, and estuaries are considered as components of the marine part of the coastal zone. The sandy beaches along with two dunes (one which runs along the seashore, and another that runs parallel but about 100 to 500 meters away from the seashore) and their vegetation are considered components of the land part. In between these dunes there lies a sandy plain, which acts as a buffer zone between the main and the sea[9].

Most of the above functions are interactive in nature. In the coastal current movement, the most important force is the tidal cycle, which drives the sea water along the shoreline, bays, creeks and upstream through the mouths of rivers and estuaries. Other important forces are the near shore and riverine, or estuarine currents. All these currents carry natural sediment load and any other marine discharge, resulting from manmade activities, and deposit them at a site defined by an equation containing parameters, such as current velocity, counter currents, topography of the seabed or riverbed and other oceanographic factors. The transportation capacity of the currents has to be understood in terms of its effect on marine biota. For example, a rise of a few degrees in temperature of a sea water body would adversely affect species occurrence and predominance among biota, which in turn could influence other life forms. Also, a sudden appearance or disappearance of a species due to anthropogenic factors may cause stress in other species. Given the instructiveness and complexities of the coastal

Figure 18: Hierarchy of a Coastal Ecosystem

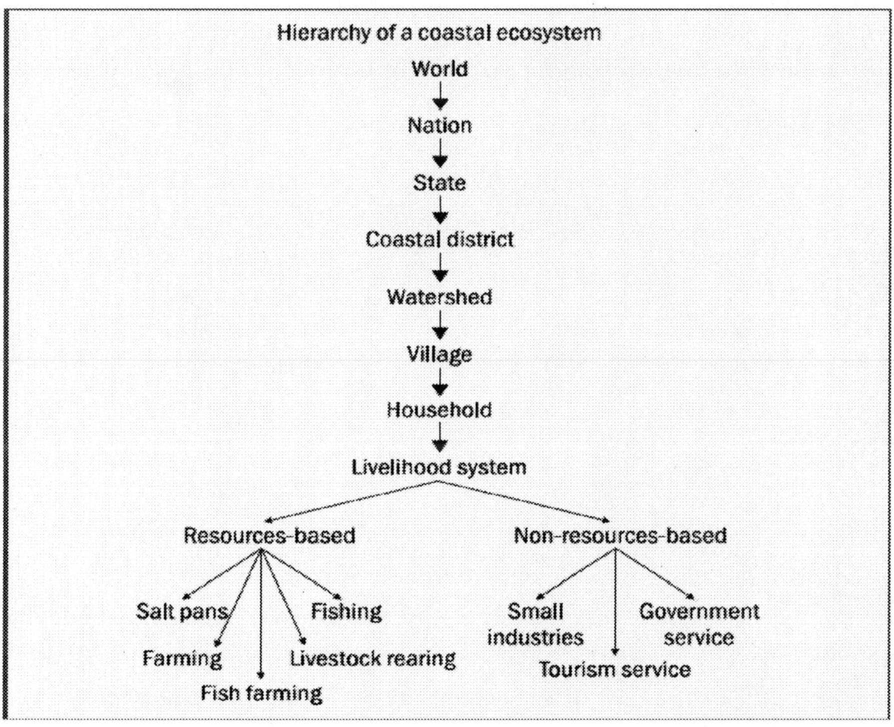

Source: Adapted from Conway and Barbier (1988)

environment, any developmental activity should to be preceded by the Environmental Impact Assessment studies to forestall environmental degradation. The following impacts on the marine part of the coastal zone have been observed while surveying the ecosensitive coastal areas of Goa.

Loss of Mangroves

Thick mangroves on the outskirts of Panaji, at Sao Pedro near Old Goa, around Talpona backwaters and at innumerable other locations are being reclaimed. In addition to the biological impacts of the loss of mangroves, the tidal waters could flood the surrounding coastal areas causing erosion and thus opening the estuarine banks to storm surges. The coastal zone of Goa has been exclusively used for agriculture, farming, shell fishing, traditional fishing and low-key recreation. Native Goans used the shoreline and the hinterland water bodies for fishing by using hand-cast and hand pulled nets, gather shells for economic and various other purposes. In earlier times traditional fishing was the main economic activity of coastal population. Goa is also very rich in diversity of Mangroves. The estimated area under mangroves is about 2000 ha in Goa with about 12 species of mangroves (Table 19).

Table 19
List of Mangrove Species Reported in Goa

Rhizophora mucronata	Avicennia officinalis
Rhizophora apiculata	Avicennia marina
Bruguiera gymnorrhiza	Avicennia alba
Bruguiera cylindrica	Sonneratia alba
Aegiceras corniculatum	Sonneratia caseolaris
Kandelia candel	Ceriops tagal

Throughout the course of Goa Rivers, one can find an intricate network of creeks and backwaters. A luxuriant growth of mangroves (some of which are degraded) and associated swamps can be observed along most of the water bodies. The most prominent and extensive backwaters with mangroves are located along the East of the capital city of Panaji. The fauna associated with mangrove ecosystem are listed in (Table 20).

Table 20
List of Fauna Associated with Mangroves in Goa

Pin tailed duck	Pond Heron	Small blue kingfisher	Common Sandpiper
Coots	Cattle Egret	Blue eared kingfisher	Green bee eater
Purple moor hen	Little Egret	White breasted kingfisher	Black Drongo
Cormorants	Large Egret	Roller or Blue jay	Grey Drongo
Shovellor	Blackwinged Kite	Night Heron	Grey headed Myna
Terns	Brahminy Kite	Reef Heron	Tree pie
Lesser wood shrike	Large cuckoo shrike	Flying Foxes (bats)	Crocodiles
Turtles	Otters	Jackls	Snakes
Crabs	Oysters	Fish	

Figure 19: A Rivulet Flanked by Diversified Mangrove Species at Carambolim (Tiswadi Taluka)

Source: *http://goaenvis.nic.in/issue*

Reduced Fish Catch and Species

A steady decrease in the total annual fish catch has been observed in Goa. The catch has declined from 105.44 thousand tons in 1993-94 to 101.90 in 1994-95 and in 1995-96, to 87.82 thousand tones21. More specifically, at Sancoale-Chicalim Bay, the decrease in production of certain varieties of shellfish and crabs, both local delicacies, is believed to be due to the land reclamation of mangrove swamps and to the construction of roads to the Sao Jacinto Island and at Talpona. More generally, one or more of the following factors may be responsible for the reduction in fish catch:

Figure 20: Mangrove cover in Goa, 1987-2007

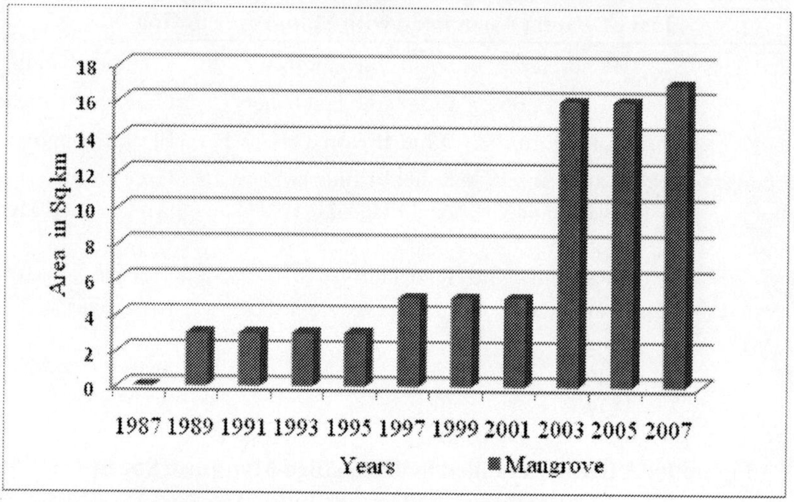

Sources: Ministry of Environment & Forests

(a) **Unscientific fishing practices**: These can include the use of nets with a mesh size smaller than permissible during spawning periods and the fishing beyond sustainable yields. These practices are pursued due to high demand for fresh seafood in the market.

(b) **Loss of spawning grounds**: Reasons for this could be mangrove deforestation, land reclamations and siltation. Short-term economic gains from the development of these areas is obviously preferred over the long-term benefits of the conservation of ecology.

(c) **Introduction of anthropogenic material**: Any disturbance at any step in the marine food web may inadvertently affect other species. The introduction of untreated sewage and waste to the environment would give rise to toxic algal blooms wiping out many species. Increased turbidity and sedimentation can also affect the benthic communities.

Table presents the total fish catch (marine and inland) for the period 1997 to 2003. The total fish catch recorded remarkable growth from a meager 17,000 tons in 1961-1962 to around 28,000 tons in 1987-88 (after Statehood). It reached an all time high in 1992-93 when the catch touched 97,014 tons. However it has not touched that point again. The fish catch shows a qualitative and quantitative drop during the period 1992 to 2003. Except for two years, i.e. 1997 and

2003, the catch remained stagnant around the range of around 70,000 tons annually.

The contribution of the fishing industry to the development of the State economy may be measured in terms of:

- Its contribution to Net State Domestic Product (NSDP)
- Its share in the total output of the primary sector.
- Table reveals that the share of fishing industry in NSDP since 1985 has never exceeded 3 per cent.

Table 21
Trends in Fish Catch (in tons) 1997-2003

Sr. No	*Year*	*Marine Catch*	*Inland Catch*	*Total*
(Base)	1987	27210	1430	28640
1	1997	91277	3270	94547
2	1998	67236	3474	70710
3	1999	60075	3365	63440
4	2000	64563	3570	68133
5	2001	69386	3749	73135
6	2002	67563	3684	71247
7	2003	90990	4321	95311

Table 22
Contribution of Fishing Industry to Net State Domestic Product

Year	*NSDP of Fishing Industry at current prices (Rs. lakh)*	*Total NSDP of Goa (Rs. lakh)*	*Share of Fishing Industry in NSDP (per cent)*
1985-86	1100	50896	2.16
1986-87	1254	60787	2.06
1987-88	1138	67048	1.70
1988-89	906	78140	1.16
1989-90	1158	91995	1.26
1990-91	1272	98651	1.29
1991-92	1336	103226	1.29
1992-93	2625	145939	1.80
1993-94	3914	188651	2.07
1994-95	4752	209554	2.27
1995-96	6864	242877	2.83
1996-97	7584	257389	2.95
1997-98	8649	312760	2.77
1998-99	12470	521215	2.39
1999-2000	10872	586212	1.85
2000-01	17456	615107	2.84
2001-02	15443	628584	2.46

Source: Statistical Handbook and the Economic Survey, Government of Goa (Various Issues)

Erosion

Dispersion of sediment load at any given point depends upon a number of parameters related to marine currents. Any activity which causes disturbances in these parameters could alter the sites of deposition and result in erosion, accretion or siltation and changes in the ecology of that area, such as land reclamations, the extraction of sand or the construction of jetties23. Consequently, there are a large number of cases where coastal stretches have been subjected to the forces of erosion. Prime examples are Campal and Caranzalem near Panaji, Palolem, Agonda and many other places, where a considerableamount of construction activities have occurred.Goa lies on the Western Coast of India and have a copious annual rainfall averaging to about 3000 mm. Goa which is also a world famous Tourist destination is famous for its natural heritage and has long and wonderful beaches. As per 2001 census, Goa had a population of 13, 47,668. About 65% of this population is concentrated along the coastal talukas of Pernem, Bardez, Tiswadi, Mormugao, Salcette, Quepem (part) and Canacona. Goa receives a floating population of more than 24 lakh Tourists (Foreign as well as domestic) Though the areal extent of Goa is about 3702 sq kms, Goa has a coastline of 105 kms. Over the years, Goa has been experiencing Sea erosion

Figure 21: Severe cliff erosion at Anjuna (Bardez Taluka)

Source: http://goaenvis.nic.in/issue

along the coasts. The sea erosion over the years has intensified to a very large extent resulting in a very huge threat not only to the coastline but also to human lives.

Impacts to the Marine Part of the Coastal Zone

- The marine part of the coastal zone provides many functions and in the present context are:
- To support marine flora including sub tidal varieties, such as mangroves. The mangrove ecosystem itself serves as a habitat for diverse types of species of birds and marine biota, in addition as the protection of the coastline from erosion, tides and storms18.
- To support a wide variety of marine organisms including mammals. The marine organisms among themselves form a very intricate, well-established food chain starting with the chemical constituents of sea water called nutrients.
- To function as a natural thermostat which balances the climate on the sub regional, regional and global scales.
- To disperse riverine load effectively in near-shore regions.

  All along the coastline of Goa, for example, between Chapora and Sinquerim in Bardez, Caranzalem and Miramar in Panaji, Salcete Coast in Central Goa and in Galgibaga, Talpona, Palolem in South Goa, there has been a boom in construction activities, most of which are for tourism or for associated purposes. To make space for and to use them as a component of cement for construction, sand is being extracted in substantial amounts. When the environmental functions are weighed against the economic services that sand performs, the fact that the former are not priced, tilts the demand in favor of the economic user-groups. There is need to quantify and monitor such sand losses and their ecological impacts. The following impacts have been observed on the coastal stretches of Goa due t o development activities:

- **Loss of sand dunes:** Sand dunes have borne the brunt of construction activities along the coastal stretches of Goa . Anjuna and Baga-Calangute-Candolim stretches in North Goa, and Salcete beaches comprising Betalbatim, Colva, Varca, Cavelossim and Mobor in central Goa, were the first beaches to lose their dunes. Our survey showed

South Goa to be the next in line as in Galgibaga, two dunes, 10 meters high, have already been flattened into plateaus at half the heights to make way for construction.

- **Endangered species**: Four species of turtles have been reported to frequent the beaches at Morjim, Miramar, Bogmalo and Palolem, covering almost the entire stretch of the Goa Coast. The .Save The Turtles. campaign of the Goa Foundation, a local Non-Governmental Organization, carried jointly with the Forest Department of the Government of Goa, reported that the number of sea turtles visiting their nesting sites on different beaches in Goa particularly in Morjim, is steadily decreasing.

  Tidal ingress: The ceaseless mining of sand and sand-dunes have effectively razed gentle slopes of sand which stop the tides from rushing further on the shore. The consequent tidal ingress has reduced the area of beach at different places, such as Miramar in Panaji, Baga-Calangute-Candolim-Sinquerim stretch and Anjuna in Bardez, and in Salcete and Mormugao on the north and central coasts of Goa.The marine part of the coastal zone provides many functions and in the present context are:

- To support marine flora including subtidal varieties, such as mangroves. The mangrove ecosystem itself serves as a habitat for diverse types of species of birds and marine biota, in addition as the protection of the coastline from erosion, tides and storms[10].
- To support a wide variety of marine organisms including mammals. The marine organisms among themselves form a very intricate, well-established food chain starting with the chemical constituents of sea water called nutrients.
- To function as a natural thermostat which balances the climate on the sub-regional regional and global scales.
- To disperse riverine load effectively in near-shore regions.

Most of the above functions are interactive in nature. In the coastal current movement, the most important force is the tidal cycle, which drives the sea water along the shoreline, bays, creeks and upstream through the mouths of rivers and estuaries. Other important forces are the near whore and riverine, or estuarine current. All these current carry natural sediment load and any other marine discharge, resulting from manmade activities, and deposits them at a site defined by an equation containing parameters, such as current velocity, counter currents, topography of the seabed or riverbed and other oceanographic factors. The transportation capacity of the currents has to be understood in terms of its effect on marine biota. For example, a rise of a few degree in temperature of a sea water body would adversely affect species occurrence and predominance among biota, which in turn could influence other life forms. Also, a sudden appearance or disappearance of species due to anthropogenic factors may cause stress in other species. Given the inter activeness and complexities of the coastal environment, any developmental activity should to be preceded by the Environmental Impact Assessment studies to forestall environmental degradation[11].

Table 23
Areas under Major Wetland Categories of the Coast

Categories	*Area (Km^2)*
Mudflat	22961
Beach/spit	1465
Shoal/bar	93
Coral reef	1270
Mangroves	3979
Marsh vegetation	370
Mudflat with vegetation	6125
Beach vegetation	290
Lagoon/backwaters	2132
Flood prone areas	3437
Coastal dunes	2509
Reclaimed areas	1212
Paleo beach ridges	434
Strand plain	1378
Salt affected area	697
Salt pans	1617

Source: SAC (Space Application Centre (1992) coastal Environment SAC report No. RSAM/SAC/COM/SN/II/ Dept. of Spazce, GOI, P. 114.

Figure 22: Coastal Zone Problems in India

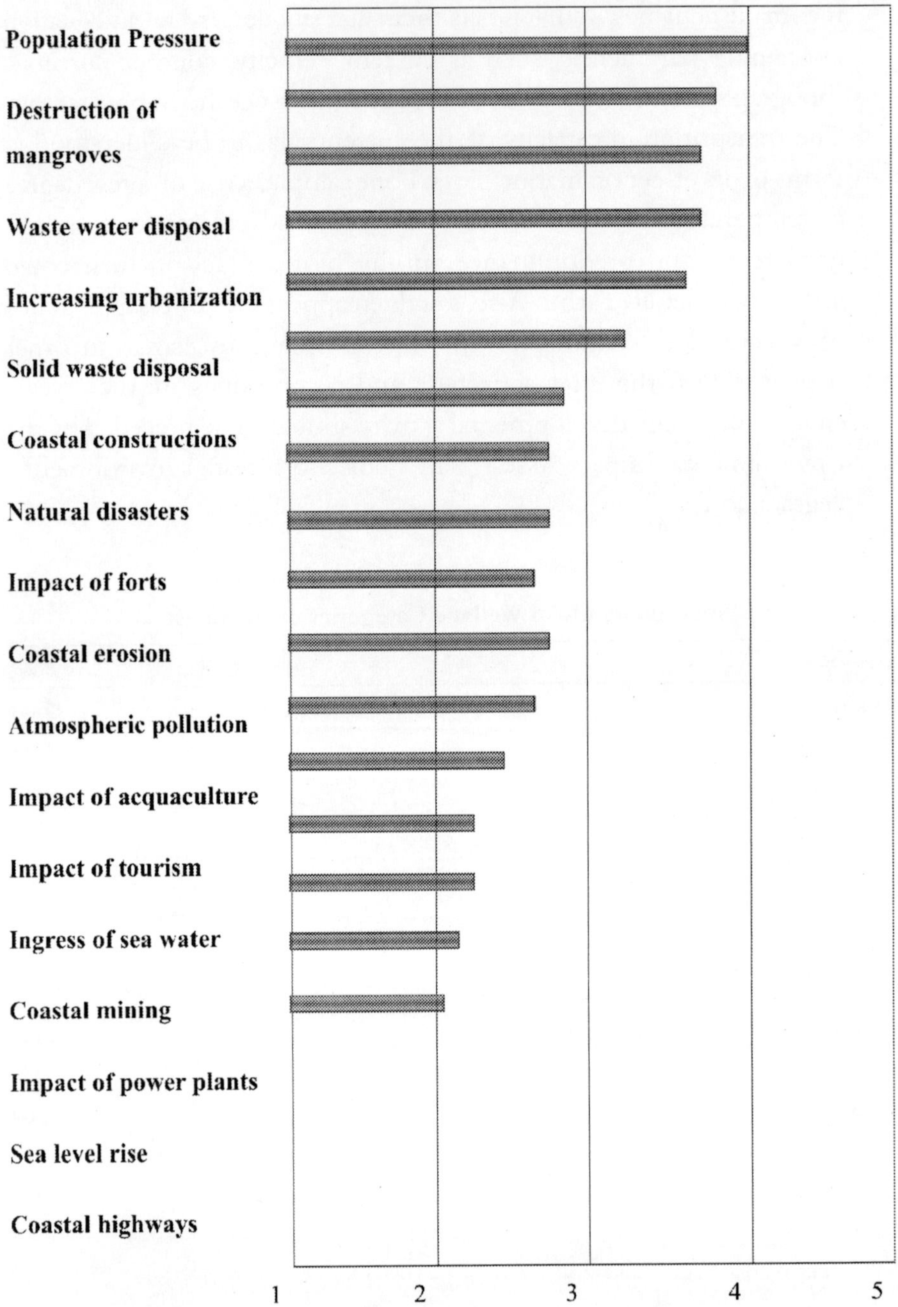

Source: Rajagopalan 1996 Coastal Zone Management in Voice for Ocean's The International Ocean Institute, Madras.

Impacts of Expanded Transport

Even though tourists in Goa almost exclusively accommodated in coastal areas, they arrive and depart Goa by some kind of transportation operating in other areas of the state. While the air and sea travel would cause negligible damage to the environment in broad terms, motor vehicles cause air pollution by their uncontrolled exhaust fumes.

Figure 23: Number of Vehicles Registered from 1999-00 to 2011-12

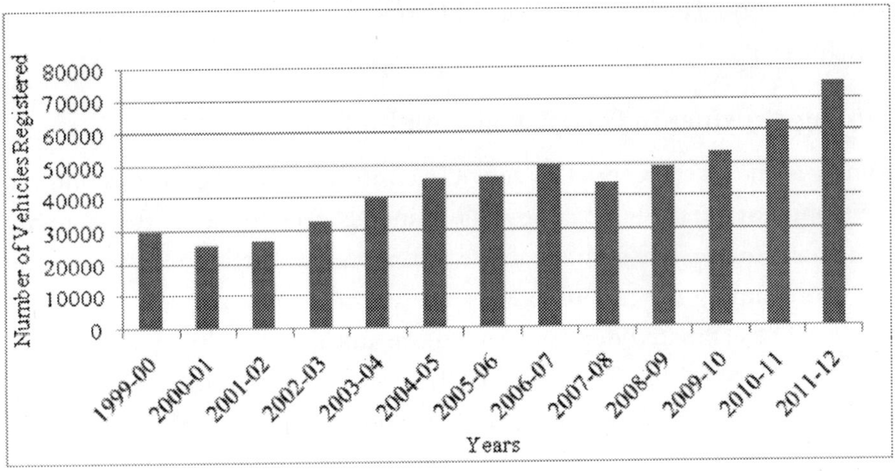

Source: Directorate of Transport, Government of Goa

Also, the alignment of the Konkan Railway has broad reaching environmental impacts. The laying of the tracks for the railway in Goa, especially through wetlands and tidal marshes and Maxem and between Bali and Mayem along with numerous bridges on the Mandovi-Zuari estuarine fronts, has been done without proper hydrodynamic and geomorphological studies[12]. The gigantic embankments, several kilometers long, supporting the rail lines along the lowlands of Goa have lead to substantial alterations in physical, chemical, biological and geomorphological setups. Blocking, dominating or increasing the tidal flow has resulted in a major redistribution of sediments giving rise to erosion/deposition or deposition/erosion with conspicuous changes in shorelines or near-shore realms. Mangrove swamps have been destroyed; tidal regimes disrupted; paddy fields flooded, and the embankments are sinking due to soft underlying strata[13]. A comprehensive analysis of the environmental impacts of the Konkan Railway alignment is needed to study such questions as the following. Is the salutation taking place in the backwaters and estuarine regions of Canacona in south Goa due to river runoffs carrying haphazardly dumped material from the digging out of the railroad? To what extent has the Konkan Railway Alignment through eco sensitive areas contributed to the environmental degradation of estuarine/coastal areas of Goa? In board terms, factors other than tourism could be responsible for the observations made above, but the contributions of the tourism industry in all these situations should be identified given the criticality of the coastal environment demands.

Mining Activities in Goa: A Pollution Problem

Mining is one of the important activities contributing to the socio economic development of the state. The main minerals ores found in the state are Iron, manganese, limestone, bauxite, silica sand, refraction clay, soapstone etc. Iron mining is predominant at present in terms of production and export. The estimated deposit of iron ore amounts to 1400 million tones. An estimate of 412 million tones of Iron ore is known to have the purity of 58 per cent iron. Ore mining is of considered economic importance in the state contributing to about 10 per cent of the economy. At present 13.5 to 15 million tons of ore is extracted every year. Each year 30 to 40 million tons of ore rejects are generated and stocked in large dumps. Ore is a non-renewable resource. With the present rate of extraction, the mining can continue till 2030. The mining involves digging of pits even below the ground water table. Digging of pits involves disturbing the ground water level in terms of quantity and quality. The pits are often filled with mining wastes. The mining wastes are also stocked as dumps. Due to rain washing of the ores dumps, the mining sediments are transported to the rivers through streams and water canals. The canals and streams are often flooded during the rainy season affecting the agriculture fields aquaculture farms causing sedimentation. The transportation of sediments also increases turbidity in the streams and rivers. There is sedimentation in the estuaries and in coastal areas. The mining rejects also effect benthic organisms in rivers, estuaries and coastal waters. As the mining is known to cause environmental impacts on land and water based activities including the coastal areas.

At present, out of the State's total surface area of 365,563 ha, about 30,000 ha, i.e., about 8 per cent of the land area is covered by mining leases numbering 274, out of these only 81 are operating covering an area of 5804 ha. Hence, the actual area under mining i.e., the broken up area would be about 2,500 ha, about 2 per cent of the total surface area of Goa. Table

Table 24
Land under Mining (in ha/per cent)

Land	*Area*	*Per cent*
Total surface area	365563	100
Mining land	70000	19
Leased out	30000	8
Operating leases	5804	2
Broken up	2500	1

Source: Department of Mines, Government of Goa.

Figure 24: Land Mining in Goa

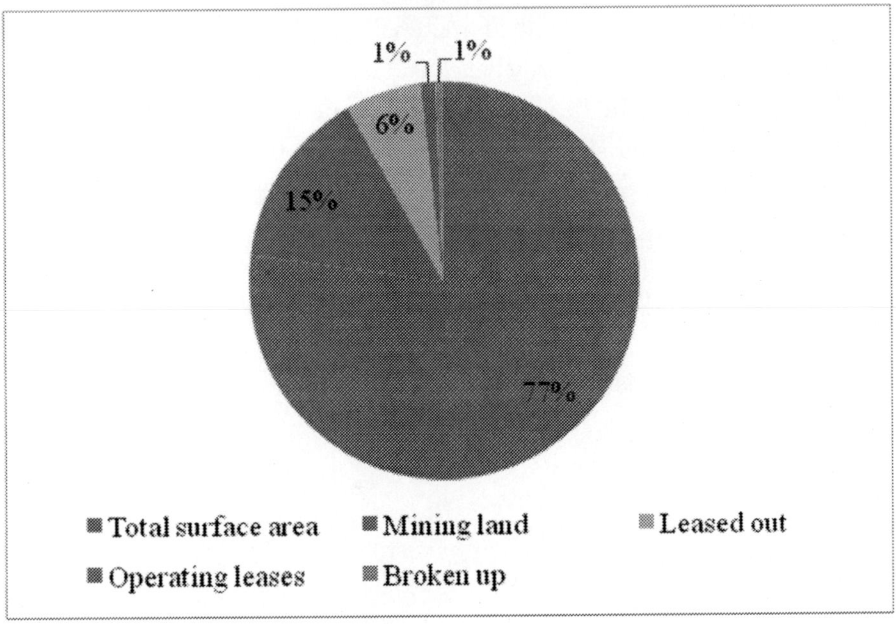

Source: Department of Mines, Government of Goa

An estimated 100,000 people living in the villages in four talukas in north and south Goa have lost their source of living. Their farms have been destroyed by mining silt and water sources have been contaminated Mining has caused irreversible damage to forests, agriculture, fisheries and water aquifers Goa has 90 operational mines spread along the Western Ghats in an area of 150 to 200 sq km. Most of the legal and illegal mines are in forest areas. Most of the mines in the state are concentrated in four talukas- Bicholim in north Goa, and Sattari, Sanguem and Quepem talukas in south Goa. An estimated 100,000 people living in the villages in these four talukas are affected. Besides loss of livelihood, they are also suffering from the adverse effects of air noise and water pollution. "Mining has caused irreversible damage to forests, agriculture, fisheries and water aquifers," The mining has also affected the Salaulim dam on the Salaulim river in Sangeum taluka, which supplies drinking water to half the state's population, besides providing water for irrigation and to industries. Over 20 mines are operating in the vicinity of the dam. Heavy silt has settled in the dam reservoir because of mining.

Environmental degradation due to mining activity includes:

- A depletion of the amount of material available for the maintenance and replenishment of nearby beaches. The extraction of sediment from the active part of the beach and/or estuarine system or from deposits that eventually nourish these systems may reduce the net availability of sand and result in beach erosion;
- Disturbance of the substrate including increased turbidity
- Loss of interstitial fauna resulting in a reduction of food items available to fishes;
- Disruptions of fish migrations through inappropriate timing of operations;
- Habitat destruction
- Potential instability of dunes, river banks and/or be and sea bed;
- Impacts on erosion and deposition cycles
- Changes to river, tidal and sea current flows
- Pollution from accidents and waste disposal

- Adverse impacts on biological communities due to build up of mud, silt and sandbanks at dumping sites
- wind mobilization of sand
- impacts on indigenous cultural values
- impact on the water table
- impacts on coastal amenity and
- Localized changes to access to coastal areas.

Table 25
Population and Related Data and Some Estimates of Pollutants Entering The Sea Around India (As of 1991)

Population	*840 million*
Coastal population (19% of total)	159.6 million
Area of the country	3.287×10^6 km^2
Agricultural area	1.65×10^6 km^2
Exclusive Economic zone	2.015×10^6 km^2
River Runoff (Annual mean)	1645 km^2
Fainfall per year (on land)	3.5×10^{12} km^2
Rainfall per year (on Bay of Bengal)	6.5×10^{12} km^2
Rainfall per year (On Arabian Sea)	6.1×10^{12} km^2
Domestic sewage added to the sea by coastal population per year (@ 60 1 per head/day)	4.6×10^9 km^2
Industrial effluents added to the sea by coastal industries per year	0.4×10^9 km^2
Sewage and effluents added by the rivers to the sea per year	55×10^6 km^3
Solid waste and garbage generated by coastal population per year (@ 0.8 kg per head/day)	53×10^6 tons
Fertilizer used per year (@ 30.5 kg/ha yr^1)	13×10^6 tons
Pesticides used per (@ 336 g/ha yr^1)	80000 tons
Synthetic detergents used per year	125000 tons
Oil transported across the Arabian Sea per year	550 MT

Source: Pollution Potential of Industries in Coastal Area of India, COPOCS/9/1995-96.

Table 26

Statewise Coastal Length, Area (Upto 25 Km Land-ward) and Industries Alongwith the Number of Industries Under 17 Categories (In Parenthesis) with High Pollution Potential

S. No.	*Coastal States*	*Coastal Length (Km)*	*Area upto 25 km from shore line (Sq. km.)*	*Industries (No.)*		*Acquaculture farms*
1.	Gujarat	1663	41,575	35	(29)	—
2.	Maharashtra	720	18,000	167	(38)	—
3.	Goa	140	3,500	2	(1)	—
4.	Karnataka	290	7,250	3	(2)	—
5.	Kerala	560	14,000	26	(12)	—
6.	Tamil Nadu	860	21,500	30	(15)	20
7.	Pondicherry (UT)	24	600	4	(4)	—
8.	Andhra Pradesh	930	23,250	30	(24)	88
9.	Orissa	450	11,250	4	(2)	20
10.	Best Bengal	200	5,000	7	(4)	10

Source: Pollution Potential of Industries in Coastal Area of India, COPOCS/9/1995-96.

Table 27

Statewise Coastal Industries (Large and Medium) and West Generation

State/Types of populant	*Gujarat*	*Maharashtra*	*Goa*	*Karnataka*	*Kerala*	*Tamil Nadu*	*Pondicherry*	*Andhra Pradesh*	*Orissa*	*Best Bengal*	*East Coast*	*West Coast*
Industries (Nos.)	35	167	2	3	26	30	4	30	4	7	75	233
Acquaculture farms (Nos.)	—	—	—	—	—	20	—	88	20	10	138	—
Aquaculture farms waste (Million m^3/d)	—	—	—	—	—	0.253	—	2.12	—	—	2.37	—
Industrial Effluent (million m^3/day	0.566	0.080	0.012	0.043	0.515	0.125	0.006	0.30	0.001	0.022	0.50	0.85
Industrial Solid waste (T/day)	95066	0.012	1.4	76	2431	9112	1.25	7191	3505	25	19834	14642

Source: National Inventory of Large and medium industry and status of Effluent Treatment and Emission Control System (Vol. 1 and 2) Central Pollution Control Board, PROBES/68/1997-98.

LAND USE LAND COVERS CHANGE OF GOA AND ITS IMPACT OF COASTAL ECOSYSTEM

Coastal environment is one of the complex phenomena, owing to its progressive or cyclic changes due to dynamic processes and it supports a variety of economic activities such as industrial, commercial and recreation, etc. In this environment, now highly disturbed and threatened due to increase of population and developmental activities (Thanikachalam and

Ramachandran, 2005). It is necessary to protect coastal environment to ensure sustainable development. Landuse/land cover is an important tool for the various planning authorities with responsibilities for the management of territory at a regional level (Marcal *et al.*, 2005). Using Land use/land cover tool allows for the identification of major processes of change and, by inference, the characterization of land use dynamics (Ademiluyi et al., 2008). Same time, the knowledge of land use/land cover map is very important to understand the coastal environment, utilization, conservation and management. Therefore land degradation is mainly due to population pressure, which leads to intense land use without proper management practices (Raju *et al.*, 2006)). These land use/ land cover changes perturb the existing coastal ecosystem (Chauhan and Nayak, 2005). Hence, studying land use/ land cover dynamics is an essential in order to examine coastal ecology and developmental consequences of landuse change over a space of time. Landuse/land cover changes have emerged as a global phenomenon and perhaps the most significant regional anthropogenic and natural disturbance to the environment. The study aided with temporal remotely sensed data for landuse/ land cover mapping in Goa Coastal area between 2000 and 2008 with reference to SOI top sheets to assess the changes that has taken place in the coastal landuse. The interpreted data were verified in the field and results were corrected. The major types of land cover area are agriculture land, plantations, settlement, salt affected land, aquaculture, land with shrub and sandy area. The results indicate that agriculture area is dominant landuse class in Goa coast and its surroundings followed by plantation. Salt affected area increased due to brackish water aquaculture and tidal inundation. The major geomorphic features identified are deltaic plain, mud/ tidal flat, pale beach ridge, beach ridge, sand dune, salt flat and coastal plain. Among these, deltaic plain covers majority of the area. The baseline information generated on land use pattern and geomorphology of the area would be of immense help for protecting the coastal environment to sustainable development.

Multi-temporal satellite data of LISS III 2008 and Landsat ETM 2000 images were used for generate landuse / land cover map. IRS P6 LISS III satellite data was acquired from the National Remote Sensing agency (NRSA) and Landsat ETM satellite image was downloaded from freely through the global land cover facility (GLCF) (http://glcf.umd.edu). Different landuse features were mapped such as settlement, agricultural land, river, land with and without scrub, plantation, salt affected land, waterlogged area, marshy/ swampy land, mudflat / tidal flat and aquaculture and their changes were analyzed with the help of GIS (Arc GIS 10.1) software environment.

Figure 25: Land use Land Cover Change of Goa, 2008

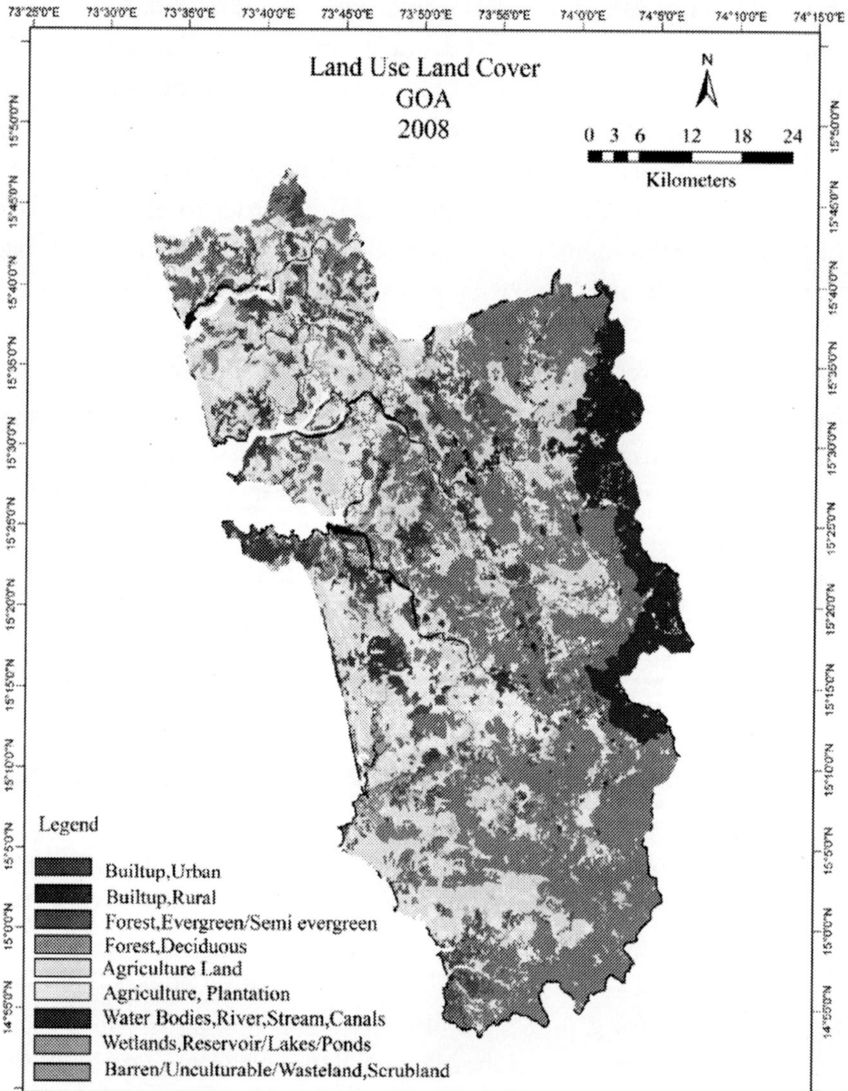

The role of tourist induced and other population movements in causing coastal ecosystem change in Goa, India. It focuses especially upon agro-ecosystems locally known as khazan lands, and sand dunes, and how they are transformed to accommodate the needs of tourists and tourism.

In Goa, human activities with an impact on the ecosystem are:

- **Changes in land-use and land cover:** Population and population movements, demands arising from remittance incomes, demand made by tourism, lower personal dependence on ecosystems, insufficient knowledge of the value of an ecosystem, lower personal as compared to community valuation of ecosystems, short time horizons, zoning rules and need to preempt their enforcement, changes in legal rules with implications for management regimes, local politics and power configurations, political economy of the state, and rent-seeking behavior as it relates to construction activities.
- **Ground water stress:** Increased demands because of population growth (both host and tourist), lack of policy to regulate access and use, improper technology of extracting equipment, economic activity, insufficient attention to the attributes of the system, development of a water market to service tourism, inadequate sewage disposal system and no-protection zoning.
- **Degradation of beaches, coastal vegetation:** Population, user behavior, rule enforcement, absence of waste management, short time horizons of the tourism industry.
- **Land form changes:** Due to natural and human factors.
- **Poor water quality in creeks:** Sewage outfalls, accumulated garbage.

The impact on ecosystems because of human activities in the area and the key societal drivers of change that this research has identified are:

- **Mangrove conversion:** Increased population pressure and use of mangroves for building houses, firewood, and fencing, some reclamation for aquaculture and agriculture, and poor rule enforcement.
- **Rising groundwater levels:** Rainfall, seepage from canals, field channels and return flow from irrigation, insufficient knowledge of the aquifer's vulnerability, absence of regulation of rising levels based on conjunctive use of surface and ground water.

- **Reduced groundwater quality:** High potassium in agricultural areas due to clay mineral dissolution or due to leaching of chemical fertilizers or both.
- **Deterioration of coastal and surface water quality:** Poor rule enforcement and direct discharges from human activities, substantial discharge of untreated effluents, increased use of nitrates and phosphates.

  In Goa, the main impacts on the ecosystem are: changes in land cover, polluted coastal and groundwater. The drivers of these changes are:
- **Change in land cover, reduced greenery:** Pressure from human activities and need for land for settlements and agriculture.
- **Polluted coastal waters:** Industrial effluents and municipal sewage, poor rule enforcement.
- **Groundwater deterioration:** Groundwater close to industries is contaminated. Large quantities of water used in industries are a threat to groundwater because of mixing in the subsurface, poor rule enforcement.

TOURISM POLICY AND COASTEL MANEGEMENT IN GOA

In the wake of the report, "Our Common Future", by United Nation's Commission on Environment and Development in 1983, India passed its own Environment Protection Act in 1986. This was followed by a Notification in February 1991, inviting the governments of India's coastal states and union territories to prepare Coastal Zone Management Plans for their respective territories. Thus the Government of Goa, in October 1988, published its Regional Development Plan, anticipating, among other activities, the growth of tourism by 2001 A.D. In this plan, a strategy is outlined[14].

"The locations of new beach resorts should be considered not only from point of view of land availability but also from the consideration of beach resource ecology, based on the Environmental Assessment Studies. Further, spreading thinly on all available sandy beach stretches from Tlerekhol/Arambol in the north to Betul/Agonda in the South is not advisable from the standpoint of conservation of resources both natural and man-made. Instead, it is suggested that beach-head developments at certain selected centers should be encouraged.

Despite these admirable commitments toward conservation and the protection of the coastal environment and ecology, the Regional Development Plan for Goa 2001. A.D. does not contain any reference to the "no development zone" of 200/200 meters from the high-tide line along the seashores, which had been much debated around the country in the early 1980s;[15] nor does it mention the Environment Protection Act of 1986 of the Government of India. Moreover, the Coastal Zone Management Plans, prepared by the Department of Town and Country Planning of Goa in 1995 and 1996 for approval by the Central Government. The current policies and relaxed enforcement thereof have led to the haphazard and uncontrolled growth of townships. Places like Calangute and Candolim in Bardez and Colva in Salcete have become over commercialized and haphazard in their development pattern. These areas have a number of unauthorized constructions, which have paid little heed to local planning rules, infrastructure supports or aesthetics. During the 1980s and the early 1990s, the rule of catering to tourists especially, international tourists and the hope of making rapid profits have led to considerable investment in resorts and apartments[16]. A quick look at the developments along the coasts of Goa and the future plans for its, reveals that:[17]

(i) These follow the ideas submitted in the CZM plan of Goa (which is yet to be formally approved) rather than its Regional Development plan; and,

(ii) The tourists are almost exclusively accommodated along the 105 km stretch of the coastline while little effort has been made to adhere to the regional plans of creating other types of tourism besides beach tourism.

Policy analysis leads us to suggest the following initiatives for more effective coastal management in Goa:

- Need for creative, decentralized forms of management within broad enabling frameworks
- Use of indicators to monitor and manage development activity and impacts
- A critical need for consultative workshops at regular intervals with stakeholders for long term success,

- A more open approach to the ill-effects of the dominant development activity
- Investment in training for the dominant activity
- Zoning (for aquaculture and industry) based on proper social and environmental assessments
- Need for effluent treatment systems which a number of small units can use
- Educating various stakeholders to alter the perceptions
- Significance and value they attach to environmental resources and change
- Strengthening of local communities and non-governmental organizations and the conjunctive management of surface and groundwater to reduce variability and to avoid rising water levels.

GOA BEACHES

The Goa coast is generally sandy except little cliffy near Panjim. The prominent river outfalls are Mandovi, Zuari, Terekhol, Chapora and Damanganga. It has extensive beach resources of international tourist interest.

Mandovi-Zuari estuarine complex on the west coast of peninsular India, comprising Mandovi and Zuari rivers, their tributaries, and the interconnecting Cumbharjua canal forms the central part of the coastal ecosystem for Goa. The estuaries are divided by extensive intertidal mudflats and adjacent rice fields. Both the rivers originate in the Western ghats, traverse a distance of 61 km and 66 km respectively, before open into Arabian sea at the Aguada and Marmagoa bays. They are more or less tidal estuaries being influenced by sea water inflow to a considerable distance inland with seasonal freshwater runoff. Zuari is the largest estuary containing 9 ha of mangroves. The upstream region is narrow (0.5 km) and subjected to intense wave action while at the mouth it is 5.5 km wide. The average annual freshwater runoff is estimated to be 9 cu. Km. Mandovi estuary and Cumbharjua canal have 7 ha and 2 ha of mangoves, respectively, occurring along the banks. Mandovi has greater freshwater influence than the other estuaries.[18] The important features of Aguada and Marmagao bays are seasonal variation in physico-chemical parameters which are greatly affected by river runoff and local mansoonal precipitation. Maximum precipitation occurs during June-September when the southwest monsoon is accompanied by stormy weather, whereas the rest of the year, the quieter conditions are prevailing. The shoreline consists of rocks and boulders with sandy beach areas.[19] In Aguada bay sand bars are formed every year during monsoon season, which change the course of tidal currents and influence hydrological factors.

Charao Island which has now been declared as reserved forest and Dr. Salim Ali bird sanctuary is situated in the Mandovi estuary. It harbors a mangrove flora comprising about 12 mangrove species and 8 associated species. The nearby area of almost 80 ha is under pisciculture.[20] There are no major anthropogenic threats. Except a fertilizer complex at Velsao, there is no major industrial development along the Goa coast. The major concern is the contamination of Mandovi-Zuari estuarine complex with mine rejects which are dumped along the shore. Further a pesticide manufacturing industry releases treated wastewater in the Cumbharjua channel connecting Mandovi-Zuari river.

Table 27

	State : Goa	*Area : Goa Beaches*
Parameters		
1.1.	The fragile coastal area is	Mangrow forest, salt water, lake, estuary, backwater etc., area of mariculture and tourist spot.
1.2.	Name of the location	Goa coast
1.3.	Area in Sq. km.	132.9 (from Trekhol to Pokm)
1.4.	a. Latitude	150^0 48' N
	b. Longitude	730^0 40' C
2.0.	Weather	
2.1.	Temperature (annual)	
	a. Maximum	31.4^{0}C
	b. B. Minimum.	23.4^{0}C
	c. C. Mean	27.4^{0}C
2.2.	Rainfall (annual in mm)	2,556
2.3.	Relative humidity (%)	
	a. Maximum	99.0
	b. Minimum	40.0
	c. Mean	60.0
2.4.	Windspeed (kh/hr)	
	a. Maximum	12.0
	b. Minimum	1.0

2.5.	Wind Direction	NE/SW	
3.	Name of the River/Drains/Discharges in and around the area	Mandovi, Zuri, Trekhol, Chapora and Damanganga rivers.	
3.1.	Possible impact on the area	Mining, municipal disposals, industrial effluents and tourism.	
3.2.	Water quality	Water quality of the rivers continue to be good except that in saline water stretches, an increase in biochemical Oxygen Demand is noticed	
3.3.	Sedimentation	The sediment input to the Zuari estuary may be from sources such as catchment area, marginal cliffs on the river banks. During onset of monsoon the estuary bears a high sediment load of which a large portion of material from the catchment area is brought into the system during the early monsoon period. Less suspended matter during heavy monsoon showed that the drainage possible comes from a lithological terrain from which loose overlying material is washed off during the initial stages of the monsoon and afterwards clear water joins the estuary	
3.4.	Types of industries located in and around the area	Fertilizers, Breweries, Pesticides, Iron ore benefaction, sugar, textiles, chemicals, distilleries, tyres & tubes pharmaceuticals of which only two are located at the vicinity of the coast. Port related operations at Marmugao including crude oil transport and municipal waste form the major sources of pollution	
3.5.	Municipal sewage discharge if any	Yes. In Mandovi estuary	
a.	Quality (CPCB data: May, 1995)	Raw sewage	Treated effluent
	Total solids (mg/1)	1,162	2,306
	Total dissolved solids (mg/1)	814	2,262
	Suspended solids (mg/1)	114	43
	Volatile solids (mf/1)	200	—
	Chloride as C1 (mg/1)	458	1,125
	-do- as NaC1 (mg/1)	756	1,856
	PH 6.9	7.4	
	BOD (mg/1at 27^{0}C3 days)	216	54
	COD (mg/1)	446	165
b.	Quantity (m^3/d)	10,200 at Panjim	

	a. Quality	NA	
	b. Quantity (m^3/d)	Fertilizers	8,640
		Breweries	290-400
		Pesticides	960
		Pellestsation	1,000
		Iron ore beneficiation	1,440
4.1.	Whether treated or untreated	Treated	
5.0.	Marine outfalls, if any	Yes	
	a. Quality	Na	
	b. Quantity	Sewerage treatment plant, Panjim – 1,440 m^3/d, treated Hindustan Ciba-Geigy Ltd. – 10,200 m^3/d treated	
5.1.	Possibility of discharge reaching the fragile area.	❖ Fertilizer to the sea through 90m long outfall with terminal diffuser ❖ Breweries – in Zuri river through a nallah ❖ Iron ore-natural drain meeting river Kalay.	
6.0.	Solid waste dumping, if any	Yes, Municipal	
6.1.	Possible impact on the area	NA	
7.0	Other Developmental Activities	Tourism, mining & hotel and allied industries. Various conservation programs such as afforestation of mangroves are in progress in Chorao island.	
7.1.	Residential tourism, construction of restaurants hotels etc.	Along the coastal belt, number of restaurants and beach resorts are located.	
7.2.	Recreational tourism (Water sports, bathing etc.)	Yes. Boating, bathing and water sports.	
8.0	Human settlements in the area	Yes	
8.1.	Socio-economic status	Fishing and tourism related	
9.0.	Coastal waster circulation pattern, possibility of reaching of sewage, effluent discharge etc.	Through tides and currents	
10.0.	Coastal water quality	See Table VII. 1.	
10.1.	Trend of water quality	Good but BOD is noticed in saline water	
11.0.	Important species available (quantitative and qualitative)	Kingfish, Mackerel, Eel fish, Mussels nad prawns. Also see Table VII. 2.	
11.1.	Concentration of contaminants in		
	a. Fish	NA	
	b. Zooplankton	NA	

11.2.	Whether the resources of the area are exploited? If yes, to what extent?	Yes
11.3.	Commercial fishing	Yes. Cat fishes, ribbon fishes and threadfin breams etc.
11.3.	Whether poaching is in practice? If yes, to what extent?	Yes.
12.	Tourist sport	Beaches all along the Goa coast (North to South)
12.1.	Number of tourists visited	About 1 million each year
12.2.	Status of beach	Clean
12.3.	Occurrence of tar balls and other solid waste on the beach	Noticed in the North beaches of Goa.
12.4.	Water quality/beach erosion/cyclones /natural calamity etc.	The Northern part of India experiences both extra-tropical and tropical cyclones. Extra-tropical cyclones occur mostly from late May to first half of June & at about the onset of northeast monsoon which extends from late October through first three weeks of November. Cyclonic storms although infrequent, occur during summer and during such events sea level increases significantly and water penetrates far inland
12.5.	Other developmental activities other than above, if any	Proposal to construct a marine Park at Shiroda. The Konkan railway which is being constructed through coastal Goa is crossing across the Mandovi-Zuari estuarine complex.

Source: (A) Kirloskar Consultants Ltd. 1994. Report on Study of Tourism Industry in Goa, December. (B) Alvares, C. 1993 "Fish curry and rice. A citizen's report on the State of Goa Environment". Ecp-form Goa, p. 260. (C) Carneiro, T. R.L. 1996 use of Hydrochemical Techniques for Detection of Sea Water Intrusion is Coastal Aquifers between fort Aquada and fort Chapora, north Goa MSC thesis Goa University.

SPATIAL ANALYSIS OF POLICIES FOR COASTAL ZONE

India has enacted comprehensive environmental protection laws to control water and air pollution. The Central Beach Erosion Board was constituted by the government of India in 1971 with following functions:

- To organize coordinated program of collection, compilations evaluation, and publication of data relating to natural phenomena and coastal process that effect the coastline through central organizations.

- To arrange general investigation, studies and research.
- To lay down general design principles and construction techniques for the guidance for the state authorities.
- To review from time to time the performance of works carried out by the maritime states and evolves improved design and techniques based on such experience.
- To render technical advice on specific problems at the request of the state.
- To draw up a program of training for the personnel engaged in coastal engineering.
- To suggest other steps necessary in tackling the problems of coastal erosion in an economic and coordinated.

So, it was the Central Beach Erosion conflicting and multiple uses of coastal zone management Authority in every maritime state India.[21]

Some of the important laws and regulations followed in India to conserve the environment are:

- The Wildlife (Protection) Act 1972 , amended in 1983, 1986, and 1991;
- Water (Prevention)and control of Pollution) Actl974, amended in 1988;
- Forest conservation Act 1986 :
- A notification on coastal zone regulation 1991.

In these Coastal Regulation Zone 1991 is most important and completely applicable to coastal zone.

Coastal Regulation Zone (CRZ)-1991

In Environment Protection Act, 1986, rule 5 (3) puts prohibition and restriction on location of industries and carrying on processes and operations different areas. This rule is in consonance with section 3 (2) (5) which read;[22]

"(5) Restriction of areas in which any industries, operations or processes or class of industries shall not be carried out or shall be carried out subject to certain safeguards."

In exercise of powers the government of India declared the coastal stretches of seas, bays, estuaries, creeks, rivers, and backwaters that are influenced by tidal actions (on land ward side) up to 500m from the high tide line as the Coastal Regulation Zone.[23]

But in 1994, the Ministry of Environment and Forest amended it.[24]

"For the purposes of this notification, the High Tide Line means the line on the land up to which the highest water line reaches during the spring tide and shall be demarcated uniformly in all parts of the country by the demarcating authority so authorized by the Central government in consultation with Surveyor General of India."

Here once again Supreme Court order dated 18.4.1996:

"The distance from the High Tide Line shall apply to both sides in the case of rivers, creeks and back waters and may be modified on a case by case basis for reasons to be recorded which preparing the Coastal Zone Management Plans . However, this distance shall be less than 100 meters or the width of the creeks, river or backwater which ever less is.[25]

Further, the Ministry of Environment, Forest and Wildlife notified 'certain activities prohibited 'and certain require 'environmental clearance' from the Ministry of Environment, Forests and Wildlife.

The 'prohibited activities 'within the Coastal Regulation Zone includes:

1. Setting up of new industries and expansion of existing industries, except those directly related to waterfront or directly needing foreshore facilities.
2. Manufacturer, handling, storage, or disposal of hazardous substance.

   But in 1997 notification govt. included that;

   "...... provide that Government of India in the Ministry of Surface Transport, on a case to case to basis, may permit storage of the petroleum products as specified in Annexure - 3 appended to this notification within the existing port that have not been classified as CRZ -I subject to implementation of safety regulations including Government of India, Ministry of Petroleum and Natural Gas after ensuring proper location of the site and availability of arising due to any accident or spillage...[26]
3. Setting up and expansion of fish processing units including warehousing, but excluding hatchery natural fish drying in permitting areas. Provided that existing fish processing units for moderation purposes may utilize twenty five percent additional plinth area required for additional equipment and pollution control measures only subject to existing Floor Space Index, Floor Area Ratio norms and subject to the condition that

the additional plinth area shall not be towards sea ward side of existing unit and also subject to the approval of State Pollution Control Board or Pollution Control Committee.[27]

4. Setting up and expansion of units and mechanism for disposal of waste and effluents, expect facilities required for discharging treated effluents into the watercourse with approval under the water (Prevention and Control of Pollution) Act 1974 and except storm water drains.
5. Discharge of untreated wastes and effluents from industries, cities or other human settlements.
6. Dumping of ash or any other wastes from thermal power stations.
7. Dumping waste from the city or town for the purpose of land filling, or otherwise.
8. land reclamation , bounding or disturbing the natural course of sea water except those required for construction of port, harbors, jetties , wharves, guys, slipways, bridges and sea-links and for other facilities that are essential for activities permissible under notification or for control of coastal erosion and maintenance or clearing of water ways, channels and ports or for prevention of sandbars or for tidal regulators, storm water drains or for structures for prevention of salinity ingress and sweet water recharge.[28]
9. Mining of land, rocks and other substrata materials, except those rare minerals not available outside the Coastal Regulation Zone areas.

   But by the notification of 31.1.1997[29] Government of India provided that the Union Territory of Andaman and Nicobar Islands, mining of sands may be permitted by the committee, which shall be constituted by the Lieutenant Governor of the Andaman and Nicobar Islands, consisting of Chief Secretary, Secretary, Department of Environment; Secretary, Department of Water Resource; Secretary, Public Works Department . The committee may permit mining of sand from non-degraded manner on a case to case basis, also the quantity of sand mined.
10. Harvesting or withdrawal of groundwater and construction of waterworks within 200m of the high tide line, in 200m to 500m zone, it shall be permitted only when done manually through ordinary wells for drinking, horticulture, agriculture and fishing.

Provided that drawl of ground water is permitted, where no other source of water is available and done manually through ordinary wells or hand pumps, for drinking and domestic purposes .zone between 50m to 200m from High Tide Line in case of seas, bays and estuaries and within 200m or the CRZ , whichever is less.

11. Construction activities in ecologically sensitive areas.
12. Any construction activity between low tide line and high tide line, except facilities for carrying activities, except in special cases and hence shall not normally be permitted in the Coastal Regulation Zone.

Treated effluents and waste water discharges into sea, facilities for carrying seawater for cooling purposes, oil, gas, and similar pipelines and facilities for essential activities.

Dressing or altering to sand dunes, hills and natural features including landscape charges for beautification, recreation and other such activities.

The following activities require environmental clearance from the Ministry of Environment, Forest and Wildlife.

1. Construction activities related to defense requirements for which foreshore facilities are essential (e.g. slipways, Jetties, except for classified operational components of defense projects for which a separate procedures shall be followed. (Residential buildings, office buildings, hospital complexes, workshops shall not come within the definition of operational requirements, except in special cases and hence shall not normally be permitted in the Coastal Regulation Zone.
2. Operational constructions for ports, has labors and light houses requiring water frontage; and Jetties, whereas, quays, slipways etc. (Residential buildings and office building's shall not come within the definition of operational activities, except in special cases and hence shall not normally be permitted in the Coastal Regulation Zone.
3. Thermal power plants (only foreshore facilities for transport of raw materials, facilities for intake of cooling water and outfall for discharge of treated waste water or cooling water); and
4. All other activities with investment exceeding 50 million rupees.[30]

In another part of Coastal Regulation Zone deals with coastal area classification and development regulations (in Annexure – 1),[31] guidelines for development of Beach resorts/hotels (in Annexure – II)[1] and list of petroleum products permitted for storage in ports areas (in Annexure – III).[32]

In annexure – I, the classification and development regulations, the coastal regulation zone has been divided into four categories and the norms of activities in those areas.

1. Categories – I (CRZ-I): In category – I, those as which are ecologically sensitive and very important, such as national parks/marine parks, reserve forests wildlife habitats and coastal reef and other marine life, areas of outstanding natural beauty/ heritage areas and areas likely to be in undated due to rise in sea level consequent upon global warming. And another part of CRZ-I is, the area between low tide and high tide line.

In these areas (or CR2-I) no new construction shall be permitted with in 500 meters of the high tide line. But in case of dispensaries, school, public rains shelters community, road, jetties, sewerage, which required for traditional inhabitants of Suderbans Biosphere reserve area, Best Bengal, may be permitted, in case to case, basis by as authority designated by the state Government.[33]

2. Category – II (CRZ-II): In this category come those areas that have already been developed upto or close to the shoreline. "Developed area", referred here, is referred to as that are within the municipal limits or in other legally designated urban areas.

These buildings shall be permitted only on the landward side of the existing road (or roads proposed in the approved coastal zone management plan of the area). These structures shall be subjected existing local town and country planning regulations including the existing norms of floor space index/floor area ratio. Same rule will be obeyed in reconstruction of authorized buildings.

3. Category – III (CRZ-III): This category includes coastal zone in rural areas, both developed and underdeveloped, and also area with in Municipal limits or in other legally designated urban areas which are not substantially built up. In these also, areas upto 200 meters from HTL is to be ear marked as ' No Development Zone' except for repairs of existing floor spaces index. In this matter State movement/UT may permit for water supply, sewerage etc.[34]

4. Category – IV (CRZ-IV): This type of category includes, the coastal stretches in the Andaman Nicobar, Lakshdweep and small islands, except those designated as (CRZ-I, CRZ-II, CRZ-III.

These are certain different norms of CRZ for this category. No new construction of buildings shall be permitted with in 200 meters of the HTL and the buildings between 20 and 500 meters from HTL shall not have more than 2 floors (ground floor and first floor), the total covered area on all floor shall not be more than 50 percent of the plot size and the total height of construction shall not exceed a meters.

Another important thing in this category has of coral reefs. Coral from the beaches and coastal water shall not be used for construction, sand from beaches may used only construction purposes up to 31st day of March, 1990 and dredging and under water blasting in and around coral formations shall not be permitted.

Annexure – II contains detail guidelines for development of beach resorts/ hotels in the designated areas of CRZ-II for temporary occupation of tourists.

COASTAL REGULATION ZONE (CRZ) : IT'S DEMARCATION AND MANAGEMENT: AN CRITICAL ANALYSIS

Environment Protection Act, 1986 Rule 5 (3) puts prohibition and restriction on location of Industries and carrying on processes and operations in different areas. This rule is in consonance with section 3 (2) (v) which reads:[35]

> "**(v) Restriction of areas in which any industries, operations or processes or class of industries, operations or processes shall not be carried out or shall be carried out subject to certain safeguards".**

In exercise of powers conferred by Rule 5 (3), coastal Regulation Zone was issued which is dated 19/02/1991 published in the Gazette 21/02/1991.[36]

As per the said Regulation, commonly known as (CRZ), the Central Government has declared the coastal stretches of seas, bays, estuaries creeks, rivers and backwaters which are influenced by tidal action (in the landward side) upto 500 mtrs. From the High Tide Line (HTL) and the land between the Law Tide Line (LTL) and HTL as coastal Regulation Zone. Further, it imposes restrictions on the setting up an expansion of Industries, operations or processes etc. in the said Coastal Regulation Zone.

The CRZ regulation, as it originally stood, and dealing with demarcation of High Tide Line reads:[37]

> **"For the purposes of this Notification the High Tide Line (HTL) will be defined as the line up to which the highest high tide reaches at spring tides".**

As per Notification dated 18/08/1994,[38] the definition of High Tide Line was modified. Aforesaid extracted portion was substituted as follows:

> **"For the purpose of this Notification, the High Tide Line means the line on the land upto which the highest water line reaches during the spring tide and shall be demarcated uniformly all parts of the country by the demarcating authority so authorized by the Central Government in consultation with Surveyor General of India".**

By notifications dated 26/11/1998[39] the Central Government constituted National coastal Zone Management Authority at the Center and also for the Coastal States. The Goa coastal Zone Management Authority is constituted by 7 members and the notification giving power to the authority reads thus:

II. The Authority shall have the power to take the following measures for protecting and improving the quality of the coastal environment and preventing, abating and controlling environment pollution in coastal areas of the State of Goa namely:

(i) Examination of the proposals or charges/ modifications in classification of coastal Regulation Zone areas and in the coastal Zone Management Plans (CZMP) received from the Goa State Government and making specific recommendations to the National coastal Zone Management Authority thereof.

(ii) (a) Inquiry into cases of alleged violations of the provisions of the said Act and/or the rules made there under, or any other law which is relatable to the objects of the said Act and, if found necessary in a specific case, issuing directions under section 5 of the said Act insofar as such directions are not consistent with any direction issued in that specific case by the National Coastal Zone Authority or by the Central Government.

(b) Review of cases involving violations of the provisions of the said Act and the rules made there under, or under any law which is relatable to the objects of the said Act, and, if found necessary referring such cases, with comments, for review to the National Coastal Zone Management Authority.

Provides that the cases under sub-paragraphs (ii) (a) and (ii) (b) or paragraph II may either be taken up suo-moto, or on the basis of complaint made by an individual, or a representative body, or an organization.

(iii) Filing complaints, under section 19 of said Act in cases of non-compliance of the directions issued by it under sub-paragraph (ii) (a) of paragraph II of this Order.

(iv) To take action under section 10 of the said Act to verify the facts concerning the issues arising from sub-paragraphs (i) and (ii) of paragraphs II of this Order

III. The Authority shall deal with environmental issues relating to coastal Regulation zone which may be referred to it by the Goa State Government. The national Coastal Zone Management Authority or the Central Government.

IV. The Authority shall identify ecologically sensitive areas in the coastal Regulation Zone, and formulate area-specific management plans for such identified areas.

V. The authority shall identify coastal area highly vulnerable to erosion/ degradation and formulate area-specific management plans for such identified areas.

VI. The Authority shall identify economically important stretches in Coastal Regulation Zone and prepare Integrated Coastal Zone Management Plans for the same.

VII. The Authority shall submit the plans prepared by it under paragraphs IV, V, VI above and modifications thereof to the National Coasts Zone Management Authority for examination and its approval.

VIII. The Authority shall ensure compliance of all specific conditions that are lad down in the approved Coastal Zone Management Plan to Goa.

IX. The Authority shall furnish report of its activities at least once in six months to the National coastal Zone Management Authority.

X. The foregoing powers and functions of the Authority shall be subject to the supervision and control of the Central Government.

XI. The Authority shall have its headquarters at Panjim.

XII. Any matter specifically not falling within the scope and jurisdiction of the Authority as so constituted shall be dealt with by the statutory authorities concerned.

In the year 1998 by notification 29/12/1998[40] again the passage introduced in 1994 was amended by substituting the worlds, as follows:

> **"For the purpose of this notification, the High Tide Line means the line on the land upto which the highest water line reaches during the spring tide. The High Tide Line shall be demarcated uniformly in all parts of the country by the demarcating authority or authorities so authorised by the Central Government, in accordance with the general guidelines issued in this regard".**

By letter dated January 8, 1999 the Central government appointed institutions and also issued guidelines for the purposes of demarcating the High Tide Line (HTL) and Low Tide Line (LTL).

The institutions authorized by the Central government by the aforesaid letter dated 08/01/1999[41] area as follows:

1. Space Application Centre, Ahmedabad.
2. Centre for Earth Sciences Studies, Thiruvananthapuram.
3. Institute of Remote Sensing, Anna University, Chennai
4. Institute of Wetland Management and Ecological Designs, Calcutta.
5. Naval Hydrographer's Office, Dehra Dun.

Broadly the guidelines issued are:

(A) Preparation f base maps 1:25,000 scale acquired from survey of India and wherever of that scale are not available they will be enlarged to 1:25,000 of smaller scale. There maps will be of the standard specifications given below:

Limits	:	7.5 minutes x 7.5 minutes
Numbering	:	Survey of India Sheet Numbering System
Horizontal Datum	:	Everest or WGS 84.
Vertical Datum	:	Mean Sea Level (MSL)
Topograph	:	topography in the SOI maps will be updated using latest satellite imageries/ aerial photographs.

Such High Tide Line mark will be then transferred to Coastal Zone Management (CZM) maps.

(B) For the determination of coastal geomorphologic signatures in the field/ satellite imageries/aerial photographs will be used for appropriate adjustments in the High Water Line/Low Water Line for demarcating the High Tide Line/Low HTL/LTL.

(C) The following geomorphologic features will be considered while demarcating High tide Line/Low Tide Line HTL/LTL.

(a) Land ward (Monsoon) Berm crest in the case of sandy beaches.

(b) Rocks, headlands, Cliffs.

(c) Seawalls, Revetments, Embankments.

(D) As per Clause 2 (v), of guidelines for demarcation of High Tide Line/ Low Tide Line in the Coastal Regulation Zone. (HTL) will also be demarcated in CZM maps along the banks of tidal influenced inland water bodies with the help of geomorphologic signature/features.

(E) Then classification of different Coastal Zones will be done as per Coastal Regulation Zone (CRZ) notification and standard national, international symbols and colour codes will be used.

(F) In the matter of local level CZM maps, the cadastral village maps in 1: 3960 or the nearest scale will be used as the base maps. High Tide Line (HTL) AND Low Tide Line (LTL) as defined in coastal Regulation Zone (CRZ) in the respective cadastral village maps and classification transferred in local level CZM maps.

Passing reference to some of the guidelines dated 08/01/1999[42] may not be out of place.

(a) Guideline V as well as guideline III (v) is contrary to clause 1 and note to clause 1 as the application of CRZ is within the belt of 500 of High Tide Line.

(b) Guideline II (1) is not clear. It is not clear whether the representation will continue to be done in the scale 1: 3960 or metric system will be used.

Later on one more agency was added to same by Ministry of Environment and Forests and that is national Institute of Oceanography (NIO), Panaji, Goa. By notification dated June 30, 1999, Goa Coastal Management Authority was reconstituted.

Again, even after that, a draft notification SO. 629 (E)[43] dated August 5, 1999 has been published for changing some features of the classification, calling for objections.

In the proposed draft notification the 'Note' to clause (1) is proposed to be substituted as follows:

"(II) The distance from the High Tide Line shall apply to both sides in the case of rivers, creeks, and backwaters and may be modified on a case to case basis for reasons to be recorded while preparing the Coastal zone Management Plans. However, this distance shall not be less than 100 metres or the width for the creek, river or backwater whichever is less. The distance upto which developments along rivers, creeks and backwaters is to be regulated shall be governed by the distance upto which the tidal effect of sea is experience in rivers, creeks or backwaters, as the case maybe and shall be clearly identified in the Coastal Zone Management Plans."

By proposing this amendment, the Note is meant to be changed as clause (ii) and for the first time a new idea is brought and in that "the distance from the High Tide Line should apply to both sides of rivers creeks and backwaters".

The purpose of the draft notification is essentially to reduce the width in the note to the main clause from 100 mtrs. To 50 mtrs. On case to case basis provided other conditions are satisfied.

The Central Government as earlier had also reduced the distance from 100 mtrs. But uniformly.

The same reduction from 100 m. to 50 m. was quashed by Supreme Court in the case of Indian Council for Enviro-Legal Action V/s. Union of India and Others 1996 (5) SCC 281.[44] Therefore, what was quashed by the Supreme Court is now sought to be restored not uniformly, but case to case basis subject to some qualifications and conditions.

This is one judgment of the Supreme Court where the scope of CRZ regulations had come for a debate.

Another judgment of the Supreme Court where the Pisciculture in the CRZ came under challenge in the case of S. Jaganath v. Union of India – (1997) (2) SCC 87 (para 4.2 and 4.6 supra).[45]

From the above it is clear, that as far as Goa is concerned, although CRZ Notification had come into force from February 20, 1991, Goa Coastal Zone Management Authority was constituted by Ministry of environment and forests only on November 26, 1998.

Prior to November 26, 1998 and after the environment Protection Act 1986 was enforced from November 1986, and after Goa was granted Statehood, the government of India decided that control of coastal stretches shall be exercised by the concerned State Governments and accordingly the Government of Goa reconstituted "Ecological Development Council" to be headed by the Chief Minister.

In this regard the judgment of the High Court of Bombay given by a division Bench at Goa in the matter of Prof. Sergio Carvalhov. State of Goa and Ors., (1989 (1) Goa Law times 276) challenging the construction carried out by 'Ramada Hotel' at Fatrade Beach, Village Varca, Taluka Salcete, requires to be notice. The matter was carried before the Supreme court. The special leave was dismissed, but all the questions decided have been left open (Special Leave Petition No. 3259/1989 with Civil Miscellaneous Petition No. 11260/1989 decided on 24/4/1989).

The events subsequent to the decisions of the Writ Petition are as follows:

(a) Government of Goa constitutes high power committee know as **Goa State Committee on Environment (GSCE),** also stating that the ECOLOGICAL DEVELOPMENT COUNCIL and ECOLOGICAL CONTROL COMMITTEE stands dissolved (July 26, 1990);

(b) Government of Goa issued a notification dated February 19, 1991 **Constituting Coastal Regulation Zone (CRZ)** regulation;

(c) Government of Goa by notification dated September 23, 1993 constitutes a fresh committee known as **Goa State Committee on Castal Environment (GSCCE)** to deal with matters pertaining to clearances of development projects within the Coastal Regulation Zone and earlier committees stand dissolved.

Notes

1. Singh K.S. (1993): People of India, Goa, Anthropological Survey of India, Popular Prakashan, Mumbai, pp. 5.
2. Wadia, E.N. (1981), Geology of India, Tata McGrew Hills, New Delhi.
4. Singh R.L. (1969) Regional Geography of India, National Geographysical Society of India, Varanasi, India.
5. Mamoria C.B. (1998) Economic and Commercial Geographic of India, Shiva Lal Agarwal and Company, New Delhi.
6. Status of Fisheries in India, special publication no. 29 CMFRI, Cochin India, 1996.

7. For example, the number of registered cars, jeeps and taxis has gone up sharply from 310,000 in 1960 to 3,330,000 in 1993.
8. The commissioning of the coastal Konkan Railway and the modernization of South-Central Railway will considerably increase the accessibility of Goa to the rest of India. A form of weekend tourism is likely to emerge from this, which may have environmental and economic impacts similar to cruise in the Carribean Islands.
9. Lobo, U. 1988. "Environmental Aspects of Silica Sand Mining from coastal Sand Dunes". Earth Resources for Goa's Development, pp. 521-523.
10. Jagtap, T.J. V.S Chavan and A.G. Untawale. 1993. "Mangrove Ecosystems of India: A Need for Protection" Ambio. V. 21. Pp. 252-254.
11. National Institute of Oceanography. 1996. Comments on the Coastal Zone Management Plans of Goa. Report submitted to India, Ministry of Environment and Forests. New Delhi.
12. Alvares, C. 1993. "Fish, Curry and Rice, A citizen's Reports on the State of the goan Environment". Ecoforum. Goa. P. 260; william, A. 1997. "Garbage, Vendors Turn Idyll into Nightmare. "the Navhind Times.3 March, p.1.
13. Alvars, C. 1993. "fish, Curry and Rice: A Citizen's Report on the State of the Goan Emvironment". Ecoforum, goa. P. 260; Gadgil. M. and S. Chandran. 1993. "Konkan Lessons- A Railway Project and the Environment". Frontline. 26 march, p. 62; Mascarenhas, A. 1992. "Our Estruaries in Peril." The Herald. 20 April, p. 4; Mascarenhas, A.K. Sawkar and O.S. Chauhan. 1997. The Coastal Zone of Goa: then and Now. Abstract 49. Seminar on Coastal Zone Environment and Management. Mangalore University, 12-14 February, pp. 50-52.
14. D'Souza, J. A. *et. al.,* 1988., The Regional Plan for Goa, 2001 A.D. India, Government of Goa, Department of Town and Country Planning, October, p. 108.
15. India, Ministry of Environment and Forests. 1991. The Gazette of India. Notification: S.O. No. 114 (E), February 20
16. Wilson, D. 1997. "Paradoxes of Tourism in Goa. Annals of Tourism Research. 21 (1), pp. 52-75 and Wilson. D, 1997, "Strategies for Sustainability: Lessons from Goa and Seychelles" in sustainable Tourism. M. Stabler (Ed) Wallingford: CAB International.
17. Wilson, d. 1997. Strategies for Sustainability: Lesson from Goa and Seychelles in sustainable Tourism. M. Stabler (ED.) Wallingford: CAB International.
18. William, A. 1997 "burgeoning construction may be epitaph to Queens of Beeches". The Navhind Times 4, March,, p. 1.

19. Wilson D. "Paradoxes of Tourism in Goa" annuals of Tourism Research 21 (1): 52-75.
20. *Ibid.*
21. *Ibid.* n.1
22. Environment Protection Act (1986) Ministry of Environment, Forest Government of India.
23. Ministry of Environment Forest (Dept. of Environment, forest and Wild life) (191). The coastal regulation zone notification. The Gazette if India S. O. No. 114E, Feb. 20. (As amended by notification dated 16.8.1994, 31.1.1997, 9.7.1997 and Supreme Court Judgment dated 18.4.1996).
24. *Ibid.* n. 2 amended by notification dated 18.8.7994.
25. *Ibid.*, n. 2, amendment to 50 meters by notification dated 16.8.1994. revised to 100 meters by Supreme Court order dated 18.4.1996.
26. *Ibid.*, n. 2 inserted by notification dated 9.7.1997.
27. *Ibid.*, n. 2, inserted dated 9.7.1997.
28. *Ibid.*, n. 2, inserted by notification dated 31.1.1997.
29. *Ibid.*, n. inserted by notification dated 31.1.1997.
30. *Ibid,* n. 2, Substituted by notification dated 9.7.1997.
31. *Ibid*, n. 2 Annexure – I, Coastal area Classification and Development Regulations.

    1 Ibid. n. 2, Annexure – II, guidelines for development of beach resorts/ hotels in designated areas of CR2 – II for temporary occupation of Tourist/ Visitors. With prior approval of Ministry of Environment and Forest.
32. *Ibid.*, n. 2, Annexure – III, list of petroleum products permitted for storage in port areas.
33. *Ibid.* No. 2, Inserted by notification dated 9.7.1997
34. *Ibid* No. 2, Inserted by notification dated 9.7.1992.
35. Ministry of Environment and Forest (1986), Environmental Protection Act.
36. India, Ministry of Environment and Forest: 1991. The Gazette o India S.O. No. 114(E), February 20.
37. *Ibid*, 2.
38. India, Ministry of Environmental and Forest (1994), the Gazette of India S.O. No. August 18.
39. India, Ministry of Environment and Forest (1998), the Gazettee of India S.O. No. 995 (E), Nov. 26.

40. India, Ministry of Environment and Forest 1998, S.O. No. 12.
41. India, Ministry of Environment and Forest 1998, S.O. No. January, 8.
42. *Ibid.*
43. India, Ministry of Environment and Forest 1999, S.O. No. 629(E), August 5.
44. Indian Council for Enviro-legal Actions Vs Union of India nad others 1996(5) Supreme court cases 281.
45. S. Jaganath V. Union of India (1997 (2) Supreme court cases 87 (para 4.2 and 4.6 Supra).

CHAPTER 4

SPATIAL ANALYSIS OF ADMINISTRATIVE ACTIONS AND PROBLEMS OF INTEGRATED COASTAL ZONE MANAGEMENT: QUEENSLAND (AUSTRALIA)

GEOGRAPHY AND THE ENVIRONMENT

Area and Position

The state of Queensland, with an area of 1,727,000 sq. kms. Occupies the north-eastern position of the Australian continent. It covers area between 10^0 and 29^0 south latitude and 138^0 and 154^0 east longitude (Figure 1). It has approximately 7,400 kms with New South Wales, 630 kms with South Australian and 1045 kms with Northern Territory. From north to south its greatest distance is 2,100 kms and from east to west 1,450 kms. The area is 22.5 percent of the Australian continent, and the occupied area 31 percent of the Australian occupied total (Table 1).

Table 1
Areas of States and Territories, Australia

State of Territory	*Area*	*Proportion of Total*
	'000 Sq. Km.	%
New South Wales	802	10.4
Victoria	228	3.0
Queensland	1727	22.5
South Australia	984	12.8
Western Australia	2526	32.9
Tasmania	68	0.9
Northern Territory	1346	17.5
Australian Capital Territory	2	—
Australia	7682	100.0

Source: Queensland Year Book, 1998. Australian Bureau of Statistics No. 56 ABS Catalogue No. 1301.3 B.

Figure 1: Location of Study Area

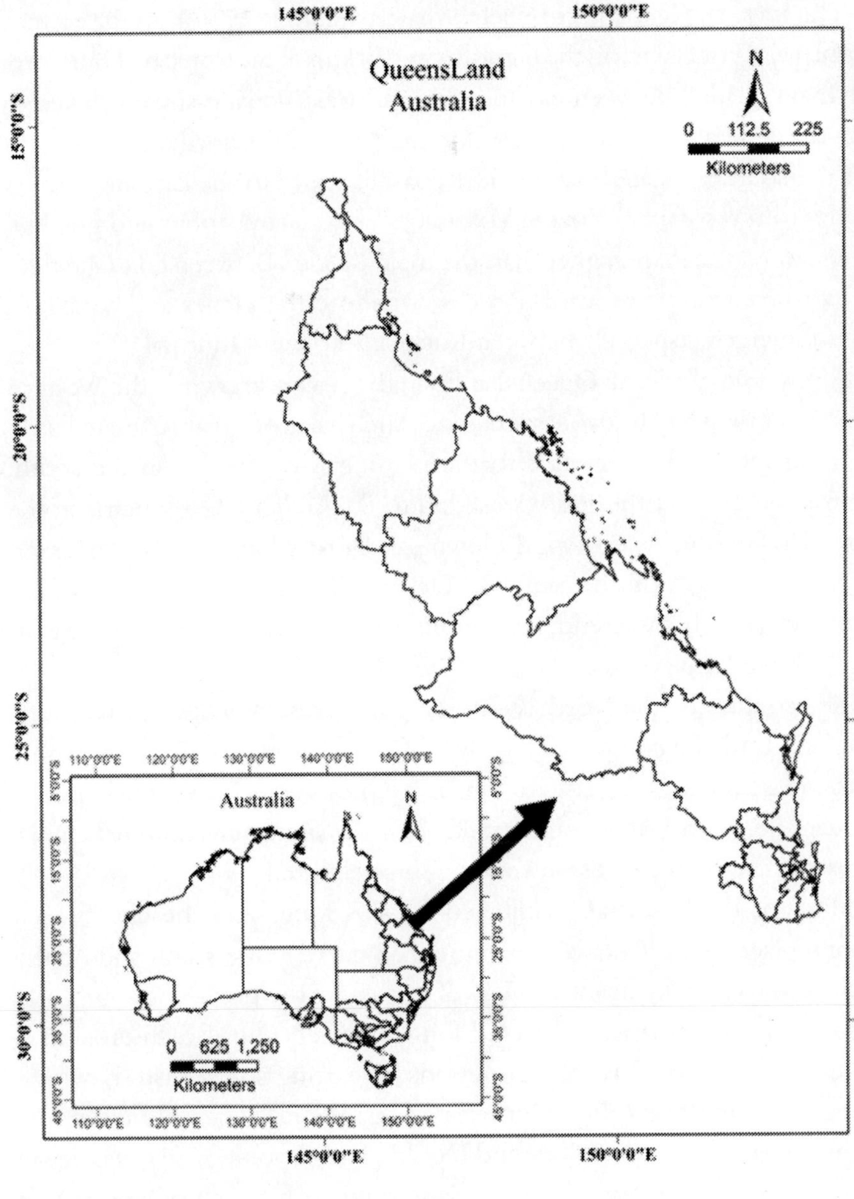

Physical Features

Queensland can be divided into four landscape regions:[1, 2]

(a) The Eastern Highlands

(b) The Western Plains

(c) The North-Western Plains

(d) The Coastal Plain with Islands and reefs.

The Eastern Highlands parallel the east, extending west from the eastern coastal plain. For 80 kms in the far north to 480 kms at the tropic of Capricorn. The main divided between east-flowing and west-flowing streams diverges from the general trend, being closest to the coast to the north of Cairns and near the southern state boarder. The coastal ranges to the east are formed mainly from resistant Paleozoic Volcanic rocks, metamorphic, and granites, and in many places are higher than the main divide.[3] Between coastal ranges are narrow corridors of weaker rocks. Offshore the ranges and corridors, now submerged, especially between Rockhampton and Innisfail.

About two-thirds of Queensland is in the region known as the Western Plains, underline by Mesozoic sandstones and shales of great Artesian basin. The drainage of this region is to the Darling River system in the south, towards lake Eyre in the south west and to the Gulf of Carpentaria in the north. Us far south-west, wind-blown sand firms longitudinal duress on the eastern margin of the Simpson Desert.[4] The red desert dons have a north-west, south-east trend, are asymmetric with steeper sides to the east, are separated by playpens.

The country of the North-Western uplands resembles parts of eastern highlands, both are composed largely of folded layers of old metamorphic rocks and granites, giving rise to rugged country. Ridges are in many places of quartzite, with north-south trend, and of similar maximum heights, representing a former erosion surface, since elevated.

Much of the Eastern Coastline consists of long, sandy beaches, which in many places are effects with pronounced curve at the south and of the beach, lose to a rocky headland. Waves caused by the prevailing south-east winds result in a northerly directed long shore current. Beach erosion is greatest in southern Australia in periods of strong south-easterly winds, and particularly affects the open ocean coastline e.g. The gold-coast, the sunshine coast (between Calour and Double Island point), and open ocean beaches of the large sandy beaches. Sand dune, some built one on top of the other to form very high sand deposits, are a feature of the coast.

Geology

The geology of Queensland is most conveniently described by referring to the present surface distribution of three structural units.

(a) Ancient rocks of the Australian Precambrian Shield exposed in the north-west and north of the state. This has been a relatively stable portion in the earth's crust during the past 1,200 million years.[5] Exposures in the Moint Island Georgetown and Cape York Peninsula areas are believed to be parts of a continuous mass extending beyond these areas beneath yonder rocks.

(b) The Tasmania Geosynclines, which extends for almost the entire length of eastern Queensland and had a complex history of dominantly marine deposition interrupted by major crustal upheavals for much of the Paleozoic Era (about 600 to 250 million years ago)[6] Subsequent continental sedimentation in this area took place under conditions of relative stability.

(c) The great Artesian Basin, a large intervening and overlapping area (nearly 2/3 of the state) filed with gently warped Mesozoic and Cenozoic sediments dating back about 200 million years.[7]

Climate

Queensland is known as 'Sunshine State' and has a typical subtropical to tropical climate, which has proved itself suitable for settlement in all parts of the state. High day-time temperatures are a normal climatic feature of

Figure 2: Daily Maximum Temperature, Queensland (1990-2007)

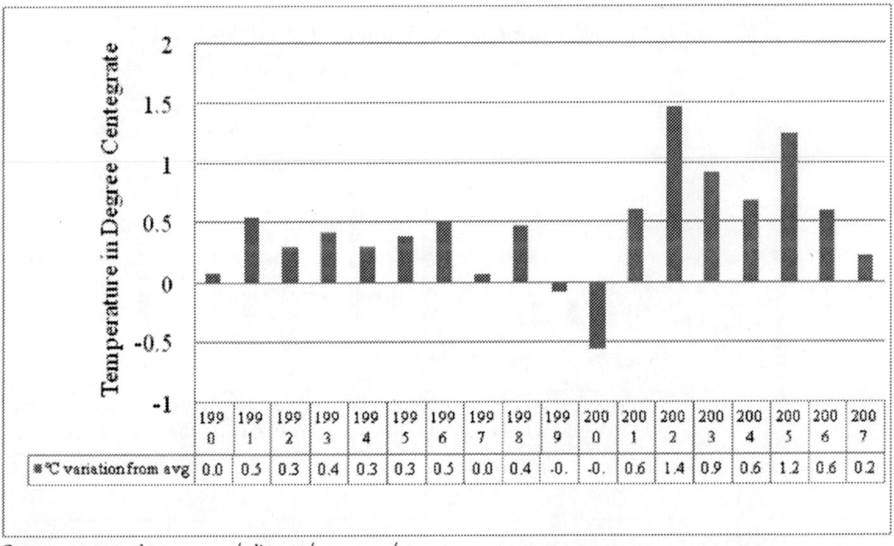

Sources: *www.bom.gov.au/climate/averages/*

the period from October to March, making in quite a short spring and a large summer. Temperature increases fairly rapidly during September and October with the temperature often exceeding 40°C in inland areas (Figure 2 and Table 2).

The sea breeze, which is an almost daily phenomenon in coastal parts, tempers conditions considerably but humid conditions in summer on the tropical coast (North of Rockhampton) can be enervating.[8] (Figure 3 and 4)

Figure 3: Daily Minimum Temperature, Queensland (1990-2007)

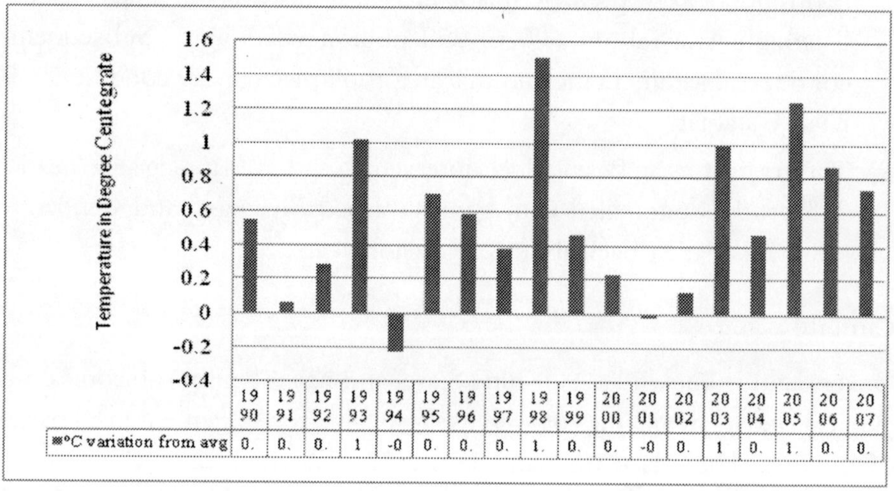

www.bom.gov.au/ climate/ averages/

Figure 4: Annual Temperature, Queensland (1990-2007)

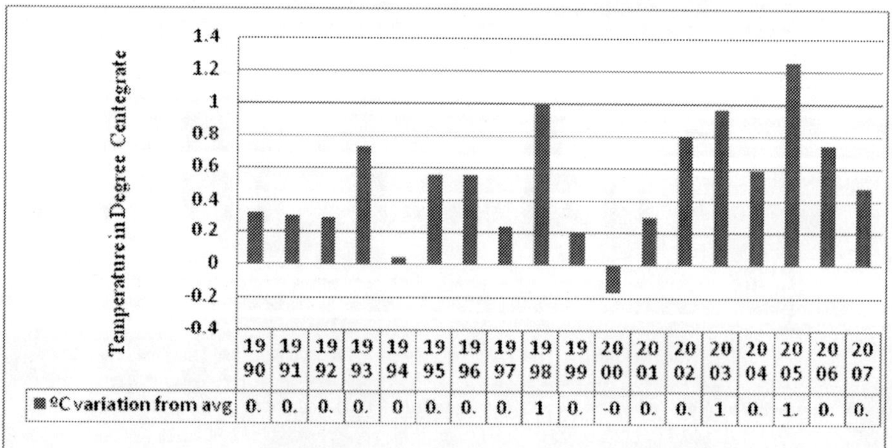

Sources: www.bom.gov.au/ climate/ averages

Table 2
Temperature for Six Typical Stations, Queensland

	1995		1996	
Station	*Mean Maximum*	*Mean Minimum*	*Mean Maximum*	*Mean Minimum*
Brisbane (A)	25.2	15.4	25.3	15.2
Rockhampt	28.7	17.3	28.8	17.0
Caims	29.4	21.4	29.4	20.9
Charleville	28.8	14.4	28.4	14.1
Longreach	31.6	16.5	31.8	16.4
Mount Isa	32.1	18.2	32.6	17.8

Source: Queensland Year Book, 1998. Australian Bureau of Statistics No. 56 ABS Catalogue No. 1301.3 B.

Day temperatures in the winter are quite mild, and the decreased coldness makes for pleasant weather May to September.[9]

With sunny days and temperatures in the last to mid twenties.

Rainfall

Average annual rainfall in Queensland varies from about 150 mm in the desert of the extreme south-western corner of the state to about 4,000 mm in parts of the sugar lands of the wet north-eastern coast; mean rainfall over the whole of Queensland is 580 millimeters a year, compared with the Australian average of 430 millimeters. However, higher rates of evaporation and run-off reduce the effectiveness of Queensland's rainfall to some extent. Every part of Queensland's receives more rain in summer 6 months (November to April) than in the winter 6 months (May to October). (Table 3) The concentration of rain in the summer months is greatest in the north and west of the state, reaching a maximum in the gulf of Carpentaria region. The area receives only 25 to 40 mm of rain and winter, or about one twentieth of the annual total. South of the tropic of Capricorn (Rockhampton-langreach) winter rainfall becomes an important part of the annual total, being about 30 per cent, while it rises to about 40 per cent along the southern border of the state. The east cost of Queensland, both tropical and subtropical portions, receives a substantial portion of its rain in winter, but on the tropical coast this is mainly due to the prolongation of the autumn rains into April and May, while July, August and September are relatively day months (Table 4).

Table 3
Climate Data

		2010			2011
Month	*Unit*	*Dec*	*Mar*	*Jun*	*Sep*
Mean daily maximum	^0C	26.8	27.8	20.3	23.6
Mean daily minimum	^0C	20.5	20.2	9.5	11.4
Rainfall, total	mm	499.4	188.6	7.4	16.4
Rain days	no.	23	16	4	7
Mean daily sunshine	hours	4.5	6.4	6.9	9.6
Strong wind days, over 50 km/h	no.	8	3	1	5

Source: Bureau of Meteorology

Table 4
Rainfall Queensland (Millimeter)

Locality	*1994*	*1995*	*1996*	*Long term average (a)*
Coastal				
Brisbane airport	840	1128	1478	1187
Bundaberg	548	1027	1270	1046
Gladstone	904	3540	996	921
Rockhampton	518	785	738	832
Mackay	1156	1090	1676	1603
Townsville	479	710	630	1111
Cardwell	1946	1436	1493	2112
Caims	1988	2075	2083	2000
Nomanton	763	616	760	910
Sub-coastal				
Toowoomba	464	1107	1247	960
Kingaroy	501	715	974	779
Gayndah	503	783	753	771
Emerald	458	475	752	640
Charters Towers	365	393	368	659
Atherton	931	1373	1312	1421
Coen	664	1036	1579	1173
Western				
Cunnamulla	241	529	364	371
Charleville	390	362	497	479
Blackall	418	346	541	522
Longreach	256	396	446	449
Boulia	139	359	186	262
Winton	484	338	330	403
Hughenden	330	355	415	488
Mount Isa	260	399	463	423
Georgetown	367	853	597	824

Source: Bureau of Meteorology (1996), Yearly Weather Review for Queensland.

Population

The first census of Queensland was conducted on April 7, 1861, when the population was 30,059 only[10], and this went on to 3,339,109 on June 30, 1996 (Table 5). On September from the colony of New South Wales in 1859, Queensland's population was 23,520, at that time the second small colony, exceeding only Western Australia. Natural increase and net migration have each been important factors in the growth of the Queensland populations. Net migration was consistently the most important cause of population growth n the state's early development and has also been the major component again since the early 1970's (Figure 6).

Since World War II, Queensland's Urban Population has grown strongly. At the 1996 population census, 80,7 per cent of people counted were in urban areas compared with 59.8 per cent of the population in 1947. Queensland's population is the least centralized of all the mainland states of Australia with 45.5 per cent of the population living in Brisbane statistical division at 30th June 1996.[11] Between 1991 and 1996, the population growth rate in Brisbane City was below the Queensland average (Figure 5).

Figure 5: Average Annual Growth Rate of Queensland and Australian Populations

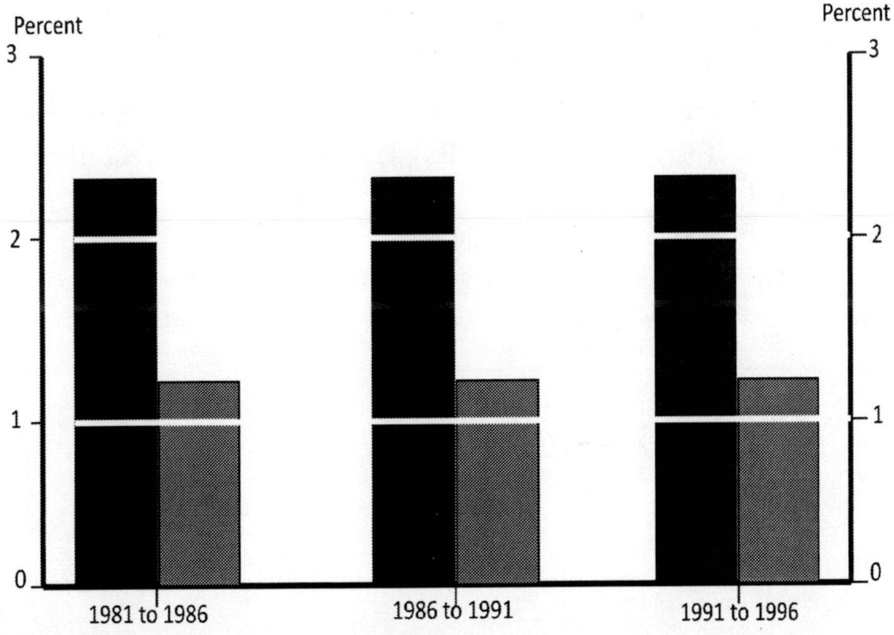

Figure 6: Population, Queensland

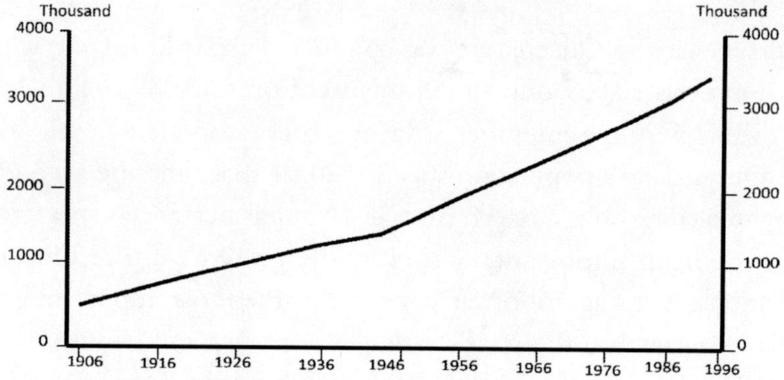

Source: Australian Bureau of Statistics No. 56, ABS Catalogue No. 1301.3, Brisbane.

Table 5
Estimated Resident Population, at 30 June 1996

State	*Total*	*Capital City Population*	*Proportion of total*
	'000	'000	%
New South Wales	6203.9	3879.4	62.5
Victoria	4560.8	3283.0	72.0
Queensland	3339.1	1520.6	45.5
South Australia	1474.4	1079.2	73.2
Western Australia	1765.7	1295.1	73.3
Tasmania	474.6	195.8	41.3

Source: Australian Demographic Statistics, (1997). ABS Publications, Brisbane

In The 2011 Census, There Were 4,332,739 People In Queensland (State/ Territory) Of These 49.6% Were Male And 50.4 per cent Were Female. Aboriginal and Torres Strait Islander People Made Up 3.6 per cent of the Population (Table 6).

Table 6
Population of Queensland 2006 and 2011

People	*Queensland 2011*	*Queensland %*	*Queensland 2006*	*Queensland %*	*Australia Australia %*	
Total	4,332,739	—	3,904,533	—	21,507,717	—
Male	2,148,221	49.6	1,935,379	49.6	10,634,013	49.4
Female	2,184,518	50.4	1,969,154	50.4	10,873,704	50.6
Aboriginal and Torres Strait Islander people	155,825	3.6	127,582	3.3	548,369	2.5

Source: Australian Bureau of Statistics

The median age of people in Queensland (State/Territory) was 36 years. Children aged 0 - 14 years made up 20.2 per cent of the population and people aged 65 years and over made up 13.1 per cent of the population.

Table 7

Different Age Group People of Queensland 2006 and 2011

Age	*Queensland (2011)*	*% (2011)*	*Queensland 2006*	*%*	*Australia (2006)*	*%*
People						
0-4 years	297,893	6.9	257,077	6.6	1,421,050	6.6
5-9 years	286,989	6.6	267,917	6.9	1,351,921	6.3
10-14 years	290,982	6.7	281,540	7.2	1,371,054	6.4
15-19 years	293,917	6.8	270,301	6.9	1,405,798	6.5
20-24 years	293,845	6.8	268,904	6.9	1,460,673	6.8
25-29 years	300,709	6.9	248,948	6.4	1,513,236	7
30-34 years	286,697	6.6	274,654	7	1,453,775	6.8
35-39 years	308,180	7.1	287,141	7.4	1,520,138	7.1
40-44 years	312,567	7.2	288,429	7.4	1,542,879	7.2
45-49 years	302,744	7	281,947	7.2	1,504,142	7
50-54 years	288,140	6.7	257,239	6.6	1,447,404	6.7
55-59 years	257,962	6	245,735	6.3	1,297,244	6
60-64 years	243,125	5.6	191,811	4.9	1,206,116	5.6
65-69 years	185,758	4.3	146,425	3.8	919,319	4.3
70-74 years	136,885	3.2	113,003	2.9	708,090	3.3
75-79 years	99,572	2.3	96,474	2.5	545,263	2.5
80-84 years	76,971	1.8	70,330	1.8	436,936	2
85 years and over	69,801	1.6	56,657	1.5	402,681	1.9

Source: Australian Bureau of Statistics

The most common ancestries in Queensland (State/Territory) were English 28.1 per cent, Australian 27.4 per cent, Irish 8.4 per cent, Scottish 7.3 per cent and German 4.7 per cent (Table 8).

Table 8

People — Cultural & Language Diversity in Queensland 2006 and 2011

Ancestry, top responses	*Queensland (2011)*	*%*	*Queensland (2006)*	*%*	*Australia (2006)*	*%*
English	1,629,463	28.1	1,380,013	26.8	7,238,533	25.9
Australian	1,587,992	27.4	1,592,702	30.9	7,098,486	25.4
Irish	484,929	8.4	413,832	8	2,087,758	7.5
Scottish	421,004	7.3	346,461	6.7	1,792,622	6.4
German	270,890	4.7	240,643	4.7	898,674	3.2

Source: Australian Bureau of Statistics

In Queensland (State/Territory), 73.7 per cent of people were born in Australia. The most common countries of birth were New Zealand 4.4 per cent, England 4.1 per cent, South Africa 0.8 per cent, India 0.7 per cent and Philippines 0.7 per cent (Table 9).

Table 9
Comparative Analysis of Population

Country of birth	*Queensland (2011)*	%	*Queensland (2006)*	%	*Australia (2006)*	%
Australia	3,192,114	73.7	2,935,259	75.2	15,017,847	69.8
Other top responses						
New Zealand	192,036	4.4	148,760	3.8	483,398	2.2
England	179,496	4.1	161,420	4.1	911,593	4.2
South Africa	35,549	0.8	22,712	0.6	145,683	0.7
India	30,260	0.7	10,972	0.3	295,362	1.4
Philippines	29,463	0.7	18,712	0.5	171,234	0.8

Source: Australian Bureau of Statistics

People Employment

The most common occupations in Queensland (State/Territory) included Professionals 18.9%, Technicians and Trades Workers 14.9%, Clerical and Administrative Workers 14.7%, Managers 12.0%, and Laborers 10.6% (Table 10 and Table 11).

Table 10
Occupation Different Group in Queensland 2006 and 2011

Occupation	*Queens land (2011)*	%	*Queens land 2006*	%	*Australia (2006)*	%
Employed people aged 15 years and over						
Professionals	385,581	18.9	312,866	17.1	2,145,442	21.3
Technicians and Trades Workers	304,563	14.9	280,340	15.4	1,425,146	14.2
Clerical and Administrative Workers	299,326	14.7	269,199	14.8	1,483,558	14.7
Managers	245,606	12	225,694	12.4	1,293,970	12.9
Labourers	215,235	10.6	217,250	11.9	947,608	9.4
Community and Personal Service Workers	202,978	10	166,399	9.1	971,897	9.7
Sales Workers	199,634	9.8	189,040	10.4	942,140	9.4
Machinery Operators and Drivers	149,322	7.3	132,113	7.2	659,551	6.6

Sources: Australian Bureau of Statistics

Table 11
Employment Status

Employment	*Queensland*	%	*2006*	%	*Australia*	%
People who reported being in the labour force, aged 15 years and over						
Worked full-time	1,302,955	60	1,180,890	61.6	6,367,554	59.7
Worked part-time	611,296	28.2	530,503	27.7	3,062,976	28.7
Away from work	125,025	5.8	113,605	5.9	627,797	5.9
Unemployed	131,798	6.1	90,950	4.7	600,133	5.6
Total in labour force	2,171,074	—	1,915,948	—	10,658,460	—

Sources: Australian Bureau of Statistics

Transport

Figure 7: Motor Vehicles on Register by Vehicle Type, Queensland, 2001 to 2013

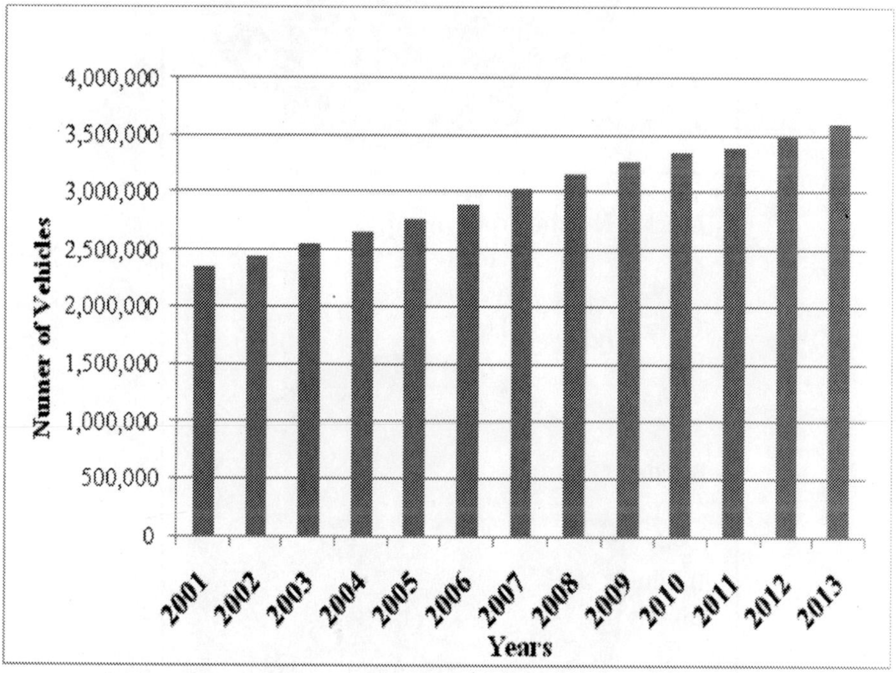

Source: Australian Bureau of Statistics, Motor Vehicle Census, Australia (cat. no. 9309.0), various editions.4.1.8 mining in Queensland

Tourism in Queensland

Figure 8: Percentage Change of Domestic Tourist in Queensland

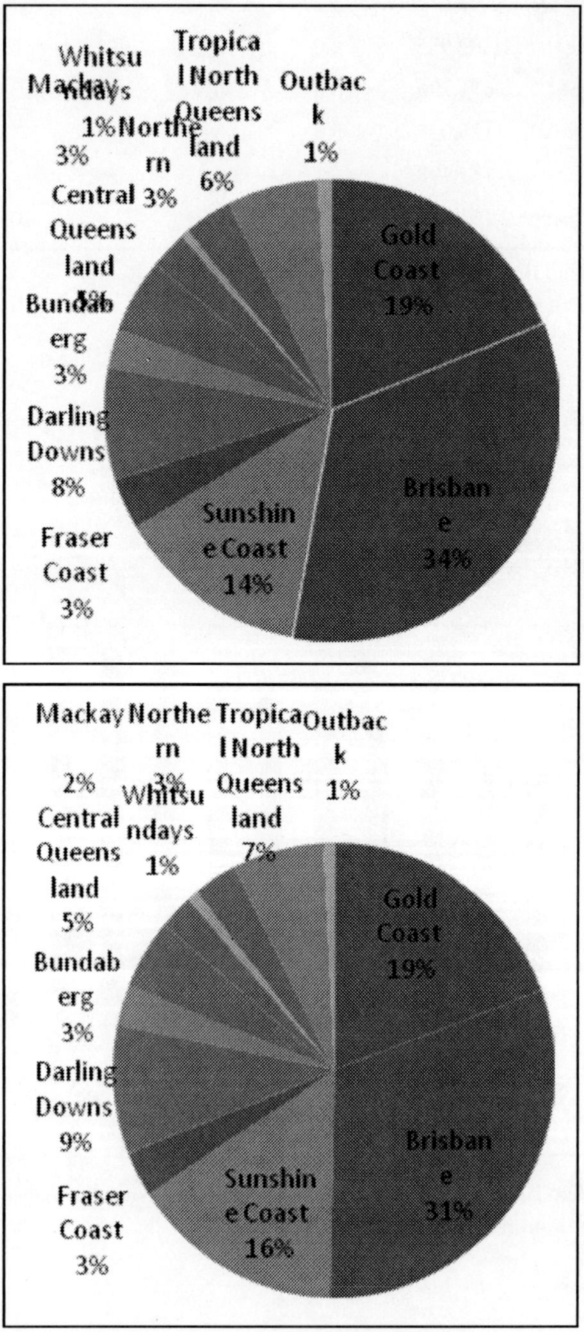

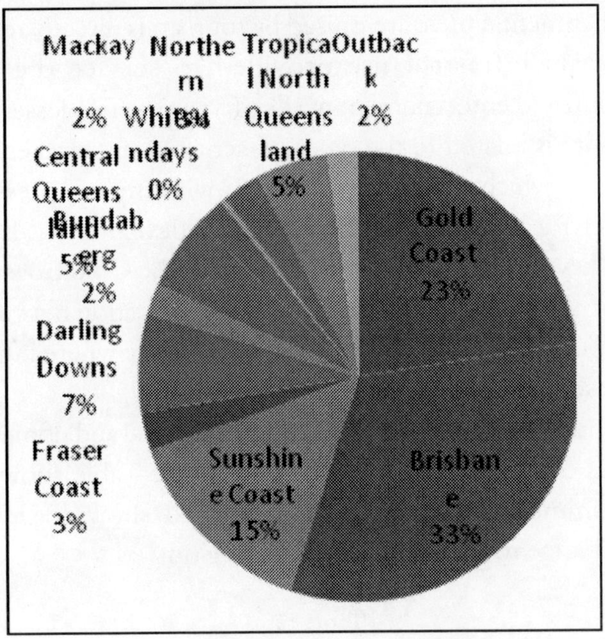

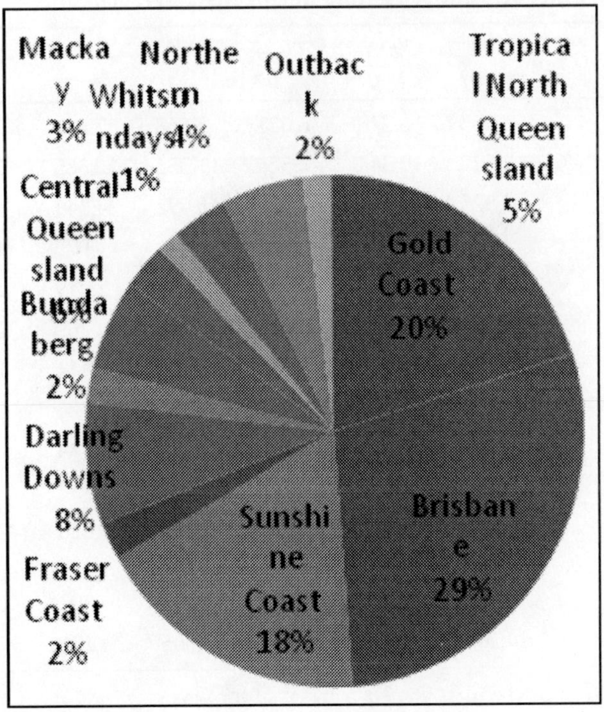

Sources: Tourism Research Australia, National Visitor Survey

The environmental pressure caused by tourism is directly related to the type of tourism infrastructure provided to service the transport, accommodation and entertainment needs of visitors. To a lesser extent, the level of pressure is related to the types of activities undertaken by visitors and the degree to which these are managed. Environmental pressure related to tourism activity and intensive infrastructure development is evident in Queensland's key coastal tourism regions such as the Gold Coast, Sunshine Coast, parts of the Whitsundays, and Cairns. Demarcation between tourism and other sources of impact, however, is problematic where infrastructure has multiple user groups.

Table 12 shows estimated numbers of international and domestic visitors to Queensland coastal regions in 2000-2013, while Table shows numbers of tourist accommodation facilities. Figure 9 and 10 shows the international visitors and Change to Queensland coastal regions

Table 12
Domestic Tourist Visitors in Queensland (2000-2013)

Domestic tourism	*2000–01*	*2003–04*	*2006–07*	*2009–10*	*2010–11*	*2011–12*	*2012–13*
Gold Coast	5,963	6,278	6,021	5,868	7,348	7,041	7,401
Brisbane	8,522	10,344	8,524	11,356	12,385	12,660	11,994
Sunshine Coast	3,825	4,811	5,329	5,092	4,344	5,094	5,993
Fraser Coast	724	960	726	976	977	1,347	1,228
Darling Downs	1,857	1,987	2,284	2,980	2,949	2,914	3,542
Bundaberg	564	788	623	945	760	1,017	1,101
Central Queensland	1,383	1,577	1,741	2,197	1,444	1,929	1,945
Mackay	567	632	835	934	726	1,018	977
Whitsundays	104	203	447	370	184	240	326
Northern	746	1,188	1,072	1,301	1,457	1,253	1,238
Tropical North Queensland	1,379	1,842	1,586	2,084	1,826	2,420	2,565
Outback	580	391	572	263	301	360	324
Total	26,262	31,001	29,761	34,365	34,701	37,293	38,634

Source: Tourism Research Australia, National Visitor Survey

Table 13
International Visitors to Australia by Country of Residence

Country of residence	*1995* '000	*1996* '000	%	*Percentage change 1995 to 1996*
Asia				
Japan	782.7	813.1	19.5	3.9
South Korea	168.0	227.9	5.5	35.6
Taiwan	152.0	159.4	3.8	4.9
Hong Kong	131.7	153.2	3.7	16.3
Malaysia	108.2	134.4	3.2	24.2
Singapore	22.4	222.8	5.3	10.1
Indonesia	135.0	154.5	3.7	14.4
Balance	192.4	226.1	5.4	17.5
Europe				
UK and Ireland	365.3	388.4	9.3	6.3
Balance (a)	378.2	401.7	9.6	6.2
New Zealand	538.4	671.9	16.1	24.8
North America				
Canada	58.4	61.1	1.5	4.7
USA	304.9	316.9	7.6	3.9
Other Countries	208.9	233.5	5.6	12.0
Total	3 725.8	4 164.8	100.0	11.8

Source: Australia Bureau of Statistics no. 56, ABS Catalogue No. 1301.3, B, Brisbane

Figure 9: Proportion of International Visitors to Australia by Main State or Territory of Intended Stay, 1996

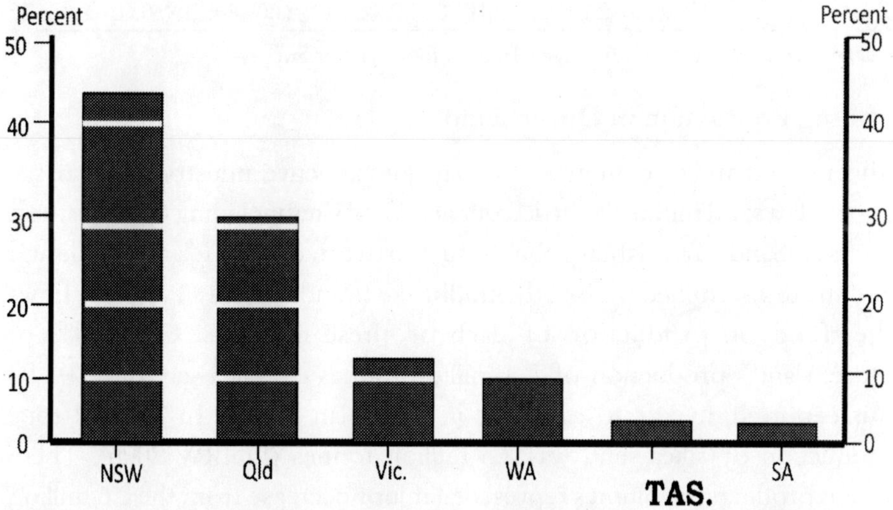

Source: Australia Bureau of Statistics no. 56, ABS Catalogue No. 1301.3, B, Brisbane

Figure 10: International Visitors by Queensland Tourism Region, 1999–00 to 2012–13

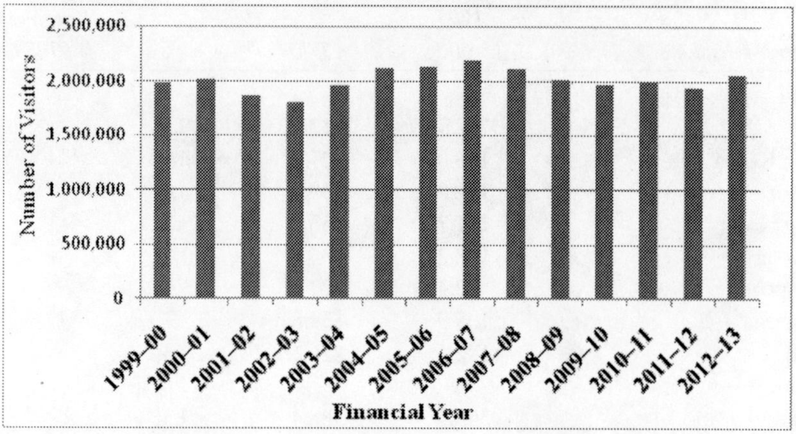

Table 14
International Visitors in Queensland (2001-2013)

Main reason of visit	*2000–01*	*2004–05*	*2006–07*	*2008–09*	*2010–11*	*2011–12*	*2012–13*
Holiday	1,483.60	1,529.10	1,472.10	1,285.20	1,185.50	1,131.40	1,206.50
Visiting friends and relatives	264.7	295.8	323.7	363.3	384.3	386.8	405.2
Business	141.1	167.6	212.7	175.4	206.3	203.6	221.3
Education	66.5	73.7	85.2	98.6	104.3	105.5	102.5
Employment	12	24.1	54.6	55.2	55.6	53.8	64.1
Other	62	47.1	47.7	51.4	64.8	69.6	65.6
Total	2,029.90	2,137.50	2,196.00	2,029.10	2,000.80	1,950.60	2,065.20

Source: Tourism Research Australia, International Visitor Survey

Mining Production in Queensland

Mineral sand mining continues to be a major extractive industry in the coastal zone; silica sand mining is carried out at several sites including Cape Flattery, Tannum Sands, Bundaberg, Ningi and North Stradbroke Island. Rutile and zircon are also mined on North Stradbroke Island. Figure 11 and 15 shows the trends in production of each of these minerals. Over 90% of Queensland's production of 2.4 million tonnes of silica sand in 2002-03 was exported, mainly to countries in the Asian region. In 2003-04 total production of silica sand was 2.5 million tonnes (DNRW 2006). These recent production volumes represent a minor decrease from the 2.6 million tonnes produced in 1999-2000 and 2000-01 (Figure 12 and 15).

Figure 11: International Tourism: Annual Percentage Change in Visitor and Visitor Nights, by Main Reason of Visit, Queensland, 2000–01 to 2012–13

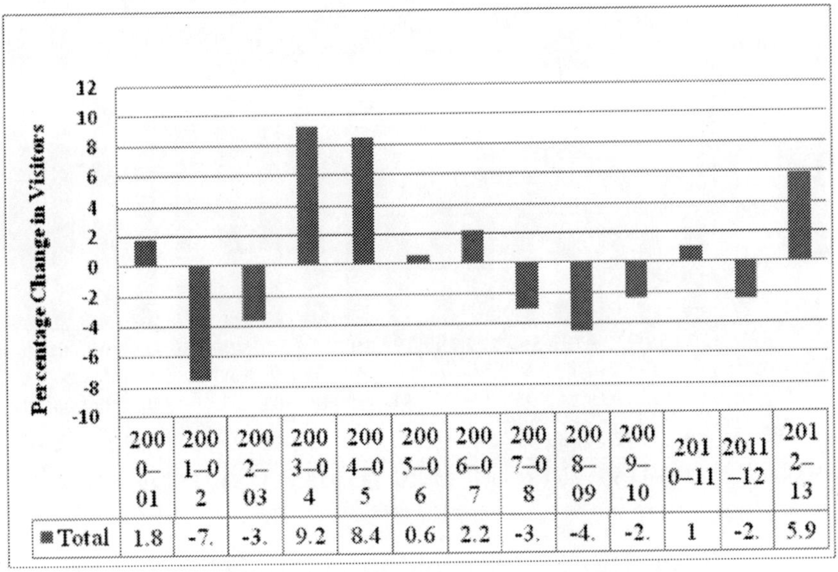

Source: Tourism Research Australia, National Visitor Survey

Table 15
Mining, Queensland (1990-2007)

Years	*Coal*	*Oil & gas*	*Metallic minerals*	*Mineral sands*
1990-91	78.363	286.656	1,724.07	320,626
1991-92	84.085	243.823	1,482.37	256,215
1992-93	85.301	261.988	1,702.21	269,253
1993-94	85.739	234.412	1,582.82	255,301
1994-95	94.496	301.337	1,645.72	313,177
1995-96	93.763	342.348	1,906.00	308,730
1996-97	99.437	354.513	1,716.37	158,000
1997-98	105.752	314.579	1,902.48	299,000
1998-99	112.634	386.3	2,051.60	233,000
1999-00	124.348	520.54	2,537.31	146,000
2000-01	138.352	622.77	3,750.89	148,000
2001-02	148.362	700.6	4,138.00	154,647
2002-03	153.602	592	3,632.00	165,200
2003-04	160.062	608	3,895.00	160,634
2004-05	172.666	777	4,944.00	209,769
2005-06	175.774	941	7,290.00	208,454
2006-07	181.257	944.42	9,396.11	309,376

Source: Registrar-General's Office, Statistics of the Colony/State of Queensland, Various Years

Figure 12: Production of Coal and Oil & Gas in Queensland 1990-2007

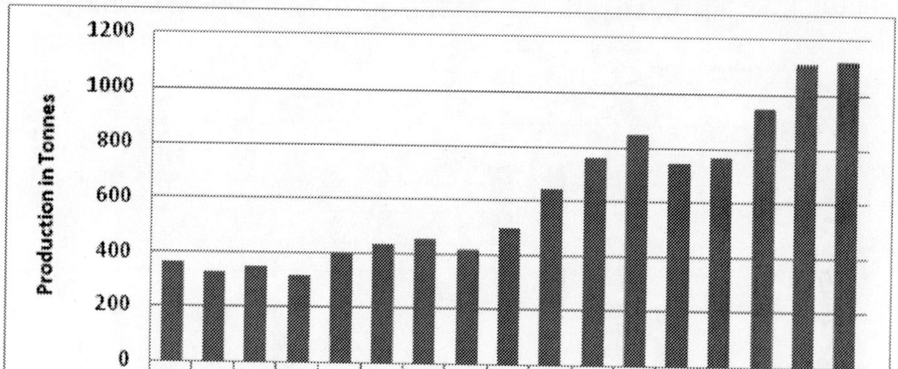

	1990-91	1991-92	1992-93	1993-94	1994-95	1995-96	1996-97	1997-98	1998-99	1999-00	2000-01	2001-02	2002-03	2003-04	2004-05	2005-06	2006-07
Oil & gas	28	24	26	23	30	34	35	31	38	52	62	70	59	60	77	94	94
Coal	78	84	85	86	94	94	99	10	11	12	13	14	15	16	17	17	18

In 2011-12, mining industry output (as measured by gross value added) represented 10.6 per cent of Queensland economic activity, 0.1 percentage point down from 10.7 per cent in 2010-11. Further, Queensland's mining industry accounted for 2.8 per cent of total employment in 2011-12. Given the contribution of the mining industry to the Queensland economy, it is important to understand the drivers of growth within this industry.

Figure 13: Production of Mineral Sand in Queensland 1990-2007

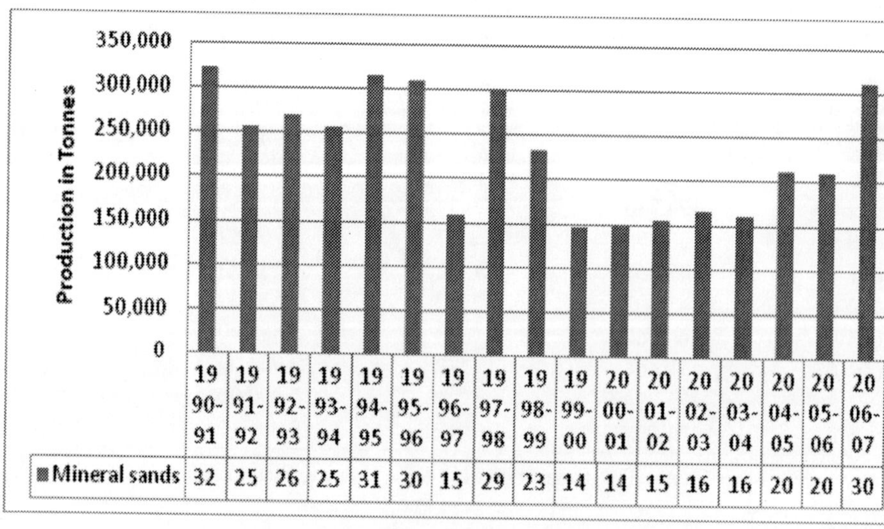

	1990-91	1991-92	1992-93	1993-94	1994-95	1995-96	1996-97	1997-98	1998-99	1999-00	2000-01	2001-02	2002-03	2003-04	2004-05	2005-06	2006-07
Mineral sands	32	25	26	25	31	30	15	29	23	14	14	15	16	16	20	20	30

The Coastal Zone: Coastal Habitats and Biodiversity

Marine Habitat Disturbance

The maintenance of marine habitats is fundamental to supporting the biodiversity of the oceans on which the fishing and marine tourism industries in coastal centres depend. Direct disturbance can result from anthropogenic activities such as intensive bottom trawling, mining and dredging, but can also be the result of extreme natural events such as tsunamis and cyclones. Marine habitats can also be degraded through subtle and chronic effects of pollution and climate change impacts.

Terrestrial Habitat Disturbance

The clearing of native vegetation and the decline in condition of remnant vegetation are closely related to the negative impacts on biodiversity through the loss of quality habitat, reduction in waterway primary productivity and the decline in the status of species and ecosystems. Ongoing impoundment of waterways has long-term implications for diversity and productivity of downstream communities.

Table 16
Oil Spill Incidents in Queensland from July 2003 to June 2006

Oil type	*No. of incidents (Total volume spilt (litres))*		
	2003-04	*2004-05*	*2005-06*
Diesel	25 (NR)	24 (2587)	27 (3465)
Bilge oil	16 (NR)	14 (665)	12 (65)
Lubricating oil	0 (NR)	0	2 (75)
Hydraulic oil	7 (NR)	0	2 (30)
Heavy fuel oil	3 (NR)	2 (40)	3 (1000)
Others (including sheens)	31 (NQ)	38 (NQ)	15 (NQ)
	82 incidents recorded, 55 within ports, 27 in coastal waters	78 incidents recorded, 43 within ports, 35 in coastal waters	61 incidents recorded, 35 within ports, 26 in coastal waters

Source: MSQ

Commercial Exploitation of Biodiversity

Queensland's commercial and recreational fisheries are managed sustainably to ensure long-term biodiversity and economic outcomes for the state. This requires the management of fishing effort, the protection of adequate areas of important fish habitats (such as juvenile feeding areas and spawning areas) and non-fished areas, and the maintenance of the quality of the oceans and coastal areas.

Pressure and Condition

The estimated total area trawled in Queensland managed otter trawl fisheries off the east coast in 2005 was 73,302 km^2, a 17 per cent reduction in the area from the 2001 estimate of 88,608 km^2.

- With a rapidly increasing human population in Queensland's coastal zone, the pressures on terrestrial, estuarine and marine resources continue to increase.
- The impacts of fishing on sea bottom communities have been removed in new protected (no fishing) areas through marine park zonings, and reduction in trawl effort has decreased the impacts in some fishing areas.
- Marine parks and declared fish habitat areas allow for enhanced management of the impacts of coastal development. In most of coastal Queensland there has not been a significant increase in the loss of terrestrial remnant vegetation since 2003.
- In the developed coastal areas the extent of natural communities is limited and the condition of these areas is often poor.
- Continuing coastal subdivision without adequate buffers to adjacent waterways increases the impacts of runoff on these waterways.
- Melaleuca and saltmarsh habitats at the interface between tidal lands and development are under the greatest threat.
- Queensland's commercial fisheries are being managed at sustainable harvest levels.
- Inshore sea grasses in Queensland appear to be in relatively fair to good condition and most impacts are generally localized. Regional

climate appears the most likely driver of observed year-to-year or long-term changes.

- Management arrangements are being implemented or being developed to restore fish stock levels for a few species of concern.
- Very limited information is available on the populations of non-commercial marine species.

Table 17

Nitrogen and Phosphorus Discharge Loads from Major Point Sources in Coastal Urban Regions for 2004-05 and the Percentage change Since 2001-02

	Nitrogen		*Phosphorus*	
	Load 2004-05 (kg)	*Change since 2001-02 (%)*	*Load 2004-05 (kg)*	*Change since 2001-02 (%)*
Gold Coast/Logan	302 923	-10	199 551	-8
Brisbane	1 491 224	-17	958 444	-10
Sunshine Coast	187 509	9	65 583	-21
Rockhampton/Fitzroy	78 020	17	46 120	-6
Mackay	165 944	na	51 569	na
Townsville	na	na	na	na
Cairns	229 028	27	100 807	25
Total:	2 454 649	-10 b	1 422 074	-8 b

Source: EPA

COASTAL GEOMORPHOLOGY IN AUSTRALIA

The Australian Coastline and Queensland Coast

Australian coastline extends from latitude 10^0s to 43^0s, and from longitude 114^0C to 154^0C and experiences several climatic and biotic type. Due to tectonic structure and a generally dry climate combine to produce a coastline which is in general free of livers continuously supplying large quantities of sediment to near shore zone.[12] Ocean graphic conditions along western and southern coasts are such as to promote the dominance of continental self derived carbonate sediments over terrigenous materials. In northeast coast, the Great Barrier Reef exemplifies the power of biotic factors in coastal development.

According Daris,[13] the latitudinal position of the continent southern sphere of influence of southern ocean swell waves, and the north east corner in the southeasterly trade wind and wave zone. While, northern coasts experience the impact of tropical cyclones which may dramatically modify coastal terrain.[14] In north western and northeastern Australia there are localities with tidal ranges in excess of 6 m, while extensive areas in southern Australia the range is 1-2 m.[15]

Coastal Classification

In Australia, there have been few attempts to classify the coast, mainly due to inadequate knowledge coupled with lack of interest by the few coastal specialists.[16, 17, 18] Davies [19 20, 21] as a part of his global review of geographical variability of coastal features, has depicted many physical and biologic properties of Australian coast and made possible a more detailed categorization of Australian coastal landscapes Bird[22] has subdivided the coast on the basis of the nature and sources of sediments which make up beach material.

The Coastline of Queensland

The coastline of Queensland has a length of 9800 km extending across 10^0 of latitude from 25^{0}10's at NSW boarders to 9^{0}15' in Torres strait. The eastern highlands which rises in places to over 100m. The NHE-SSW trend of the coastline is determined by the structure of the Tasmania Geosynaline and its associated basins, which forms the axis of the Highlands. Cenozoic uplift and a complex history involving deep weathering and regolith removal ensure a massive yield of sand and silt size sediments to the east coast.[23]

According to Hopley, the Australian shield remain tectonically a region of relative stability, even over the last 6000 years earth movements have occurred around the Queensland coast, possibly the result of the water loading are the continental shelf as sea level rose from its lowest level of about –150m, 18000 B.P. This has affected the relative sea level pattern and influenced many coastal landforms. a marked reduction in wind and wave energy conditions takes place north wards. Significant wave height exceeded 50 percent of the time is 15m at gold coast, 0.8 m near Rockhampton and 0.5.m at Cairns, while occurrence of gale force winds seas a similar reduction from 0.7 per cent at Brisbane to 0.1 percent at Cooktown.[24 25]

The whole of the Queensland coastline is prone to tropical cyclones during summer months, and on average, three cyclones per year are experienced in both the gulf of Carpentaria an off eastern coast. Any part of the coast can experience storms with central pressures of 960 mb and wind speeds in excess of 150 km/hours. But the coastal zone most prone to intense storms stretches from Princess Chalottle Bay to Fraser Island. In coastal areas sheltered by the Great Barrier Reef Cyclonic Seas may rise wave heights to 8m or more, thus producing occasional high energy events in direct contrast to prevailing conditions.[26]

The coast is where the ocean meets the land. Queensland's mainland coastline is over 9500 kilometers long and extends from west of Karumba on the Gulf of Carpentaria to the Queensland– New South Wales border at Coolangatta. Queensland coasts are diverse, comprising a mix of sandy beaches, rocky headlands, low-lying mud and sand islands, coral atolls and rocky islands. The interaction of coastal processes with the various landforms creates a very complex and dynamic natural system. The most characteristic of these landforms are the gently sloping, sandy beaches which make up 66 per cent of the Queensland coastline. The sandy areas are often backed by beach-ridge plains (a broad sequence of beach ridges)1and usually bordered seaward by rocky headlands or tidal inlets, or fringed by coral reefs. Culturally and economically, these sandy beaches are the most valued feature of the coastal zone, but they are also the most dynamic. Queensland is internationally renowned for these sandy beaches. In 2006, the gross tourism value of the Gold Coast beaches was estimated at between $106 million and $319 million. Queenslanders also enjoy living close to the ocean—85 per cent of the state's population (3.8 million people) lives within 50 kilometers of the coast. This coastal population is growing. In 2009, the Gold Coast, Moreton Bay and the Sunshine Coast experienced the largest population increases (after Brisbane) in Queensland4. Coastal areas further north, most notably Cairns, Townsville and the Fraser Coast (Hervey Bay), have also recorded large population increases. Although a coastal lifestyle may seem idyllic, this complex and dynamic environment poses risks to coastal communities from hazards including storm tide inundation, coastal erosion, cyclones and sea level rise inundation.

The Queensland coast is constantly changing due to both naturally occurring processes (e.g. variations in sediment supply, sea level, weather patterns) and, more recently, man-made changes to the coasts (e.g. sea walls, groynes and channel dredging). Natural processes, such as coastal erosion, become 'problems' when they threaten property and infrastructure. As coastal processes are often not well understood, the 'solutions' may create even more problems. Careful, considered management is needed to accommodate the needs of the community and maintain the natural environment.

The geomorphology of the coast (the way it looks and how it functions), its vulnerability to certain hazards and their relative impacts at a given location, are the product of a complex interplay of physical factors. Sediment inputs, the exposure to waves, the tidal range and climatic forces (prevailing winds and cyclones) vary along the length of the Queensland coast.

Queensland Coastline Regional Subdivision

As according to the combination of structural variation, recent history and variations in energy levels produces sizes fold regional division of Queensland coastline (Table 18 and Figure 14).

Table 18
State Marine Parks, Queensland 2013

State marine park	*Area(km2)*
Great Barrier Reef	344,400
Great Sandy Marine Park	6,000
Moreton Bay Marine Park	3,400

Source: Queensland Government, Department of Natural Resources

Figure 14: Percentage of Marine Park, Queensland, 2013

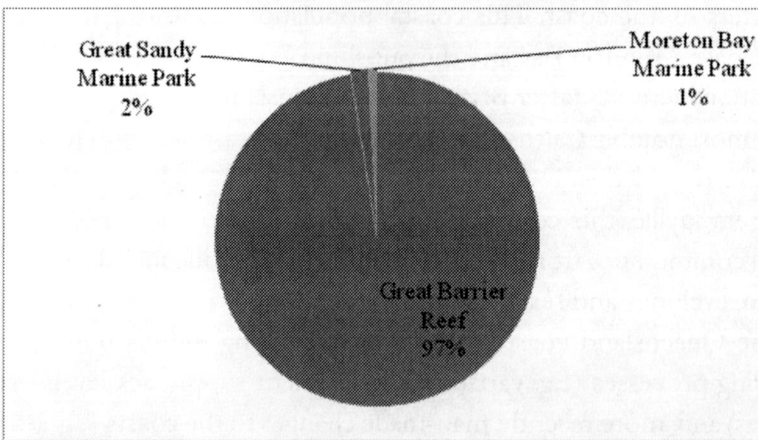

Source: Queensland Government, Department of Natural Resources, Recreation, Sport and Racing

The Gulf of Carpentaria

From the Northern Territory to boarder to the Norman River the coastal plain, almost 40 km wide, consists of silty deposits and self flats with occasional low beach ridges termed Cheniers.[27] It is drained by numerous meandering tidal weeks and rivers hired with manpower. The depositional coastline of eastern gulf of Carpentaria is divided into two parts by the lateritic cliffs of Albatross Bay. To the south the Chenier and salt flat environment of further west is continued but the plain is narrower (up to 20 km) and series of sandy beach ridges occur close to river months. North of albatross by the coastline consists of a series of beach ridges derived jointly from the sands of the Jardine River and form the tidal delta at the western exist of Torres Strait.[28]

Torres Strait to Cook Town

Reduced wave energy due to the proximity of the great Barrier Reef makes this a low energy coastline characterized by sandy beaches with narrow zone of low beach ridges about 1 km wide separated by rocky headlands. The headlands have convex rocky slopes showing little modification by marine processes except for the removal of regolith developed during low sea level stands.[29] The most impressive coastal done in tropical Australia occurs in this region notably around New Coastal Bay, Ordered Bay, Cape Granville (500 km^2) and cape Bedford.[30] princes Charlotte Bay completely protected from the south eastern and a Chenier 25 km wide occurs here. An outer fringe of mangroves is backed by upto 5 km of bare saline mod flats with isolated Cheniers.

Cook Town to Hinchinbrook Island

This sub-division of Queensland coast concedes with the high-test rainfall region in Australia, annual totals exceeding 2000mm, while exceeding over 400 mm near Innisfail[31] down to the high tide level. The most extensive mangrove systems are found in the Hinchinbrook channel and behind Ransay Bay. The intertidal zone is rocky with massive boulders, washed from the regolith. Minor forms of chemical weathering are seen on the rocky out crops.[32]

Hinchinbrook Island to Gervey Bay

Due to deposition of sand brought by rivers of central Queensland to the coast. So, much of the coast is depositional with series of beach ridges trailing northwards from south of almost every stream. Typically the coastline compromises ten or more ridges up to 500 m wide but close to major rivers the sequence may widen to over 5 km.[33]

The ridges are higher in the northern part of each sediments compartment due to the addition of a dune cap where the beach is more exposed to the prevailing south easterlies but the dunes are rarely more than 10m high. The only major dune accumulations on this coast occur on Whitsunday Island, Curtis Island and north of Rockhamton.[34] The largest rives have buildup deltas or large extensive sediment in fills. The Burdekin, draining 129,000 km^2 has built Australia's largest cuspata delta with over 150m of deltaic sediments. The northwest, cape Bowling green, extending sewards for 18 km, is Australia's largest emergent sand spit.[35] The most extensive rocky coasts are found opposite the Whitsunday islands but similar forms found on many of the offshore islands.

Harvey Bay to the NSW Border

This is a high energy swell dominated coast of southern Queensland and there are massive sand barriers formed from the northward drift of sand from the NSW coast.[36] This region contain parabolic dons aligned to south east winds. On fraser island the dunes rise up to 240m and incorporate some 40 proceed takes many of them in a rainforest setting.[37] Most of these large sand masses are Pleistocene in Age and have been weathered into a range of coloured sands. The largest high done system frazer, cooloola and Moreton-Stradbroke, are separated by coastlines with lower linear coastal beach ridges. Australia's major tourist resort, the gold coast, has been developed on low beach ridges of southernmost sections of the barrier coast.

The Great Barrier Reef

From 9^{0}15' South the great Barrier Reef extends southwards along a perimeter of 2300 km to Pady Elvolt Island at 24^{0}07's. The outer reef varies greatly in distance from mainland appreciating within 23 km of 14^{0}S to a maximum of 260 km at 21^{0}S.[38] The whole reef province incorporates an area of approximately 230,000 km^2 within which lie over 2500 reefs., varying in size from isolated pinnacles to massive structures upto 25km long and 250 km^2 in area.[39] North of cairns the outer reefs form a continuous barrier with only narrow passes. Mid-shelf reefs are large and oval in shape whilst small inner self reefs wither have vegetated cays or are capped by complex low wooded islands containing sand cays. The largest refs are those of the Pompey complex. They are separated by narrow passes up to 90 m deep and form a broad belt upto 23 km wide.[40]

Potential Environmental Problems

The Queensland coast is essentially disposition sand barriers making upto 45 percent of the coastal area, as like much of the eastern Australian coastline. These sand deposits have build up in the last 6-6500 years since sea level first reached its modern position, the earliest deposits on the barriers being derived from the continental shelf and moved onshore by the marine transfusion. At least in southern Queensland and NSW, because of the tectonic history of the coastal some, there has been no supplementation since from new fluvial sources. Shoreline retreat of upto 50 m is single events may occurs but is not always acknowledged in the continuing pressures to allow commercial development on or near the shoreline.

The coastal zone is not independent of its hinterland and the potential for shoreline and nearshore response to poor management practices in the coastal catchmetns is particularly high in Queensland. Solar radiation levels are being highest in the tropics and form the energy input for most geomorphic processes. However, the level of energy transfer by the tropical rainforest ecosystem, at their most productive period, is thought to approach the maximum possible under natural conditions. A high proportion of energy is thus used in the development of the plant community and not in erosion or removal of debis by streams. Removal or modification of the plant cover may have a spectral response in terms of sediment yield. According to Doughlas, in a natural rainforest catchment denudation rates of between 6 and 45 m^2.km^2/yr have been demonstrative. Expecting logging may accelrate erosion rates two to three fold and clearing can produce a tarfold increase in sediment yield.

Human Activities That Impact on Coastal Environment

Many human activities can contribute to declining water quality in the Great Barrier Reef. Some of these activities include

- Coastal Development
- Agriculture
- Aquaculture
- Mining and industry
- Shipping

1. ***Coastal Development:*** Increasing population combined with the popularity of living near the coast has resulted in the expansion of towns, cities and other developments along the Queensland coast. In fact, over the last 200 years this expansion has seen the loss of significant areas of wetlands and important vegetation areas within the Great Barrier Reef Catchment. Today the coast adjacent to the Great Barrier Reef Marine Park contains marine tourism infrastructure, ports and harbours, urban and resort development and industrial development. These developments may result in sediment, nutrients, chemicals and other pollutants being discharged to local waterways and the Great Barrier Reef. With more people living in the Great Barrier Reef Catchment and using the Reef for recreational and commercial activities like boating, fishing, tourism and shipping, there is potential for more human impact on the Great Barrier Reef into the future.

2. ***Agriculture:*** Agricultural industries, including grazing and cropping, are the largest users of land in the Great Barrier Reef Catchment. Today 80% of the land adjacent to the Great Barrier Reef Marine Park supports agricultural production, primarily beef cattle grazing and intensive cropping.

   Extensive clearing of vegetation in the Great Barrier Reef Catchment has occurred to allow for cattle grazing. This, combined with over-stocking on farms, can result in widespread soil degradation, particularly during drought conditions. This degradation results in soil erosion and the transport of eroded material to the Great Barrier Reef during times of heavy rainfall.

Sugarcane cropping covers the largest area in the Great Barrier Reef Catchment. Other major crops grown in the catchment include a variety of grains, cotton, bananas and other fruit and vegetables. Cropping involves the application of fertilisers (such as nitrogen and phosphorous) and pesticides. Use of these has increased significantly since the 1950s. Some of the fertilisers and pesticides are taken up by the crop but a significant portion applied to the land may end up in coastal waters. Poor agricultural practices may result in soil erosion and the discharge of sediments, nutrients and pesticides into rivers, estuaries and eventually the Great Barrier Reef.

3. ***Aquaculture:*** Aquaculture facilities located within and next to the Great Barrier Reef Marine Park produce a range of marine and freshwater species including pearl and edible oysters, prawns and barramundi. Aquaculture in Queensland is a growth industry with most facilities utilising pond-based operations to produce prawns.

   Traditionally, aquaculture farms have often discharged high concentrations of suspended solids and nutrients to nearby waterways. However, this situation is improving with the implementation of new techniques such as settlement and bio-filtration ponds that contain algae, bivalves or fish in new and some existing aquaculture farms. Today, discharges from aquaculture farms are regulated to ensure they protect the water quality of local waterways and the Great Barrier Reef.

   Environmental risks from aquaculture include nutrient loading of estuarine systems, the introduction of exotic diseases and possible threats to wild populations through genetic alteration and disease. All of these risks are associated with transfer of aquacultured animals into natural waterways. The major pressures associated with aquaculture relate to a farm's location and the amount and quality of its waste discharged into tidal waterways. Many of Queensland's aquaculture facilities do not discharge to natural waterways. Freshwater aquaculture operations (species other than barramundi and prawns) are not permitted to discharge directly to natural waterways. Prawn and barramundi farms that discharge into tidal waters are required to adhere to strict discharge limits. In addition, recirculation technology is constantly improving. Many prawn and barramundi farms have high rates of recirculation (up to 95%), so that very little water exchange with natural waterways is required.

Table 19 shows trends in total ponded areas under aquaculture, which peaked in 2003-04 (Lobegeiger and Wingfield 2005, 2007).

Table 19
Total Ponded Area of Aquaculture Facilities (ha), Queensland, 2000-01 to 2005-06

Statistical Division	*2000-01*	*2001-02*	*2002-03*	*2003-04*	*2004-05*	*2005-06*
Brisbane	0	0	0	0	0	0
Moreton*	198	181	181	172	180	171
Wide Bay	158	153	143	149	143	131
Darling Downs	19	13	11	22	17	18
Fitzroy	30	22	30	19	22	13
Central West	0	0	0	0	0	0
Mackay	147	293	289	262	239	225
Northern	190	274	277	345	267	255
Far Northern	323	264	296	262	309	309
Total	1065	1200	1227	1231	1177	1122

Source: Lobegeiger and Wingfield 2005, 2007

Figure 15: Total Ponded Area of Aquaculture Facilities (ha), Queensland, 2000-01 to 2005-06

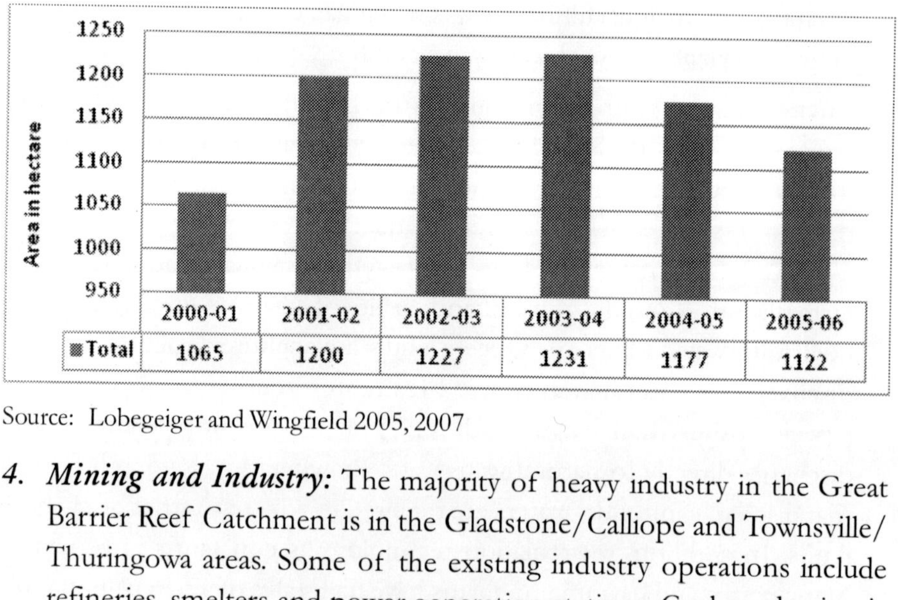

Source: Lobegeiger and Wingfield 2005, 2007

4. ***Mining and Industry:*** The majority of heavy industry in the Great Barrier Reef Catchment is in the Gladstone/Calliope and Townsville/Thuringowa areas. Some of the existing industry operations include refineries, smelters and power generation stations. Coal production is

the major mining operation carried out in the Great Barrier Reef Catchment, with mines in the region producing approximately 96% of Queensland's 95 million tonnes of annual black coal production. Other mining operations close to the coast include shale oil, silica and magnesium.

5. **Shipping:** Ships regularly transit the inner shipping route of the Great Barrier Reef Marine Park carrying a wide range of cargoes including bauxite and alumina, manganese, iron ore, coal, sugar, silica sand, general container freight and petroleum products. These ships transport these and other products to and from ports and communities along the Queensland coast.

   Oil or chemical spills released from ships following an incident have the potential to cause serious environmental damage to the marine environment. However, waste products and garbage from the day-to-day operation of a ship can also pollute the waters of the Great Barrier Reef. These wastes include oils, chemicals, sewage, garbage, toxic compounds released from anti-fouling paints and ballast water. Shipping presents a number of environmental risks including oil spills, introduction of exotic organisms through ballast water discharge, and potential pollution from sewage, anti-fouling paints and waste disposal; it also contributes to air pollution.

   The potential risk of oil spills at or around ports can be estimated by examining the volumes of petroleum products shipped through Queensland ports, although this risk can be alleviated by increased safety measures to avoid spills, and development of response plans in the case of an oil spill

   Three major oil spills in or adjacent to Queensland waters have been recorded since 2002-03, two from shipping incidents and one from a land-based spillage at the Port of Brisbane (Table 6.6). The spill at the Port of Brisbane was the largest spill reported to date and required a major emergency response by relevant government agencies. Booms and sand and clay barriers were used to contain the spill, and oil was physically removed. The company involved was later prosecuted, was fined $300 000 and paid almost $500 000 for clean-up costs (EPA 2004).

Table 20
Oil Spills in Queensland and Nearby Waters, 1997-98 to 2005-06

Year	*Number of oil spills*	*Number of significant incidents*		*Notes*
1997-98	61	2	*	
1998-99	108	2		
1999-2000	5	0		
2000-01	68	2		
2001-02	96	2	*	
2002-03	86	3		The grounding of the bulk carrier Doric Chariot on Piper Reef on 29 July 2002 (no oil spill)Pacific Quest- oil spill in Australian waters near Border Island (near Hayman Island in the Whitsunday Islands group), 25 December 2002. The initial extent of the slick was reported to be about 1 km long with a sheen trailing for 50-100 km and up to 2 km wide in some places. In March 2003 almost 2000 tonnes of light crude oil seeped from a ruptured pipeline at Lytton near the mouth of the Brisbane River into 5 ha of reclaimed riverside land, drainage channels and nearby small creeks.
2003-04	82	1	*	A 42 m hopper dredge, the Karma , ran aground approximately 10 km south of Agnes Waters on 14 November 2003.
2004-05	78	0		
2005-06	NA	1		Just before midnight on 24 January 2006, approximately 25 tonnes of heavy fuel oil was spilt from the bulk carrier Global Peace while berthing at the RG Tanner coal loading facility in Gladstone.

*No oil spill. NA = not available
Source: AMSA 2001, 2002, 2003, 2004, 2005, 2006

The Coastal Erosion Problems in Queensland

According to Ford (1977)[41]

"Beach erosion is a natural part of beach behaviour and becomes a problem only when it threatens property and improvements. The essence of the problem is not that beaches erode but that development has occurred within the zone of these natural beach movements".

In Queensland, man's activities may accelerate these natural processes. Destruction of done vegetation by grazing of stock, burning of fredunme vegetation, timber cutting or afford vehicles may lead to depletion of sand reserve held in the foredune and accelerate erosional events. Sand mining has the potential to aggravate erosional problems. An example of human contribution to natural north Cairns. Erosion has been very pronounced on Machan's Beach and yorkey's Beach, particularly since the early 1960s. Machan's Beach, for example receded upto form in the 30 years period 1935-1968 most of the after 1963. Cook (1981)[42] and Bird (1969)[43] has investigated that upto 1932, Thomatic Creek outed as a flood overflow of the Barrn but in the floods of that year became a permanent distributory. The creek now carries 30 percent of the flood flow to the sea.

Rates of coastal erosion along the Queensland coast are expected to increase as sea level rises. The Bruun Rule estimates the extent of erosion in relation to sea level rise. However, it is still uncertain exactly how the coast will respond to the changing environmental conditions projected under climate change. In addition to rising sea levels, projected changes to atmospheric circulation systems may also cause changes to wave patterns. Changes in wave direction may alter the sediment budgets of coasts, causing increased erosion or realignment of the coast36. Increased numbers of severe tropical cyclones combined with stormier conditions during 'cool' phases of the IPO may also contribute to increased rates of erosion. If the severity or frequency of erosion events increases, there may be insufficient time between events for natural processes to replace eroded sediments. This results in a retreating coastline. An increased rate of coastal erosion is a significant risk for coastal areas. In Queensland there are approximately 15 200 residential buildings located within 110 metres of 'soft', erodible coastlines, of which approximately 5400 are located within 55 metres3. The Gold Coast has the highest number, with approximately 2300 residential buildings within 55 metres, and 4750 within 110 metres of 'soft' coastlines3. The fate of the Great Barrier Reef (GBR) under climate change is uncertain, but the GBR is currently an important factor influencing wave conditions along the Queensland coast. The GBR shelters the Northern and Central Queensland coasts and creates low-energy wave conditions. The GBR as we know it is only 6000 years old and during that time sea level has been relatively stable. If reef building fails to keep up with sea level rise or if large parts of the reef die, then these previously low-energy coasts may be subjected to high-energy swell waves27. Such changes to the physical

Figure 16: Coastal erosion impacting on during TC Structures at Tully Heads, Cardwell North Queensland 2006 debris well

Source: DERM

Figure 17: The 5.33 metre storm surge Yasi, 3 February 2011, damaged the esplanade and deposited sand and above normal levels

Source: DERM

structure of the GBR would occur over long time frames, and may not necessarily result in increased coastal erosion. This is because swell waves, in addition to causing erosion, can also transport large quantities of sand onto the coast.

One of the expected impacts from climate change is accelerated coastal recession due to rising sea-levels, although rates and location of recession are highly dependent on several factors. These include the inherent susceptibility of differing coastal landform types, regional variations in the processes driving erosion/recession or instability (for example, sea-level rise and wave climate), and local factors such as topography and sediment budgets.

The number of residential buildings in Queensland (by local government area or LGA) located within 55 and 110 metres of 'soft' shorelines is shown in Figure. Across Australia, nearly 39 000 residential buildings are located within 110 metres of potentially erodible shorelines, with nearly 40 per cent of those buildings located in Queensland. There was no consideration of any cxisting, planned or future protective structures associated with the estimates of buildings at risk by 2100. Local sediment processes, such as accretion, were not considered.

Figure 18 a and b: Number of residential buildings (by state and territory) located within 55 and 110 metres of 'soft' shorelines (simulating the average and maximum extents of coastal recession by 2100)

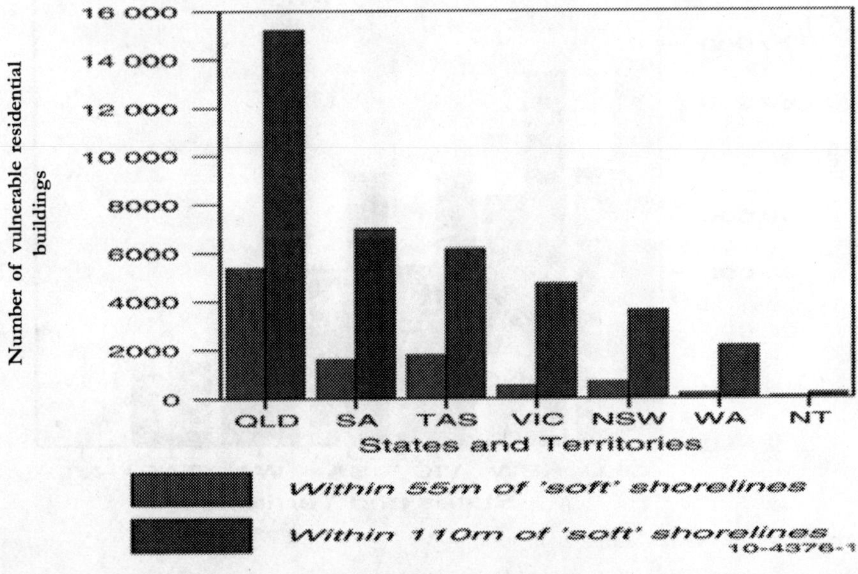

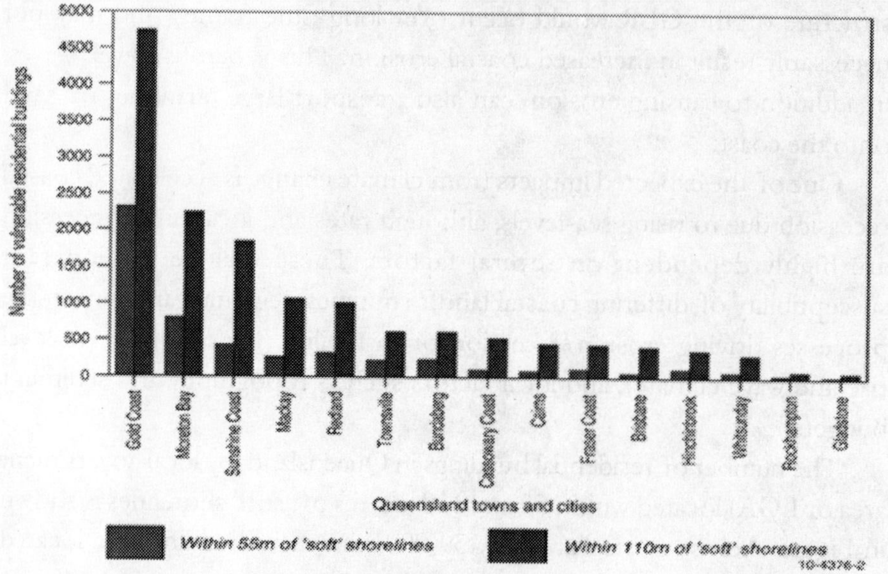

Sources: Aus Geo News March 2011 Issue No. 101

Queensland have the greatest vulnerability when considering both the value of the infrastructure and also the number of buildings affected. Figure shows the number and replacement value of potentially vulnerable residential buildings (by state and territory) considering the combined impacts of both inundation and recession.

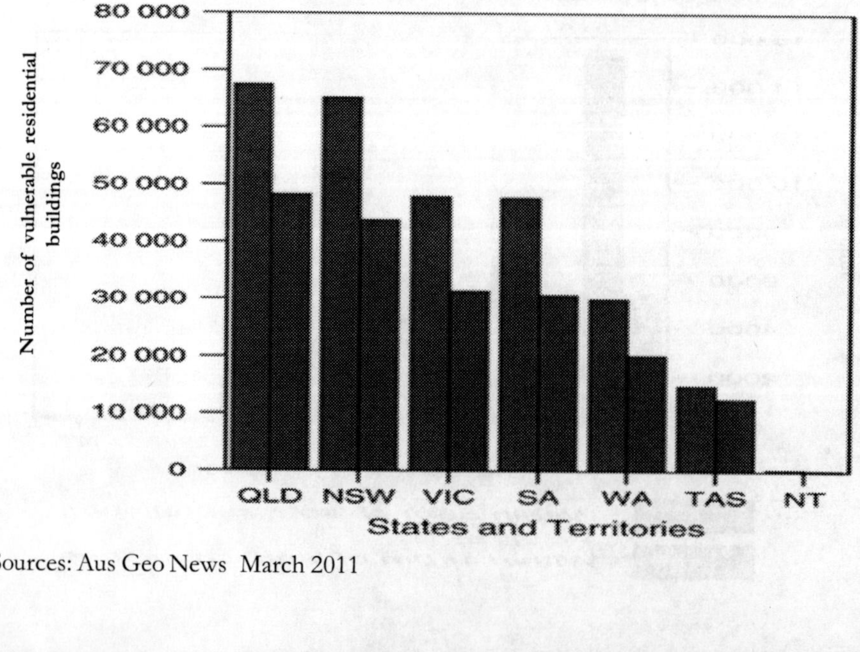

Sources: Aus Geo News March 2011

Coastal Vulnerability

Figure 19 shows the number of vulnerable residential buildings (from inundation and recession) under the 2100 projected sea-level and current (2008) population as well as the ABS Series A, B and C population projections. Potential vulnerability is significantly increased by the ABS Series A and B population projections. In fact for the Series A projection the increase in sea-level has a smaller impact on the vulnerability compared to the increase in population (see figure 20; note the additional part of the bar above the level for 2100 sea-level and 2008 population). For the Queensland region, Figure shows the number of vulnerable residential buildings (from inundation and erosion) for the most impacted LGAs (considering the 2100 sea-level with the 2008 population, and also ABS Series A, B and C population projections). The south-east corner of Queensland where most of the vulnerability for residential infrastructure is located is currently

Figure 19: Length (in kilometers) of vulnerable roads/railway (by state and territory) considering the combined impacts of both inundation (1.1 meter SLR and storm tide) and recession (Bruun rule; 100 times SLR). Values are based on the 'upper' and 'lower' estimates derived by localized validation/comparison with utilizing elevation data.

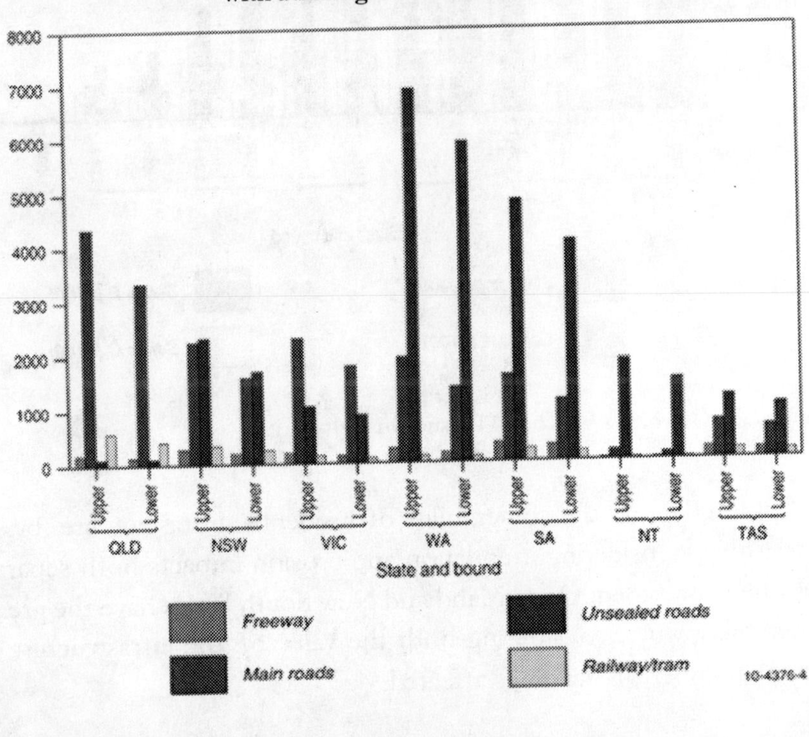

experiencing large population growth and an associated building boom. All along the entire eastern seaboard, including South East Queensland, adaptation to rising sea-levels is becoming a priority for local councils battling to implement sound controls as increased population puts greater pressure on the coastal zone.

Figure 20: Number of vulnerable residential buildings (from inundation and recession) under 2100 sea-level using the current (2008) population and also the ABS Series A, B and C population projections

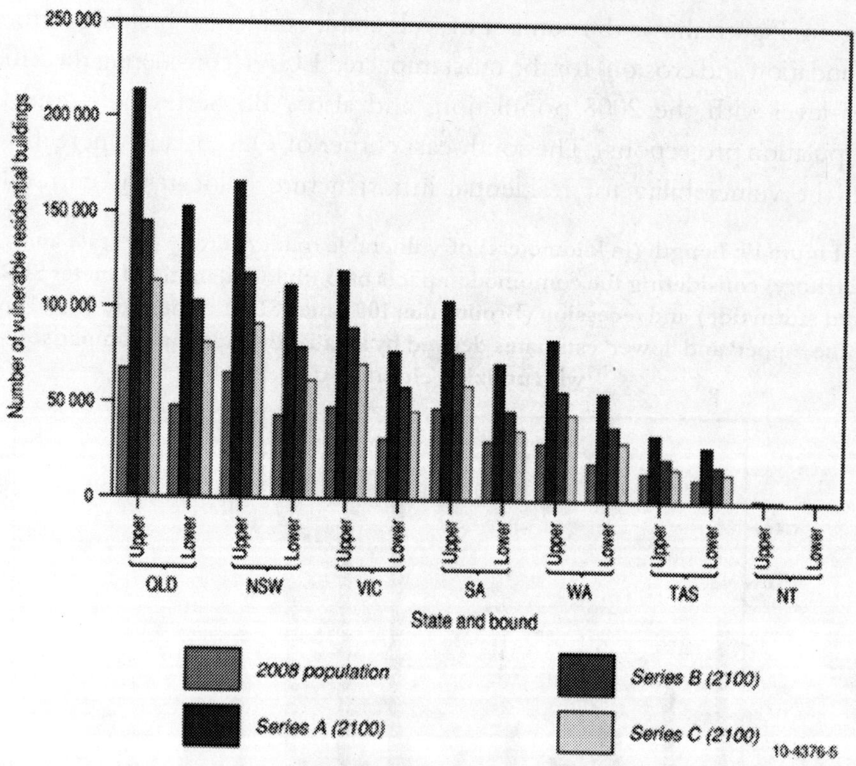

Sources: AusGeo News March 2011 Issue No. 101

Table 21 shows the vulnerability of residential infrastructure (by state or territory) considering inundation and erosion impacts both separately and when combined. Queensland and New South Wales have the greatest vulnerability when considering both the value of the infrastructure and also the number of buildings affected.

Table 21
Number and Value of Residential Buildings Vulnerable to the Impacts of Coastal Inundation, Recession and the Combination of Inundation and Recession for all States and the Northern Territory

State	*'Inundation' only*		*'Recession' only (Zone of Potential Instability)*		*Inundation + Recession (Zone of Potential Instability)*	
	Number	*Value ($mil)*	*Number*	*Value ($mil)*	*Number*	*Value ($mil)*
New South Wales	62 400	19 000	3 600	1 260	65 200	19 800
Northern Territory	200	60	200	80	400	130
Queensland	56 900	16 000	15 200	5 800	67 700	20 500
South Australia	43 000	7 400	7 000	1 300	47 800	8 300
Tasmania	11 600	3 300	6 100	1 800	14 900	4 300
Victoria	44 700	10 300	4 700	1 450	48 000	11 400
Western Australia	28 900	7 700	2 100	600	30 000	8 000
AUSTRALIA	247 700	63 760	38 900	12 290	274 000	72 430

Sources: AusGeo News March 2011

In Queensland shoreline recession is concentrated in the summer months when tropical cyclones induce rough seas. These are called "culminating storm" when the sediments swept from the beaches is lost to deeper water where it is not available for return to the beaches during normal lower energy conditions. Such events have taken place on southern Queensland beaches in 1989, 1929, 1936-7, 1950 and 1974, resulting in up to 425 m^3 of sand per metre length of beach being eroded, with beaches receding by up to 50 m.

In addition to the problems caused by erosion, low lying areas of many of Queensland's coastal towns and cities are vulnerable to flooding. Even predicted king tides may cause minor disruption in the lowest parts of settlements, including cairns and Towsville, but with such flooding occurring at least once a year, the predictable frequency influences the nature of land use in these areas. A greater hazard is the flooding which may result from the passage of a tropical cyclone.

The whole of the Queensland coast is surge prone but the hazard varies considerably around the coast.

(i) Southern Queensland: The continental shaft is narrow and deep water is close inshore, most cyclones reaching these latitudes are of reduced strength, surges above one metre are unlikely.

(ii) Central Queensland: Fraser island to Whitsunday Passage: this zone has a high risk of major cyclones, the continental shelf is wide and shallow thus increasing the surge height.

(iii) North Queensland: Whitsunday to Hinchinbrook; a high cyclone risk, a moderately wide and shallow contribute shelf and only a moderate tidal range produce a very high surge risk for this coastline.

Figure 21: P-S-I-R Framework Continuous Feedback Process in Coastal Areas

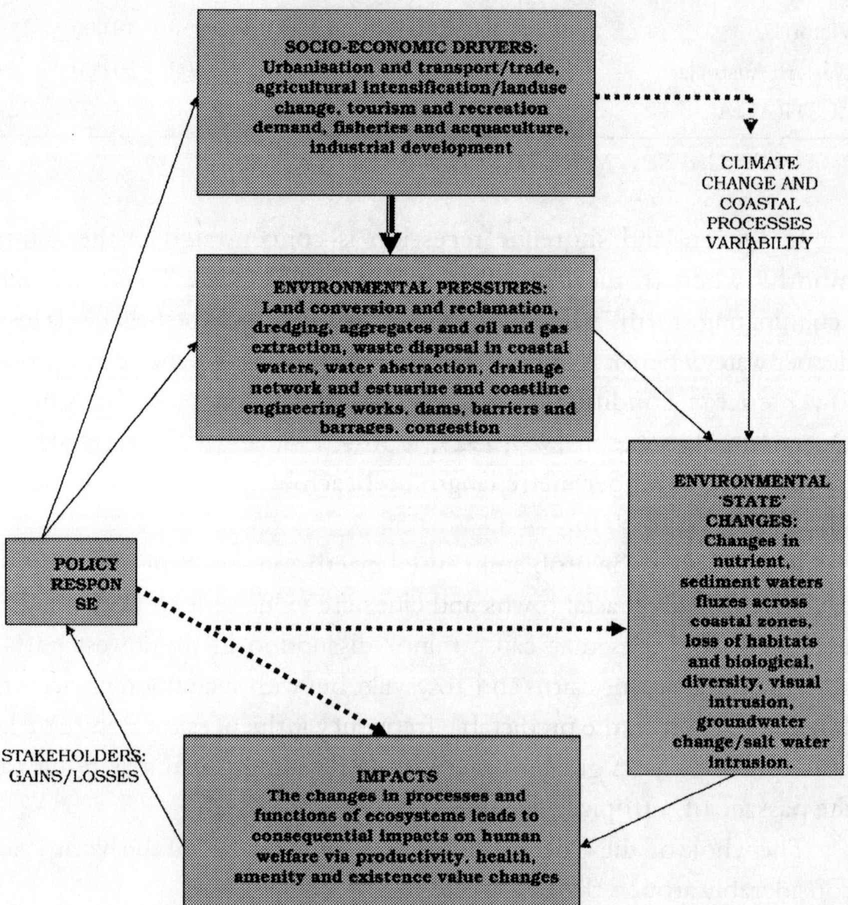

Figure 22: 1.2. P-S-I-R Cycle, Continuous Feedback Process

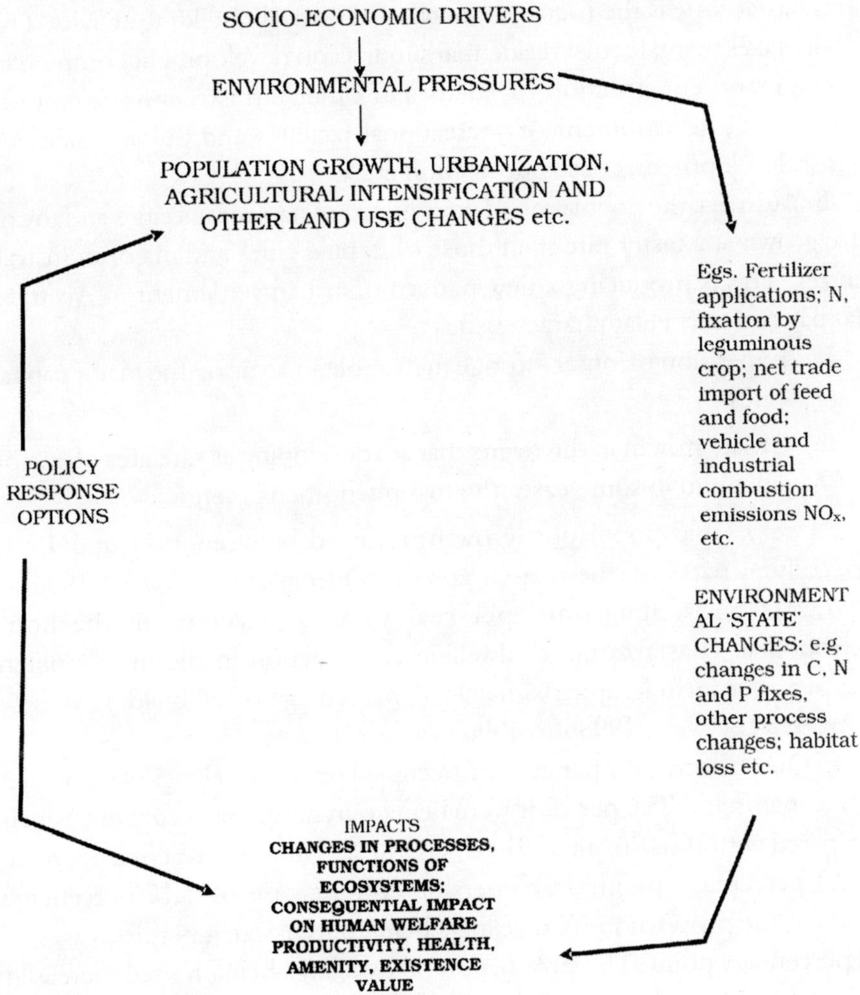

Source: Turner R.K. (1997). Pressure, Trends and Impacts in the Coastal Zones: Interactors between Socio-Economic.

(iv) Far North Queensland: Hinchinbrook to Cape York, a slightly lower tidal range here is offset by a reduction in cyclone frequency and possibly intensity.

(v) Gulf of Carpentaria: The shallow nature of the gulf and frequency of cyclones gives this area a high surge risk, offset only by a slightly higher tidal range in the south east gulf.

Urban and Building Development along Coastal Zone

The coastal zone is the focus for much of Australia's building activity. This activity takes many forms: residential subdivision development commercial development, construction of roads and other infrastructure (e.g. water and swages), development of recreational facilities and public amenities, tourist development; coastal protection etc.

In Australia, the population of non-metropolitan coastal cities and towns have grown at a faster rate than those of capital cities and major industrial centres. This is producing a new pattern of urban settlement in Australia that has two particular characteristics

(a) Expansion of outer – fringe metropolitan areas of the major capital cities;

(b) Urban growth in the reigns that are developing as satellites of major cities and in some cases the two phenomena merge.

At very rapid population growth occurred between 1971 and 1991, especially in parts of the coastal zone in Queensland. Between 1986 to 1996, 50,000 dwelling units per year were constructed in the non-metropolitan coastal zone. If dwelling construction in the metropolitan coastal area is include, approximately 90 percentage of all building activity in Australia between 19986 to 1996 (Table 22).

In Queensland, 38.2 per cent of occupied private dwellings were owned by occupants and 25.6 per cent were being purchased by occupants. When compared with those from 1991 census, these figures represent a decrease of 2.3 percentage points in ownership and increase of 1.12 percentage points in the proportion of dwellings being purchased, a net decreases of 1.2 percentage point. The proportion of dwellings being rented increased 3.7 percentage points over some period.

Table 22
Home Ownership, Queensland

	1986		*1992*		*1996*	
Dwellings	*Number*	*Percentage*	*Number*	*Percentage*	*Number*	*Percentage*
Owned	325,581	39.1	399730	40.5	443338	38.2
Being purchased	238442	28.6	241843	24.5	297049	25.6
Rented (b)	223148	26.8	279731	28.4	372456	32.1
Other (c)	46332	5.6	64655	6.6	47433	4.1
Total	833503	100.00	985959	100.00	1160276	100.00

Source: Queensland Year Book (1998), Australian Bureau of Statistics No. 56, ABS Catalogue No. 1301.3. B, pp. 239.

Land Tenures in the Coastal Zone

Land tenure is an important considerations in managing the coastal zone. To a large extent the use of coastal lands determined by the tenures in which those lands are held. In Australia's coastal zone, about 57 percent of the zone is private land, 16 percent is held under indigenous tenure, and less than 5 percent is occupied under each forestry, defence, reserves and other tenures; mining activities occupy less than 1 percent of the area.[44] (Figure 23 and Figure 24).

Figure 23: Distribution of Land Tenures in the Coastal Zone

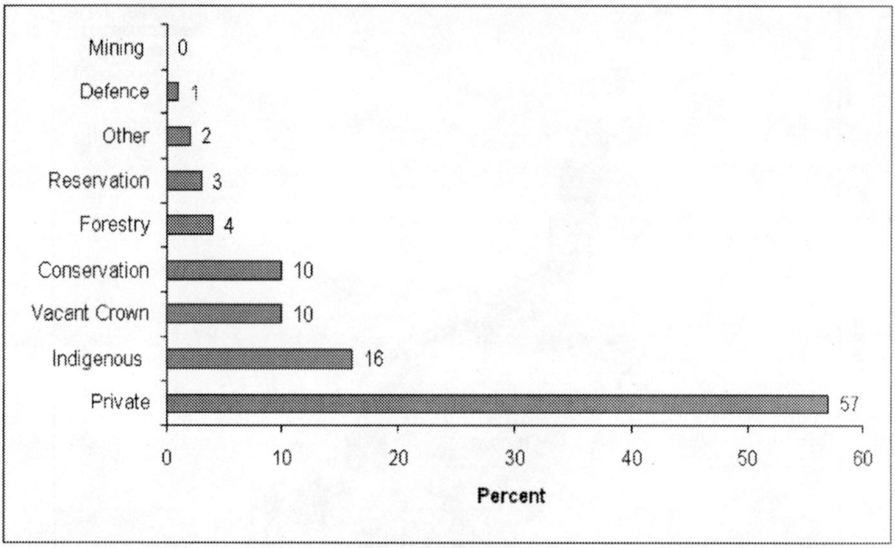

Source: Resource Assessment Commissioner, Coastal Zone Inquire Final Report 1993, PP. 19.

In Queensland under the Aboriginal and Torres Strait Islanders (land holding) Act 1985, deeds of freehold title were granted in the trust for the benefit of Aboriginal and Torres Strait Islands inhabitants of former reserve areas, now call trust areas.[45] By April 1990, 31 Deeds of Grant in Trust (DOGIT) had been made over an area of 2,000 sq km. Aboriginal land (existing leases on DOGIT Lands) comprises 3.4 million hectares (1.8 percent of the state). A further potential two million (1.2 percent o the state) is available for claim, but must first be gazetted as claimble land. To date, 13 national perks and 14 pockets of vacant crown land have been gazetted, with the national perks above totaling 2.4 million hectars.[46]

And about sea right, only limited potential sea right exists in Queensland with respect to ideal lands.[47] The only areas that Aboriginal people can claim as marine estates are tidal lands (meaning land that is ordinarily covered and uncovered by the flow and ebb of the tide at spring tide) and such claims are at the discretion of the Queensland government.

Figure 24: Land Use Land Cover of Queensland Coastal Area (2006)

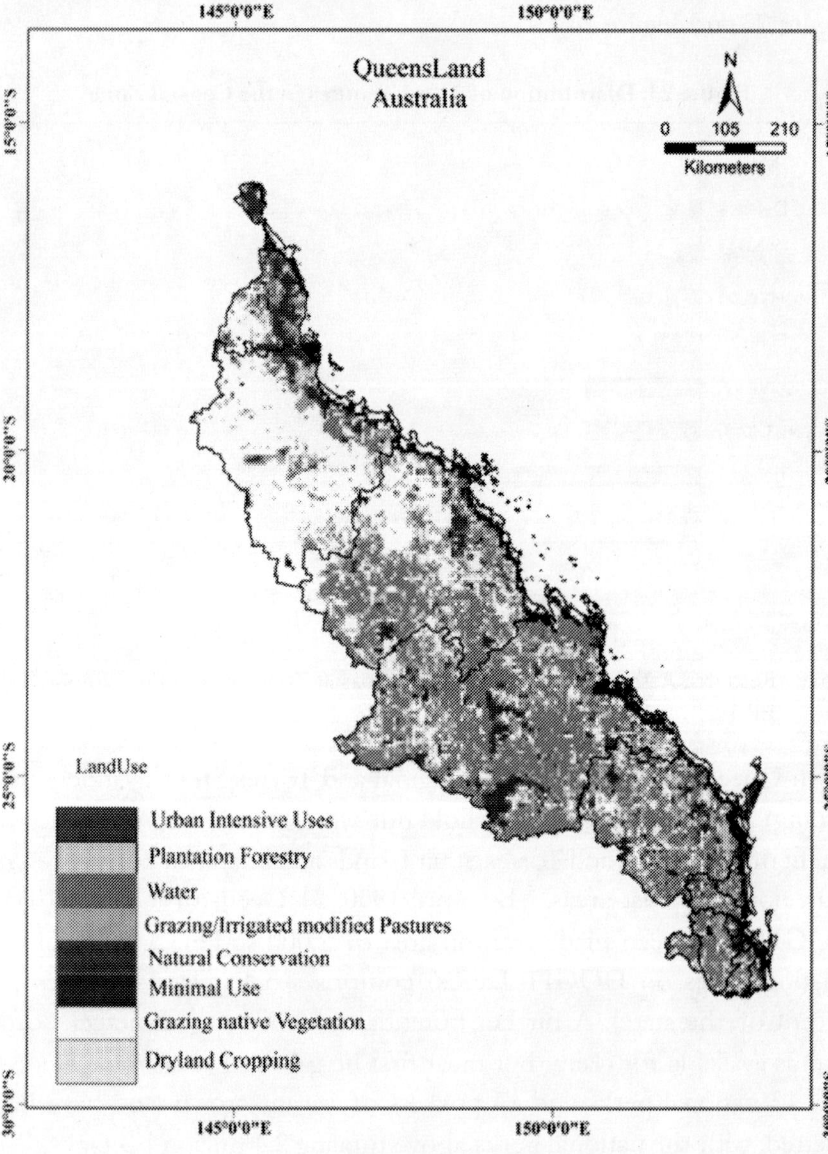

SPATIAL ANALYSIS OF ADMINISTRATIVE ACTIONS AND PROBLEMS

Coastal planning in Queensland is currently administered by state, local and in the case of great Barrier Reef Marine Park, Commonwealth authorities. Jurisdiction over coastal planning and management matters is exercised by a number of agencies in each region. For example, there are some 32 agencies with authority touching on coastal management issues in Moreton Bay area.[48]

The Department of Environment and Heritage administers a programme that focuses on the management of the state's coastal area thorough the investigation of coastal processes and the formulation of policy. One of the first initiative was Canals Act 1958 towards land based coastal development.

Canal Act

After coming of 'Canal Estate' in mid 1950s a new form of coastal land subdividivision in gold coast area, problems of land transfers, maintenance of newly created water ways and the sale of building blocks before the canal development was complete, arose. The two local authorities who were dealing with there canal estates Gold coast City and Albert shire, approached the state government for assistance with these problems. It was resolved to prepare new legislative dealing specifically with canal estate development along the coast, and the Canals Act was proclaimed in 1958.

The Act was divided into two main areas of interest.[49]

1. Approvals required
2. Maintenance responsibilities for the canal water ways. The Act stipulated that a provision Approval was mandatory for a canal development. This approval looked at the concept of land usage and the desirability of a canal estate proceedings in a particular locality. A final approval was subsequently required to permit the actual construction of a canal estae, and covered the design to details of development.

Marine Park Act 1982

Complementary state and Commonwealth legislation has been enacted, namely the great Barrier Reef Marine Park Act 1975 (Commonwealth) and the Marine Park Act 1982 (Old). The Marine Park Act 1982 provides for State Marine Parks to be managed as multiple use areas. It was agreed between the two governments that complementary Marine Parks under State and Commonwealth Jurisdiction would be declared in the Great Barrier Reef region to ensure effective management and protection of the area. This cooperative approach adopted between the federal and Queensland government's was an important initiative in the protection and management of this important area of the coastal zone.[50]

Beach Protection Act 1968

Due to this crisis of beach erosion on the gold coast in the late 1950s was to lead to another significant change in coastal management policy in the state. A series of cyclonic events suddenly placed many buildings at risk, particularly at Surfers paradise in 1964, the then Queensland Government, acting on the advice of the co-ordinator General, commissioned the Delft Hydraulics Laboratory of the Netherlands to examine the beach erosion problems of the gold coast to recommend appropriate investigation programs . Thus, in 1968, The Queensland Government first legislated for the protection of the coastal zone.[51] The major aim of the Beach Protection Act 1968 was to deal with beach erosion. To fulfill this, it established a Beach Protection Authority (BPA) to advise on activities affecting the coast and to make recommendations for specific erosion presentation work.[52]

In 1984 the Beach Protection Act received major amendments.[53] these broadened the scope of the Act and increased powers of the BPA. In particular, they empowered the Governor in Council, on the recommendation of the BPA, to declare any part of the coast to be a Coastal Management Control District.[54] The BPA may prepare a Coastal Management Plan for any Coastal Management Control District.[55] In Coastal Management Control Districts, applications to develop land must be forwarded to the BPA and approved by the Governor in Council.[56] Unless a developer has a permit granted under the Beach Protection Act, any approval, consent or permission granted by a local authority is of no effect.[57] Compensation is available to those whose interests in land are affected by a refusal of the governor in council to grant a permit under the Beach Protection Act.[58] In addition to Coastal Management Control Districts, the

BPA was given power to prepare Erosion Prone Area Plans for any part of the Queensland Coast.[59]

In these areas, land owners could be required by the BPA or a relevant local authority to construct and maintain coastal protection works at their own costs.[60] They (by BPA) could be prohibited from pasturing stock, damaging vegetation or interfering with the surface of the land.[62] Beach Protection Act in 1984 got amended but still there lacked a comprehensive framework for coastal planning and management in Queensland. For example,

(a) It failed to take into amount the multifaceted nature of coastal planning.

(b) It created a separate approval system for control districts that had little respect for existing local government procedures.

(c) Its limited purpose and objectives did not quarantine public access to the coast nor adequately provide for the conservation and protection of the coastal environment for future generations.

Marine Perks Act 1982

Complementary state and Commonwealth legislation has been enacted, namely the Great Barrier Reef Marine Park Act 1975 (Commonwealth) and the Marine Parks Act 1982 (Old). The Marine Parks Act 1982 provides for State Marine Parks to be managed as multiple use areas. It was agreed between the two governments that complementary Marine Parks under state and Commonwealth Jurisdiction would be declared in the great Barrier Reef region to ensure effective management and protections of the area. This cooperative approach adopted between the federal and Queensland Governments was an important initiative in the protection and management of this important area of the coastal zone.[63]

Coastal Zone Inquiry

Under the terms of Reference established by the Commonwealth Government Act 1989, the Resource Assessment Commission understood its inquiry into the management and use of Australia's coastal zone resources between February 1992 and November 1993 (Publication of its Final Report). The issues and outcomes of this inquiry are too wide and in

Figure 25: Major Pieces of Queensland Environment Legal System

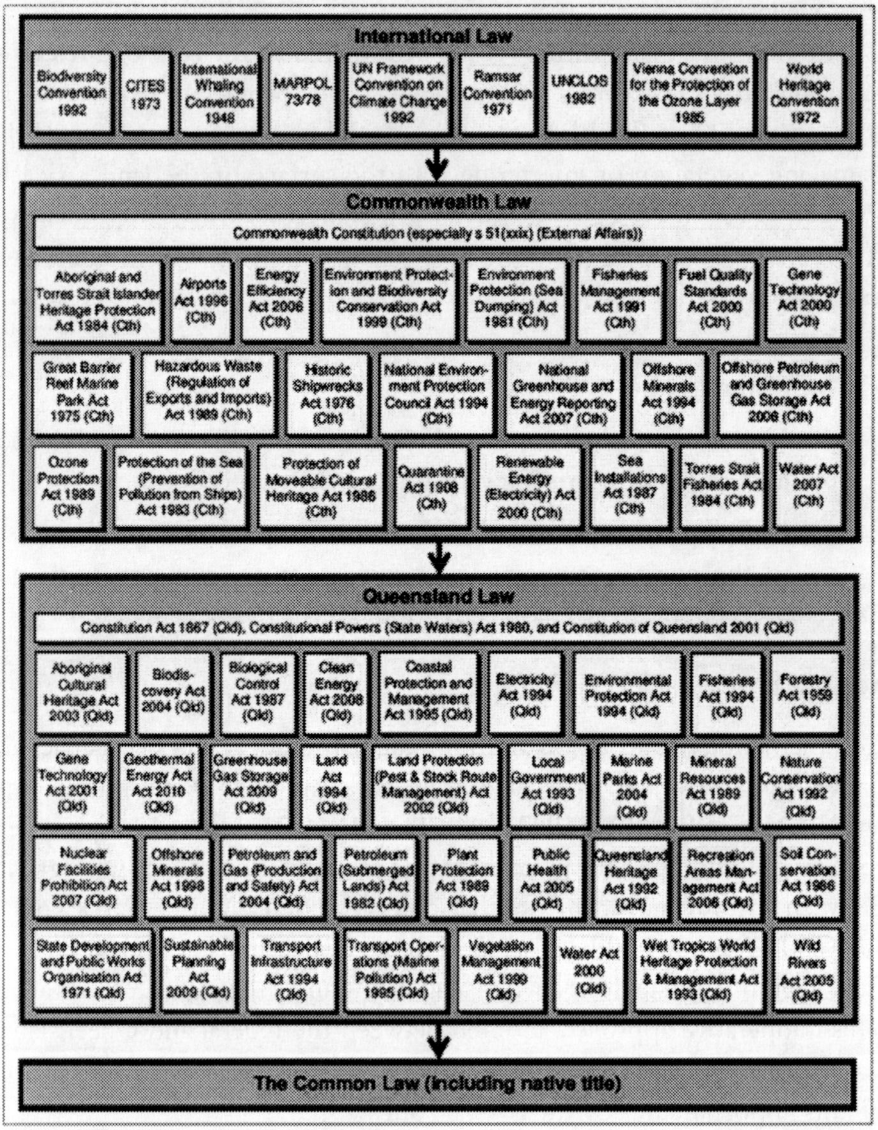

Sources: http://www.envlaw.com.au/sqels5.pdf.

volumes. But main out come of those issues relating to how coastal management is evolving in different areas of Queensland can be sited.

In the field of Urban development, the inquiry found that over half of Australia's total population growth during the past 20 years occurred in non metropolitan parts of the coastal zone, particularly on the sunshine coast and gold coast in Queensland, in SW of western Australia, n far north Queensland, and on the central and north coasts of NSW (New South Wales). This rapid urban expansion often occurred in the areas that were previously dominated by rural activities.[64]

One of the consequences of this urbanisation was the pollution of the coastal waters by stromwater run off and effluent disposal. Degradation of beaches and other natural environments also occurred from improper and excessive use, with a reduction in the extent of bushland and wetlands and depletion of coastal habitat. The inquiry concluded that we need to change the coastal zone resources were used to prevent the loss of ecosystems, degradation of recreational amenity of the coast, and decreasing economic growth and employment opportunities.[65]

And about legislature issues, the inquire found that regulatory responsibility for management of coastal zone resources lies primarily with state and local government. Although state governments had attempted to better co-ordinate and update legislation. The inquiry concluded that existing legislative mechanism did not provide for the coastal zone and that coastal management policies in the three spheres of government needed to be more integrated and better reflect social, economic and environmental issues.[66]

And about local and regional focus, the inquiry noted that local government played a critical role in coastal management but that many local authorities were limited in financial and technical expertise resources.[67] It also considered that many non-traditional areas including: information systems; data acquisition and assessment, monitoring; review and evaluation techniques; and resource and environmental indicators. Inquiry also stated that a more regional approach was needed for effective and integrated coastal management since many of natural systems and processes extends beyond the jurisdictions of individual local governments. Regional strategies enabled resources to be managed more effectively and efficiently.[68]

Among the Principal Legislation used to Manage Coastal, Zone Resources is the Following

- Local Government Act 1936
- Harbours Act 1955

- Camals Act 1958
- Queensland Marine Act 1958
- Beach Protection Act 1968
- Clean Waters Act 1979
- Fauna Conservation Act 1974
- Building Act 1975
- Great Barrier Reef Marine Park Act 1975 (Commonwealth)
- National Parks and Wildlife Act 1975
- Fisheries Act 1976
- State Development and Public Works Organisation Act 1981
- Marine Parks Act 1982
- Integrated Resort Development Act 1987
- Mineral Resource Act 1989
- Aboriginal Land Act 1991
- Nature Conservation Act 1992
- Queensland Heritage Act 1992
- Coastal Protection and Management Act 1995

The early 1990s have been described as a "Watershed" for coastal management in Australia. This was because of increased interest by the Commonwealth and State Governments in coastal management resulting in major national and state reviews, and the updating or creation of coastal programs across Australia.

Since 1980, Commonwealth government has conducted at least 29 inquiries into coastal management or aspects of it, and various state governments at least 34.[69] The most significant of these were management of the Australian Coastal Zone, a report from the House of Representatives Standing Committee on Environment and Conservation (HORSCEC, 1980).[70] The Inquired Coastline: Protection of the Coastal Environment by the House of Representatives Standing Committee on Environment, Recreation and the Arts (HORSCERA; 1991)[71] and Resource Assessment Commission Coastal Zone Inquiry.

The recommendations from HORSCEC (1980)[72] included that

The Commonwealth Government, in consultation with the states, (should) develop and promulgate national policies and objectives for the conservation and preservation of Australian Coastline … (p.38).

The Commonwealth government, jointly with the states, established an Australian Coastal Management Council (ACMC) … (p.39) (and)

(ACMC) determine guidelines for allocation of any Commonwealth funds that may become available to the states for programs in accordance with national policies … (p. 41).

The Commonwealth government subsequently did not out on the recommendations of the HORSCEC report and its findings, although it was "systematic to the thrust" of its recommendations.[73]

HORSCERA (1992)[74] had similar terms of reference to the previous HORSCERA in unique and recommended that

The Commonwealth develop without further delay a national coastal zone management strategy …. (p. 84).

The Commonwealth designate the proposed Environment Protection Agency as the federal body responsible for coastal matter ….. (p. 85).

Effective public participation in coastal zone management be encouraged ….. (p. 86).

Table 23
Summary of Recommendations of Federal Coastal Management Inquiries Related to Institutional Arrangements

Elements	*Horscec 1980*	*Horscera 1991*	*RAC 1993*
A national coastal strategy	1	1	1
Commonwealth Coastal Zone Legislation		1	1
Commonwealth Coastal Agency			1
Specific Ministerial Council	1		
An Intergovernmental agreement		1	1
Integration of Commonwealth and State Management	1	1	1
Financial assistance to state and local governments	1	1	1
Integration of local government		1	1
Regional basis to management			1
Community and citizen participation		1	1

Source: Haward, M. (1995). Institutional design and policy making "Down Under". Developments in Australian and New Zealand Coastal Management. Ocean and Coastal Management 26:87-117.

(a) HORSCEC - House of Representatives Standing Committee on Environment and Conservation.

(b) HORSCERA - House of Representatives Standing Committee on Environment, Recreation and the Arts.

(c) RAC - Resource Assessment Commission.

Green paper on Coastal Protection Strategy 1991 and the Coastal Protection Bill 1993.

In April 1991, the Queensland government released a discussion paper on a Coastal Protection Strategy for the state.[75] In much the same vein as the Commonwealth Coastal Policy (CCP) and the national reports that proceeded it, the Green Paper identified a need for better husbandry of resources and clear directions for coastal developers, users and administrators.[76] In particular the Green Paper set the following goals and values for coastal management in Queensland:

- To conserve and enhance the coast, its native flora and fauna, its heritage places, habitats and natural processes.
- To allow orderly and environmentally responsible use of coast having regard for long term community benefit and natural occurrences such as tropical cyclones
- To maintain the public right of access to the coast and beaches and, where possible, obtain development free areas adjacent to beaches and foreshores for public and coastal management purposes.
- To ensure policies are in place to deal effectively with the coastal consequences of any greenhouse effect.[77]

The green paper favoured a management strategy that combined local responsiveness with in a framework of regional and state requirements.[78] It made proposals for a Coastal Protection Act to replace the Beach Protection Act and a Coastal Protections Authority to replace the BPA.[79] Other recommendations in the green paper included the need for coastal buffer zones to help reduce the adverse effects of sea level rise and the composition of state wide and regional coastal plans to guidelines and management guidelines. These would place the onus of proof on the developer to show that any proposed development would be in accordance with the principles of ESD and in compliance with the guidelines.[80]

In 1993, the gross government published a Draft Coastal Protection Bill. The 1993 Bill closely followed the recommendations of the green paper and included provisions related to a coastal protection Advisory Council (CPAC)[81], state and regional coastal management plans, environmental impact studies and control districts with separate development approval processes.[82]

Coastal Protection and Management Act 1995: Key Provisions and Critique

The 1993 Bill underwent a length process of public consultation and revision.[83] Two years after the publication of the first draft Coastal Protection Bill, and four years after the publication of the Green Goss government finally succeeded in passing the CPMA in December 1995. Its main provisions can be dealt with under seven headings:

COASTAL DEFINITIONS USED IN THE QUEENSLAND COASTAL PROTECTION AND MANAGEMENT ACT (1995)

- Foreshore means the land lying between high water mark and low water mark as is ordinarily covered and uncovered by the flow and ebb of the tide at spring tides.
- The coast is all areas within or neighbouring the foreshore.
- Coastal management includes the protection, conservation, rehabilitation, management nad ecologically sustainable development of the coastal zone.
- Coastal resources means the natural and cultural resources of the coastal zone.
- Coastal waters are Queensland waters to the limit of the highest astronomical tide.
- Coastal wetlands include tidal wetlands, estuaries, salt marshes, melaleuca swamps (and any other coastal swamps), mangrove areas, marshes, lakes or minor coastal streams regardless of where they are of a saline, freshwater or brackish nature.
- The coastal zone is:

(a) Coastal waters; and

(b) All areas to the landward side of the coastal waters in which there are physical features, ecological or natural processes or human activities that affect, or potentially affect, the cost or coastal resources.

Objects, Definitions and Application

The objects of the Act differ slightly to the goals originally outlined in the Green Paper. They include a commitment to the goal, core objectives and guiding principles of ESD, as in the CCP, and a reference to biological diversify but no reference to global warming or maintaining pubic rights of access to the cost.[84] Section 3(C) states that integrated management of the coastal zone will be "in conjunction with other legislation", an addition which indicates that changes pending in the PEDA Bill have now been taken into account. As in the CCP, a further goal is to improve our knowledge of coastal resources and effects of human activities on the coastal zone.

The Act adopts a number of new definitions. The "coast" is now defined as "all are a within or neighbouring the foreshore",[85] a considerable simplification of the definition formerly provided by the Beach Protection Act.[86] The "coastal zone" is defined as "coastal waters and all areas to the landward side of coastal waters in which there are physical features ecological or natural processes or human activities that affect, or potentially affect, the coast or coastal resources.[87] These definitions were criticized for being "vague and ambiguous" in the Legislative Assembly but their loose terminology allows the many diverse factors which impinge on the health of the coastal zone to be taken into account when applying the Act.

The Act binds all persons, including the State[88]

Institutions

Following the 1993 Bill, the Act establishes a Coastal Protection Advisory Council (CPAC) whose membership has grown from eight in the 1993 Bill to 12 including the chief executive as chairperson.[89] All members are to be appointed by the Minister. The Explanatory Notes indicate that the CPAC will consist of representatives of local government, conservation, tourism, industry, fishing and Aboriginal and Torres Strait Islander interests.[90]

The function of the CPAC is to advise the Minister on coastal management issues, some of which, are listed in the Act.[91] the list is not exhaustive and it is clear that the CPAC will advise on a much large range of issues than its predecessor, the BPA. The advisory function of the CPAC is only bounded by a requirement that, in performing its functions, it must: (i) monitor the integration of coastal zone management; (ii) have regard to existing interests in land in the coastal zone, including (iii) liasing and consulting with Aboriginal people and Torres Strait Island's particularly concerned with land in the coastal zone and having regard to their traditions and customs.[92]

In addition to the CPAC the Act requires the Minister to appoint a regional consultative group whenever a regional coastal management plan is being prepared.[93] Its principal function is to advise the Minister on issues relating to the regional plan.[94] Its membership must include representatives of local government tourism, conservation, industry and Aboriginal and Torres Strait Islander interests.[95]

During the second reading of the Bill, a number of criticisms were raised by the Opposition about the composition and functions of the CPAC and regional consultative groups. These were:

- Membership of the CPAC should be dealt with in the Act and not the Explanatory Notes accompanying it;[96]
- Membership of both committees emphasizes expert and special interest representation rather than active participation by elected local government officials;[97]
- Membership of both committees will be decided solely by the Minister and need not include representatives of regional interests in Queensland;[98]
- The advisory powers of both committees (e.g., in responsing to submissions on draft coastal plans) undermine local governments' planning powers;[99]
- Together they create a "convoluted bureaucracy" that duplicates existing committes.[100]

These criticism demonstrate an underlying concern that local government powers are being steadily encroached upon by a centralized government bureaucracy that places too much faith in technocratic, paternalistic styles of government.

Coastal Management Plans

Following the recommendations of the Green Paper» the Act provides for State and regional planning in the coastal zone- The State coastal management plan will state principles and policies to guide coastal zone management and include map(s) showing coastal resource information.[101]

Regional coastal plans will also include a policy framework and resource information maps.[102] Regional plans may also identify, and describe schemes of coastal management works and key coastal sites retiring special coastal management.[103] Both State and regional plans may prescribe offences for their contravention[104] and take effect as subordinate legislation upon approval by the Governor in Council.[105]

Public participation in the preparation of State plans is heavily qualified. The Act requires the Minister to give notice to the public once a draft State plan has been prepared.[106] Submission on the draft State plan has been prepared. Submissions on the draft plan must be considered first by the CPAC and then by the Minister who must take into account the CPAC's advice on each submission.[107] The preparation of regional plans follows a more complex procedure in which public notice inviting submissions must be given at two stages – when the plan is first proposed and when a draft has been made. At each stage, the Minister must consider these submissions and the advice given by the CPAC and the regional consultative group about them.

To implement the provisions on State and regional planning, the Goss government allocated $5 million to State and regional planning over the next five years.[108]

Integrated planning is a key objective of the CPMA.[109] The Explanatory Notes endeavour to show how State and regional coastal planning will be fully integrated with other planning legislation.

It appears that the State coastal management plan will include a set of policies which the government will make into a State Planning Policy (SPP)[110] Local authorities must have regard to SPPs when preparing planning studies, amending planning schemes and deciding various development applications.[111] The coastal SPP will be the "primary tool for incorporating State coastal policy into planning schemes. In addition, a head of power will be incorporated into the PEDA legislation to ensure that State and regional coastal management plans will be treated in the same way as SPPs outside of control districts[112].

It is arguable that unnecessary complexity is introduced in to the planning system by giving coastal management plans the same status as SPPs, thereby forcing local authorities to have regard to three different documents when dealing with planning matters in the coastal zone.

Figure 26: South East Queensland Coastal Plan

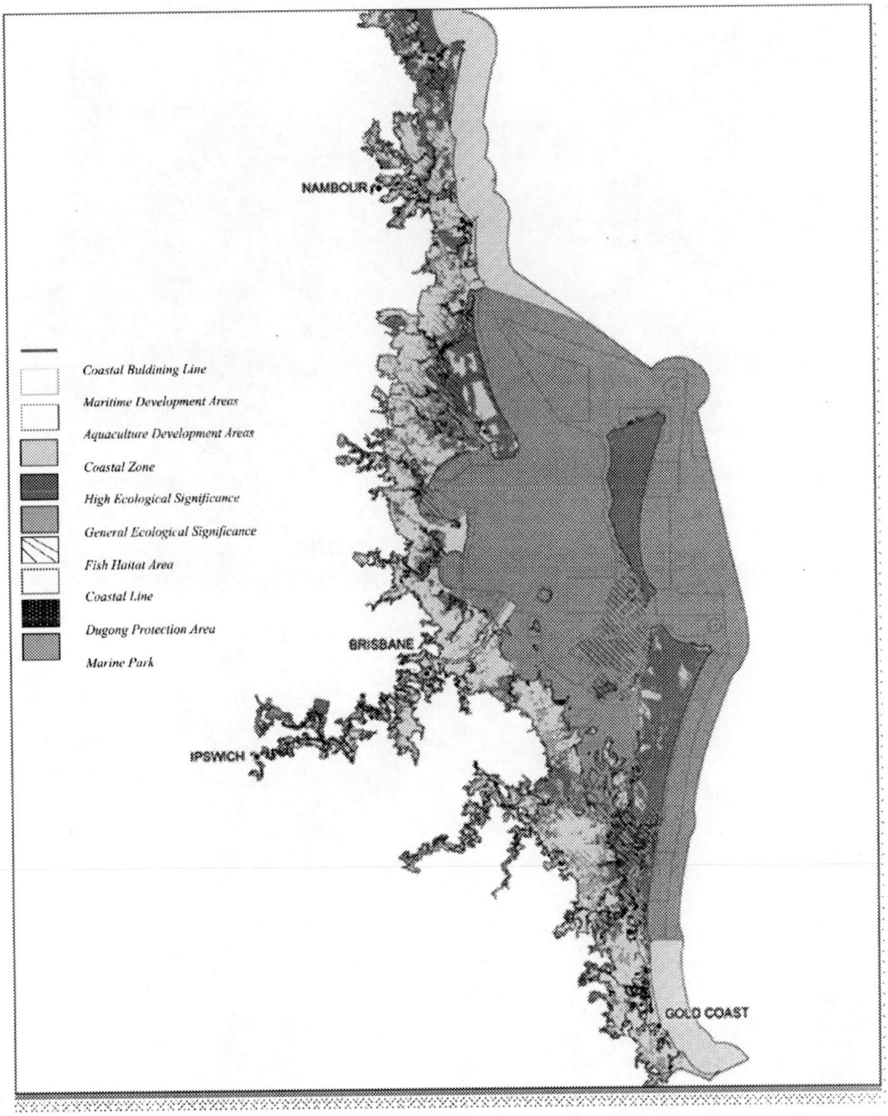

Source: Department of Environment and Heritage Protection, Queensland Government

Figure 27: Wide Bay Burnett Coastal Plan, Queensland

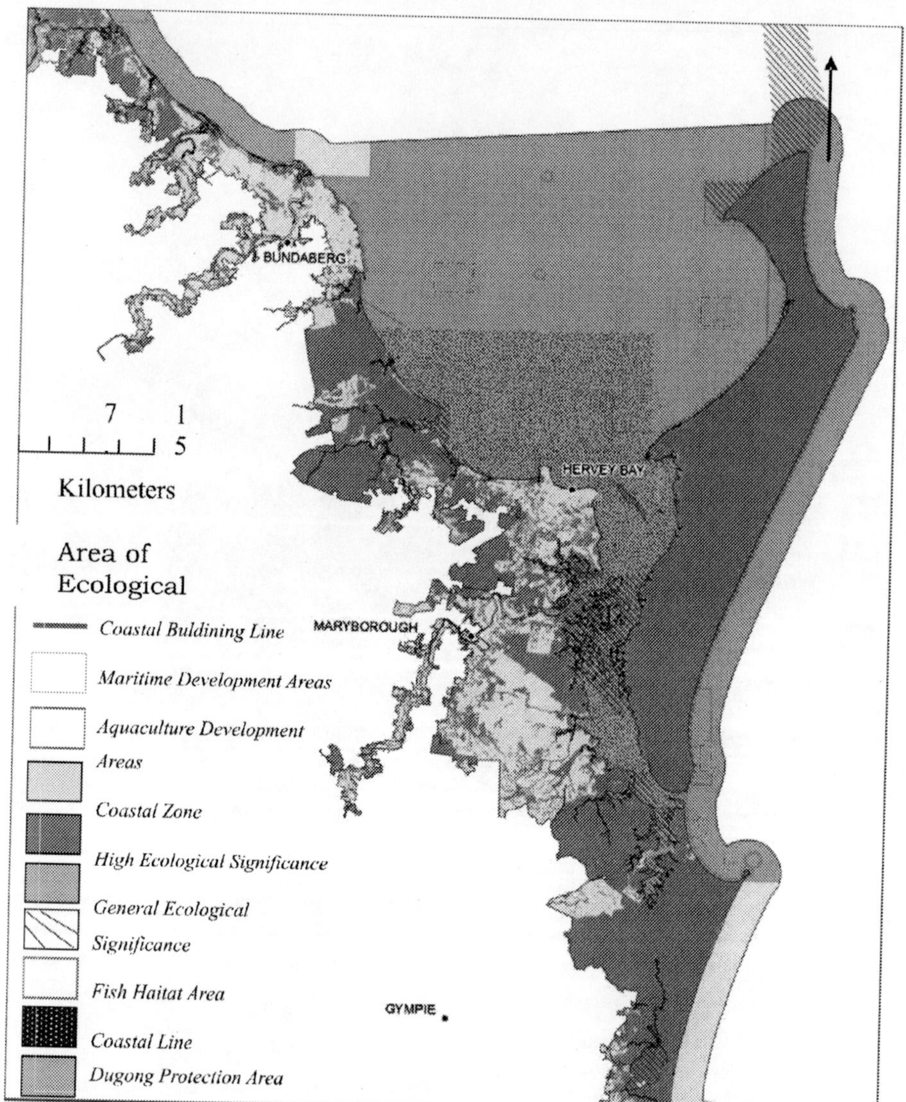

Source: Department of Environment and Heritage Protection, Queensland Government

Figure 28: Central Queensland Coastal Plan

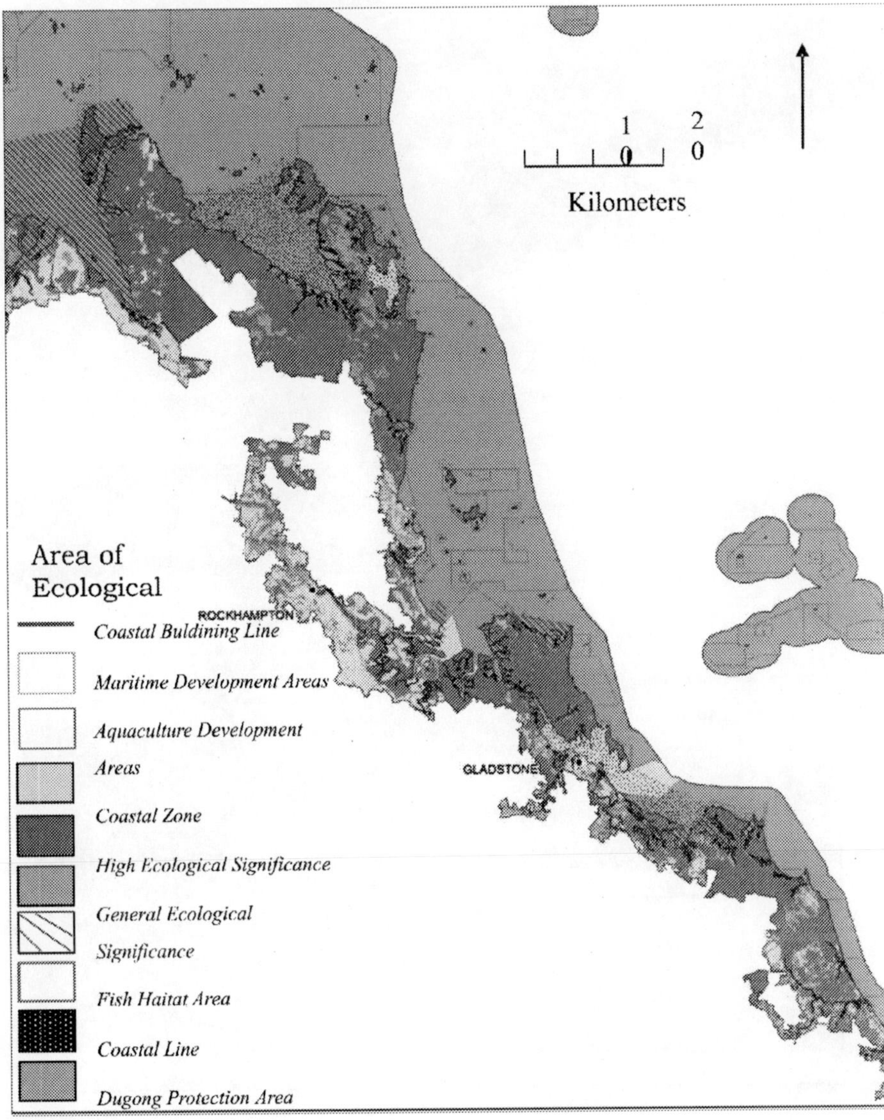

Source: Department of Environment and Heritage Protection, Queensland Government

Figure 29: Whitsunday Hinterland and Mackay, Queensland Coastal Plan

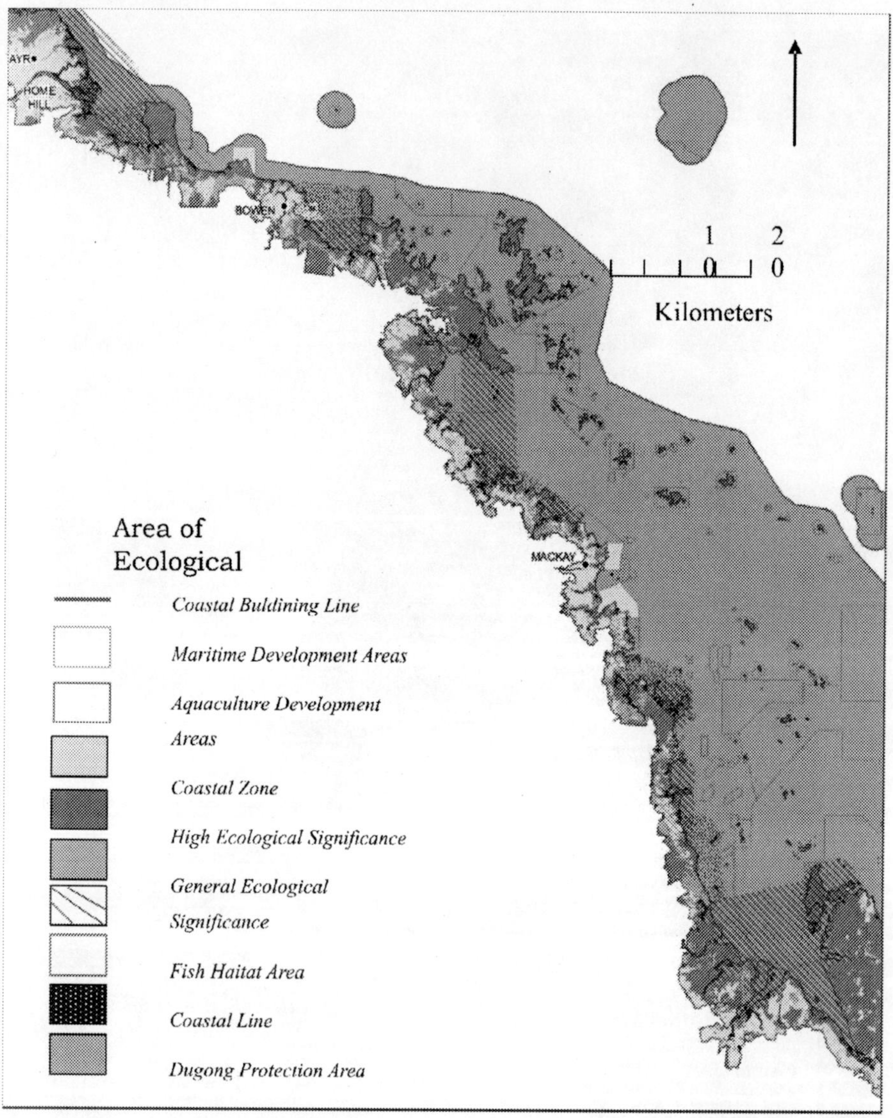

Source: Department of Environment and Heritage Protection, Queensland Government

Figure 30: Townsville–Thuringia Queensland Coastal Plan

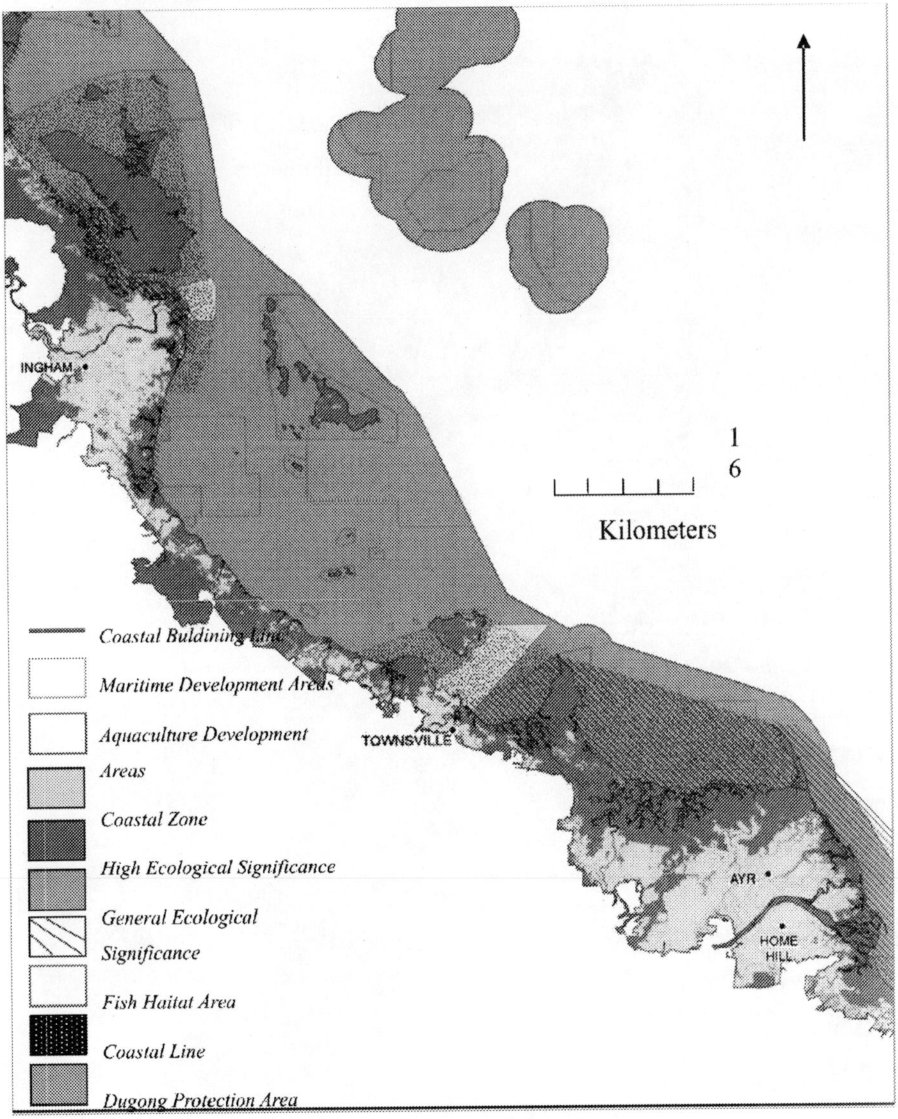

Source: Department of Environment and Heritage Protection, Queensland Government

Figure 31: Far North Queensland Coastal Plan

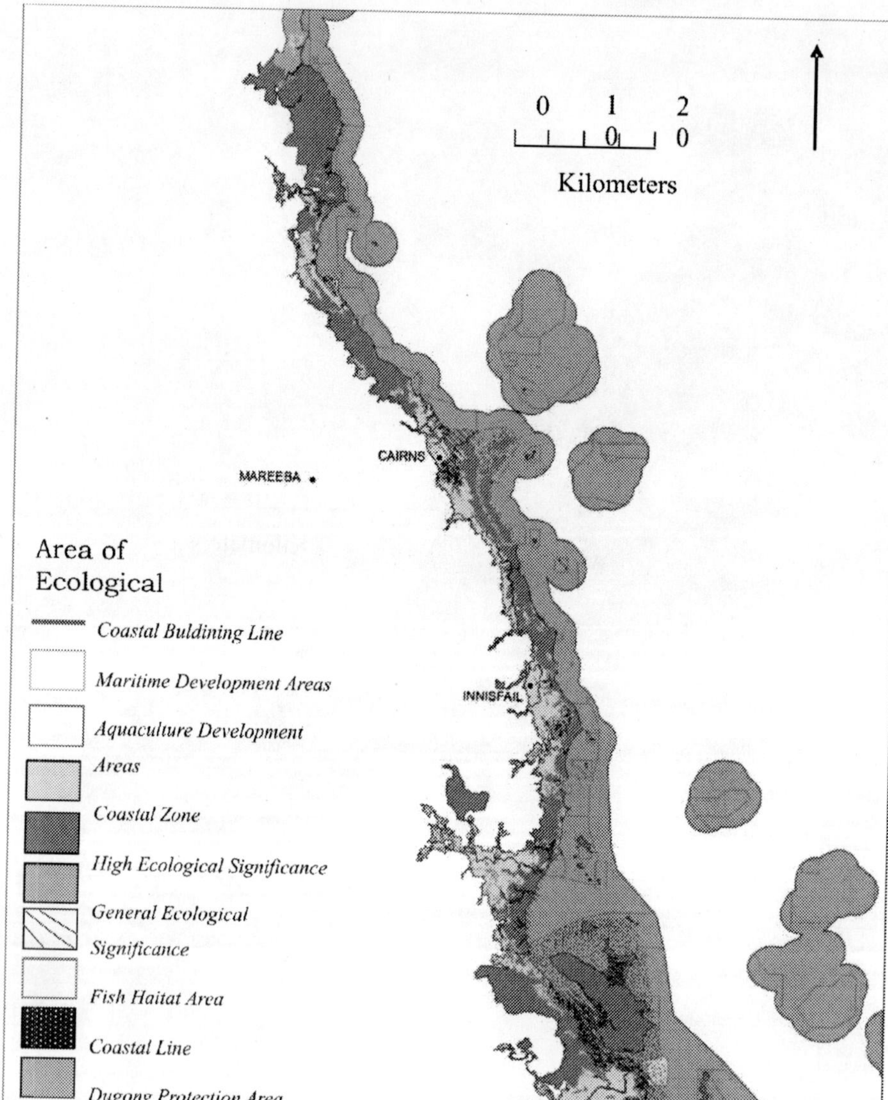

Source: Department of Environment and Heritage Protection, Queensland Government

Figure 32: Cape York and Torres Strait Coastal Plan, Queensland

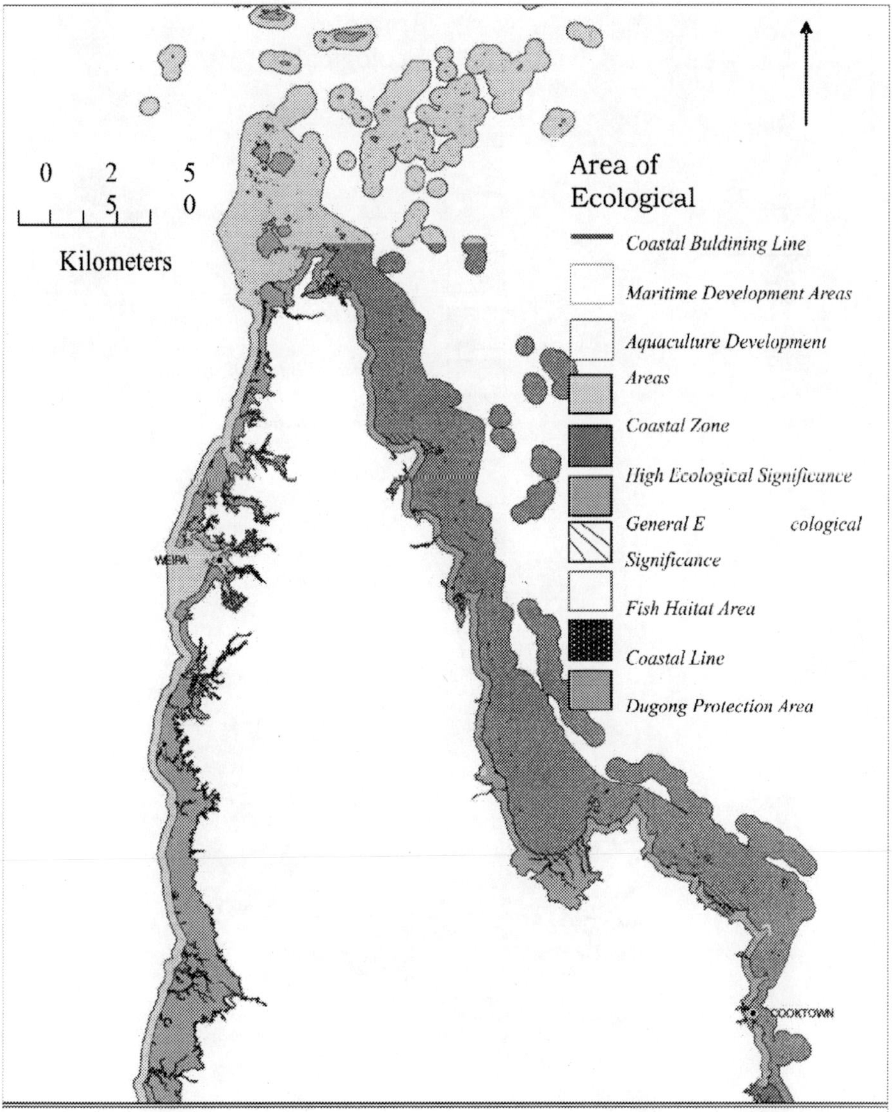

Source: Department of Environment and Heritage Protection, Queensland Government

Figure 33: Gulf region Coastal Plan, Queensland

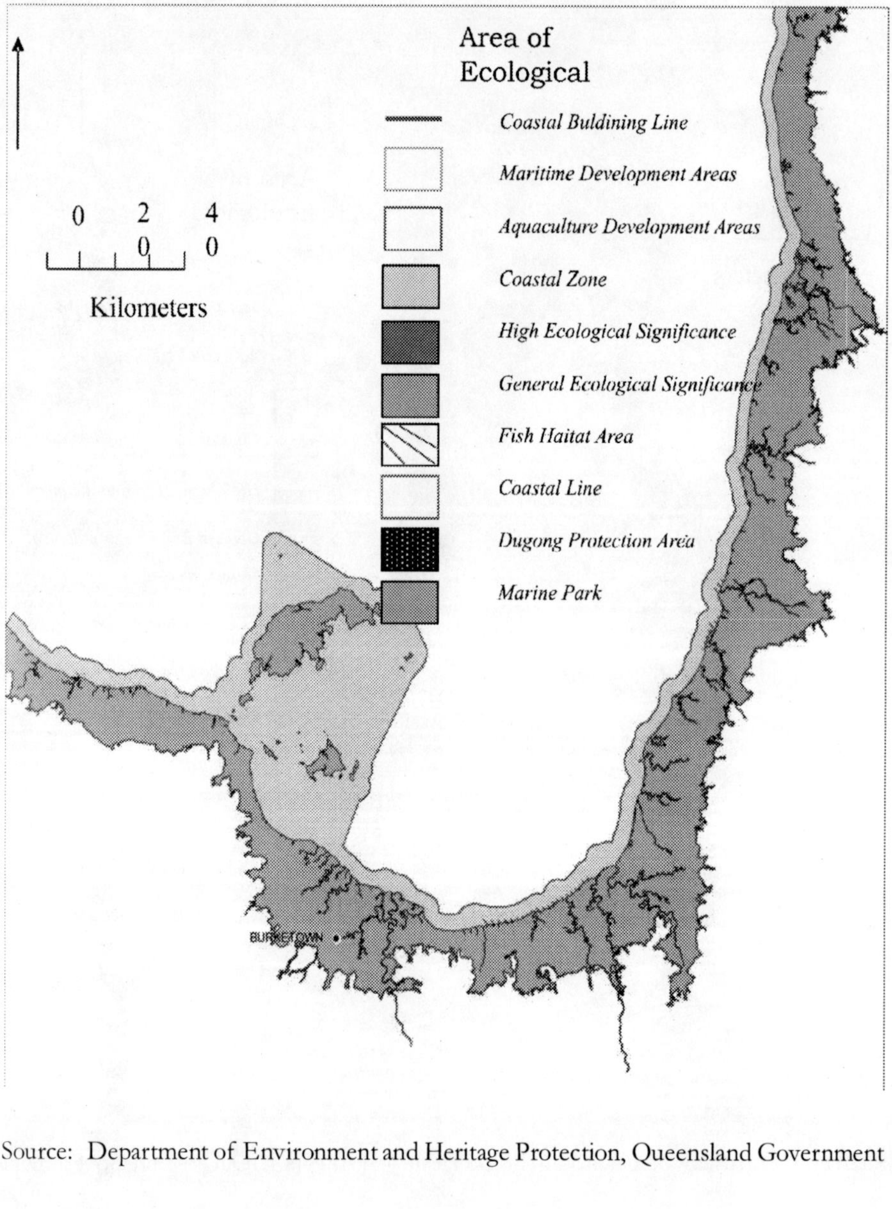

Source: Department of Environment and Heritage Protection, Queensland Government

The State Coastal Management Plan has standing equivalent to that of a State Planning Policy, which means that local governments' IPA planning schemes must consider the policies in the state and regional coastal plans. However, of the 36 coastal councils that have IPA planning schemes in place at 21 August 2007, only seven appropriately reflect the state and regional coastal plans. The EPA is currently finalising guidelines that advise local government on how to appropriately reflect the coastal policies in future reviews of their schemes. Growth and development in South East Queensland are also guided by a statutory regional planning strategy, the *South East Queensland (SEQ) Regional Plan 2005-2026* (DLGPSR 2005).

More recently, the development of a statutory Far North Queensland 2010 Regional Planning Project has commenced to guide decision making related to growth, development and management of that region, including the coast, over the next 20 years or more. In addition to the statutory regional plans and state and regional coastal management plans, a range of other legislative tools are used to manage coastal use and development. These are summarized in Table 24.

Table 24
State legislative responses to pressures from coastal land use change and infrastructure development

Pressures	*Response mechanism*	*Legislation*
Land use change	Integrated Development Assessment System (IDAS); State and Regional Coastal Management Plans; SEQ Regional Plan	Integrated Planning Act 1997
Protection of fish habitat	Declaration of fish habitat areas; development approvals, self-assessable codes and environmental authorities	Fisheries Act 1994
Aquaculture development		Environmental Protection Act 1994
Leasehold land management road, granting easement	Leases and approvals	Land Act 1994
Regional vegetation management	Codes; guidelines; approvals	Vegetation Management Act 1999

Tree clearing on private land		
Water for consumptive use-town supplies, irrigation and riparian access	Water resource plans, resource operations plans; water allocations or licences; approvals	Water Act 2000
Removal of vegetation or quarry material from a watercourse		
Works, reclamation and dredging on tidal land or water	Sanctions, authorities and approvals	Coastal Protection and Management Act 1995
Canals	Approvals	Coastal Protection and Management Act 1995
Development in erosion prone areas and coastal management districts	Land surrender approvals	Coastal Protection and Management Act 1995
Works in and removal of material or discharging of wastes into a marine park	Permits	Marine Parks Act 2004
Pollution of water, air, land	Environmental authorities and development approvals	Environmental Protection Act 1994
Major developments (dams and weirs, port construction and major aquaculture)	Impact assessment and approvals	State Development and Public Works Organisation Act 1971

Sources: http://www.envlaw.com.au/sqels5.pdf.

TOURISM AND RECREATION

The Queensland Ecotourism Plan 2003-2008 (QEP) provides a framework for planning, developing, managing and marketing Queensland's nature-based tourism industry. Tourism Queensland is responsible for the implementation of this plan, in partnership with other relevant state and local government agencies, the tourism industry and the wider community.

The Queensland Government and the Queensland tourism industry have completed the development of a new ten-year vision for tourism. The Queensland Tourism Strategy (QTS) charts an integrated whole-of-government and industry approach to achieving sustainable tourism targets.

The QTS aims to improve the performance, competitiveness and structural efficiency of the industry and deliver a range of long-term benefits to both business and government. A central theme of the strategy is recognition of the significance of the environment in the Queensland tourism experience.

Improved planning and regulatory frameworks are ensuring that recently developed areas of Queensland's coastal zone are being approached in a sustainable manner. Visitor management in state-controlled protected areas will now be managed under the Tourism in Protected Areas (TIPA) framework established by the EPA (EPA 2007). TIPA's commercial operating agreements manage latent visitor capacity, and encourage the uptake of sustainable practice and ECO Certification, an accreditation program of Ecotourism Australia (EA 2007).

Queensland had 17 ECO Certified operators recognised among the 2006 Queensland Tourism Awards finalists. This provides an indication of the tourism industry's willingness to adopt a more sustainable approach and the increasing focus on the fundamentals of ecotourism throughout the industry. Sustainable nature-based tourism continues to make a strong contribution to the protection of Queensland's natural heritage and by its very nature fosters conservation.

Control Districts

The act gives special powers to the chief executive (or his or her delegate) in control districts. First, he or she may serve a coastal protection notice on any person requiring that person to take reasonable action to protect land or stop any activity which the chief executive is satisfied is likely to have a significant effect on coastal management or cause wind erosion.[113] Secondly, he or she may serve a tidal works notice on a person responsible for works in or over the foreshore or on land under tidal water,[114] A tidal works notice may require the person to repair or remove the works.[115] If a person fails to comply with a coastal protection or tidal works notice, the chief executive may take the required action and recover the costs incurred from that person.[116] Thirdly, the chief executive may temporarily occupy and use land in a control district for the purpose of building, maintaining or repairing works in aid of a coastal plan.[117]

A person who has been served with a coastal protection or tidal works notice may appeal to the Planning and Environment Court (PEC).[118] The court may confirm, vary or set aside; the noticed.[119] There is no indication in the Act of the factors which the court must take into account when deciding appeals of this type.

A regional a plan regulation or notice that declares a control district may fix a coastal building tine for the district No building approval can be given over land lying seaward of the coastal building line.[120]

Control districts, coastal protection and tidal works notices are the principal management tools of the new Act. They bear close resemblance to the mechanisms provided in the Beach Protection Act. 1968-1986,[121] giving some credence to the Opposition view that this Act "is all about reinventing the wheel".[122] However, unlike the Beach Protection Act and the 1993 Bill, the Act does not include a separate approval process for new developments in control districts. This is a clear and logical concession to the integrated development approval system (IDAS) that the heart of the PEDA Bill. This proposed legislation provides for the referral of particular types of development application to concurrence agencies that will have power to determine the application.[123] If the PEDA is passed (Department of Environment (DOE) will act as a concurrence agency or development manager for applications to develop private land in control districts.[124] This will, it is hoped, help solve the problem of fragmented management responsibilities, identified as a major impediment to coastal Management).

Compensation

The basic principle governing compensation is that owners of interests in land will only be eligible for compensation of the existing use that may be made of their land is changed by a prohibition imposed by coastal plan or the declaration of a control district.[125] Further qualifications on this right apply. In particular, an owner who has suffered in this way is only entitled to compensation if he or she makes an "application for the land"[126] within two years of the change and the application is refused only because of this Act.[127] The application must indicate that a compensation claim may be made if the application is refused.[128]

Claims for compensation must be lodged with the chief executive who must decide the reasonable compensation payable, if any, within 60 days of receiving the claim.

Enforcement

The PEC has a wide discretion to make whatever orders it considers appropriate to remedy or restrain offences against the Act.[129] Restraint orders may be issued by the court on the application of the Minister, the chief executive, "someone whose interests are affected by the subject matter of the proceeding or by "someone else with leave Of the court." Persons falling within this last category need have no proprietary, material, financial or special interest in the subject matter of the proceeding.[130] This liberal approach to standing is qualified in two ways. First, before granting third parties leave to bring proceedings, the court be satisfied that a number of conditions are met including that harm has been or is likely to be caused to the coastal zone, that it is in' the public interest that the proceeding and that if would not be an abuse of the process the court.[131] Secondly, the third party may be required to give security for the payment of costs or an undertaking about damages.[132] These conditions may forestall third party enforcement of the Act.[133]

Miscellaneous

Part 3 of the Act permits the chief executive to delegate his or her powers under the Act[134] and gives the Governor in Council power to make regulations relating to coastal management.[135]

In addition to these administrative affairs, Pt 3 of the Act commits the chief executive to publishing a report on the state of the coastal zone at least every four years. This will assess the condition of major coastal resources. "identify trends in coastal values", review significant programs in relation to the coastal zone and evaluate coastal management strategies implemented in pursuance of the Act.[136]

Queensland Coastal Legislation

The Queensland Government has a range of legislation and policies relating to management of the coastal zone. However, the assessment of most coastal development applications has been devolved under legislation to local councils. In these cases, the local council acts as assessment manager and the Queensland Government acts as a concurrence agency providing advice on the applicability of Queensland coastal policies to the proposal. If a coastal development application is likely to have a 'significant impact' on a matter of national environmental significance, it requires approval from the Australian Government under the Environment Protection and Biodiversity Conservation Act 1999. The primary Queensland coastal legislation is the Coastal Protection and Management Act 1995 (the Coastal Act). The Coastal Act establishes the framework for coastal management in Queensland through:

- protection, conservation, rehabilitation and management of the coast including its resources and biological diversity
- ecologically sustainable development of the coastal zone
- coordinated and integrated management and . administration for developing the coastal zone
- a land surrender provision that applies to new . subdivisions. The Queensland Government may require that the area of land in the erosion-prone area be surrendered for coastal management

A review of the previous State Coastal Management Plan recognised the need to increase its provision for climate change. The new Queensland Coastal Plan 24 includes an updated sea level rise figure and planning period of 0.8 metres by 2100, based on the upper limit of the most recent projections released by the Intergovernmental Panel on Climate Change in its Fourth Assessment Report18. This figure is used for determining coastal hazard areas which guide land-use planning and development decisions to reduce the risk to persons and property. Under the new Queensland Coastal Plan coastal hazard risk assessments are to be based on:

- a planning period of 100 years for coastal development
- a sea level rise factor of 0.8 meters by 2100 due to climate change
- the 100 year average return interval for extreme storm event or water level
- a 10 per cent increase in cyclone intensity (relative to maximum potentialintensity) due to climate change.

The new Queensland Coastal Plan also contains coastal hazard maps that show areas at risk from storm tide inundation. The default storm tide inundation area is based on a 0.8 meter sea level rise by 2100 due to climate change and represents an increase of 0.5 meters from the default level of 0.3 meters used in the State Coastal Management Plan (excluding areas with existing development commitments). The hazard maps also indicate erosion-prone areas based on this 0.8 metre figure. Large-scale regional maps, as well as property scale maps, are available for Coastal Plan Mapping and Coastal Hazard Area Mapping on the DERM website. The new Queensland Coastal Plan requires that development in areas vulnerable to storm tide inundation be located, designed and operated to mitigate against the potential impacts of a storm tide (e.g. by raising floor heights of habitable rooms). In future, land-use planning decisions will be required to consider the likely impacts of storm tide inundation and place new zones for urban purposes outside areas vulnerable to storm tide inundation.

Notes

1. Stevens, N.C. (1985) Geology and Landscape of Queensland, Brisbane.
2. David. Sir T.E. Browne, W.R. (1960). The Geology of the Commonwealth of Australia, Arnold, London.
3. Op.cit. n. 1, pp. 23.
4. Op.cit. n.2, pp. 15.
5. North cote, K.H. (1975) A Description of Australian Soils, C.S.I.R.O.
6. *Ibid*, 5.
7. Stevens, N.C., (1990) Geology and Landscape of Queensland, Brisbane.
8. Auliciems, A. and Kalma, J.D. (1979), A Climatic classification of Queensland, Human Thermal Stress in Australia. J. Appl. Meteor 18, 616-126.
9. Australian Bureau of Meteorology (1985), the climate of Brisbane Queensland. Capital City Series, Government Publishing Service Canberra.
10. Demographic History of Queensland (3104.3). ABS Publication, Brisbane, Queensland.
11. Queensland Population (3234.3), ABS Publication Brisbane, Queensland.
12. Bird, E.C. (1978). The Nature and Source of Beach Materials of the Australian Coast. In /Davies, J.C. and Williams, M.A.J. (eds.) Land from Erowtion in Australian A.N.U. Press, Canberra, 144-157.
13. Davis J.I. (1977). The coast in Jeans, D.M. (ed.), Australia, a Geography University of Sydney Press, Sydney, 134-151.
14. Hopley, O. and Harvey. N. (1979): Regional variations in storm surge characterizing around the Australian coast: a preliminary investigation,

natural hazards in Australia, Australian Academy of Science, Canberra, 164-185.

15. Easton, A.K. (1970). The tides of the continent of Australia. Australia Horace Lamb Centre Research Paper 37, Flinders University, 326 pp.
16. MoM, B.G. (1978). Future trends in Coastal Geomorphology. *Australian Geographer* 14, 64-65.
17. Immam and Nodsterm C.E. (1971). On the tectonic and morphologic classification of costs. *Journal of Geology* 79, 1-21.
18. McGill, J.T. (1958). Map of Coastal forms of the World. *Geographical Review* 48, 402-405.
19. Davies, J.L. (1972) Geographical Variation in Coastal Development. Oliver and Boyd, Edinburgh, 204 pp.
20. Davies, J.L (1974). The Coastal Sediment Compartment. *Australian Geographical Studies* 12, 139-151.
21. Davies, J.L. (1977). The Coast. In Jeans, D.M. (ed.), Australia, a Geography, University of Sydney Press, Sydney, 134-151.
22. Bird, E.C.P. (1978). The Nature and Source of Beach Materials on the Australian Coast. In Davies, J.L. and Williams, M.A.J. (eds.) landforms evolution in Australia, A.N.V. Press, Camberra, 144-157.
23. Coventey, R.C. (1980). The Qvanternary of North-Eastern Australia. In Henderson R.A. and Stephenson P.J. (ed.), the Geology and geophysics of North-East Australia, 375-417.
24. Cook, P.J. and Mayo, W. (1977). Sedimentology and Holocene history of a tropical estory (Based Sound, Queensland), Buyr. Min. Res. Geol. Geophysics Bell 170-206 pp.
25. Roads, E.G. (1982). Depositional model for a Chenier Plain, Gulf of Carpenteria, Australia, *Sedimentology*, 29, 201-221.
26. Hopley, D. (1974) coastal Changes produced by topical cyclone Althea in Queensland, December 1971. Australian Geographer 12, 445-456.
27. Rhodes, E.G. (1981). Depositional model for a Chenier Plain, Gulf of Carpentaria, Australia. Sedimentology, 29, 201-221.
28. This is predominantly a steep coast with tropical rainforest extending.
29. Coventry, R.C. *et al.* (1980), the Quaternary of North-Eastern Australia. In Henderson R.A. and Stephenson P.J. (eds). The Geology and Geophysics of North East Australia, 375-417.
30. Pye K. (1982). Morphological development of coastal dunes in a humid tropical environment, cape Bedford and Cape Flattery, north Queensland. *Geogr Annals* 64A. 213-227.

31. Bird E.C.F. and Hopley. (1969) Geomorphologic features on a humid cropical sector of Australian coast. *Australian Geomorphologic Study*, 7, 89-108.

32. Bird E.C.F. (1970), The step Coast of the macalister Range, North Queensland, Australia, *J Trop Geog.*, 31, 33-39.

33. Hopley, D. (1971). The origin and significant of north Queensland Island spits. *Australian geographer* study, 12. 90-106.

34. *Idbi.*, 3.

35. Op.cit. n. 1, 1999.

36. Hails, J. R. (1964). The coastal depositional features of southeastern Queensland, *Australia*: Geo, p, 207-217.

37. Orme G.R. and Day R.W. (eds) 1978, Handbook of recent geological studies of Moreton Bay, Brisbane River and Stradbroke Island, University of Queensland, 8 (2), 104 pp.

38. Hopley D. (1982). Geomorphology of the Great Barrier Reef: Quaternary Development of Coastal Reefs, Wiley – Interscience, NY.

39. Idbi, n. 1, pp. 79

40. Idbi, n. 1, pp. 79

41. Ford L. (1977), Alternative means of combating beach erosion. *Beach Conservation*, 29, 2-4.

42. Cook D. (1981). Barron River Investigation. *Beach Conservation,* 44, 1-3.

43. Bird E.C.F. (1969). The deltic castline near Carins, Queensland,m *Auster Egeogs,* 11, 138-147.

44. Resource Assessment Commissioner, Coastal Zone Inquire Final Report 1993, p. 819.

45. Altmas A., T.C., D.C. Smith (1993), Existing and Potential Mechanisms, Camberra – Act 2000, pp. 8.

46. *Ibid.*, pp. 8.

47. *Ibid.*, pp. 9.

48. Coastal zone inquiry governmental approaches to coastal zone reserve management information pager 6, Camberra ACT.

49. *Ibid*, p. 5.

50. Perkins, D. (1990) National and Marine Parks within the Great Barrier Reef Region – The legislative framework for development and conservation, engineering in Coral Reef Regions, Townsville.

51. Beach Protection Act 1968 (Old), Act No. 17, 1968. This Act was reprinted in 1988 as the Beach Protection Act 1968-1986.

52. *Ibid*, title, Section 5, 34.
53. Beach Protection Act and Another Act Amendment Act 1984, Act No. 65, 1989.
54. Section 36(1)(9). In 1989 there were 25 Coastal Management Control Districts.
55. Section 37(1).
56. Section 44.
57. Section 44(IB).
58. The level of compensation is determined by the BPA with a right of appeal to the Planning and Environment Court: 546.
59. Section 41 A.
60. Section 43.
62. Section 47 (2)
63. Coastal Zone Inquiry, Resource Assessment Commission Coastal Zone Inquiry Draft Report, 1992, Canberra.
64. Coastal zone Inquiry, Resource Assessment Commission Coastal Zone Inquiry Draft Report, 1992. Canberra.
65. Resource Assessment Commission, Coastal Zone Inquiry (1993) Coastal Zone Inquiry Final Reports, Canberra, Commonwealth of Australia..
66. Op. Cit. n.1.
67. Op. Cit. N.1.
68. Op. Cit. N.1.
69. RAC, Coastal Zone Inquiry, 1993.
70. House of Representatives Standing Committee on Environment and Conservation (HORSCEC), (1980). Management of the Australian Coastal Zone. Canberra, Australia: HORSCEC.
71. House of Representatives Standing Committee on Environment, Recreation and the Arts (HORSCERA) (1991). The Inquired Coastline. HORSCERA.
72. Op. Cit., n.2.
73. Op. Cit. N. 3.
74. Ibdi, 1.
75. Queensland Department of Environment and Heritage (QDEH), Coastal Protection Strategy – Proposals for Managing Queensland's Coast (Green Paper BP 541-1) Queensland Government, Brisbane, (1991).
76. Idbi.

77. *Ibid*, p. 10
78. *Ibid*, p. 2
79. *Ibid*, p. 25.
80 *Ibid*, p.21.
81. Coastal Protection Bill 1993 (Old).
82. *Ibid*
83. The Bill that was eventually submitted to the Legislative Assembly was the forty ninth redraft of the original Bill, Legislative Assembly, Minister's Second Reading Speech, Brisbane, 31.10.95. Queensland Parliamentary Debates, p.768.
84. CPMA, s.3.
85. *Ibid*, s.6.
86. In the Beach Protection Act 1968-1986, "coast" is defined as "All and, including the bed and banks of any rivers, stream, watercourse, lake or other body of water – (A) that is situated above mean high water markers at spring tides of any tidal water and within 400 meters, measured by the shortest distance of that mark; (b) that is situated below mean high water makers at spring tides of any tidal water ..." op. cit n 19. S. 3
87. CPMA, s. 11.
88. Section 14.
89. Section 17, 18.
90. Explanatory Notes, Coastal Protection and Management Bill (1995), p. 16.
91. CPMA, s16(1)
92. Section 16(3).
93. Section 19.
94. Section 20.
95 Section 21.
96. Queensland Parliamentary Debates, op. Cit. N. 41, p. 743.
97. *Ibid.*, p.755.
98. *Ibid.*, p.743.
99. *Ibid.*, p.757.
100. *Ibid.*, p.755.
101. CPMA, s 26(2).
102. Section 31(2) (a), (d)
103. Section 31(2) (b), (c).

104.Sections 29, 36, 37 – 44 provide for the review and amendment of coastal plans.

105.Sections 29, 42.

106.Section 27.

107.Section 16(I) (g), 28 (I).

108.As announced by the Minister for Environment and Heritage in his Second Reading Speech, op. Cit. N. 41, p.530.

109.CPMA, s. 3(c).

110.Queensland Parliamentary Debates, op.cit. n. 41, p. 529.

111.Local Government (Planning and Environment) Act 1990, ss. 2.7, 2.19, 4.7, 4.13, 5.1, 5.9, 5.11

112.Explanatory Notes, op.cit. n. 48, p. 4.

113.Section 52(2).

114.Section 53(1).

115.Section 53(3).

116.Section 54(1).

117.Section 61(6). Power is also granted to take or deposit materials on the land and to build temporary structures on the land.

118.Section 95.

119.Section 100.

120.The Minister may make an exception if the structure is not contrary to the coastal plan and the building is not likely to have a detrimental impact on coastal management: s 59(3).

121.The Act provides for each coastal management control district and erosion prone area declared under the Beach Protection Ac to be treated as a control district and for setback requirements to be treated as coastal buildings line; s. 104.

122.Queensland Parliamentary Debates, op cit., n.41, p.741.

123.Op cit n. 8, cl. 3.2, 13.

124.Queensland Parliamentary Debates, op. Cit. N 41, p. 531. Until the PEDA becomes law the separate approval procedures contained in the Beach Protection Act 1968-1986, remain in force.

125.CPMA, s 86(1).

126."Application for the land" means an application to build a structure that was as of right under a pre-existing planning scheme or an application for subdivision of land that is consistent with the planning schemes; 86(4)

127.Section 82(2) (b), (c), (e)

128.Section 86(2)(d).

129.CPMA, ss 84(5)-(12), 85. Such orders may, inter alia, restrain the use of plant or equipment or a place, require the demolition or removal of a structure or the rehabilitation of the coastal zone: s84(9). The court may exercise its powers whether or not there is danger of substantial damage to the coastal zone if the person engages or continues to engage in the activity: ss 84(7), 85(3).

130.Section 84(1)

131.Section 84(2)

132.Section 84(4)

133.As occurred in Central Queensland Speleological Society incn. Central Queensland Cement Ply. Ltd (1989) 2 Qd R 512. See further, B. Gates, Environmental Law in Australia (4th ed. Butterworths, Sydney, 1995), pp. 461-516.

134.CPMA's 101.

135.Section 103.

136.Section 102.

CHAPTER 5

IMPLICATION OF INTEGRATED COASTAL ZONE MANAGEMENT ENFORCEMENT: INDIA AND AUSTRALIA

PROCESS OF ENFORCEMENT

Once the Integrated Coastal Master Plan has been agreed to and approved by the government, and the individual projects have been evaluated for their environmental consequences, implementation begins. Implementation is carried out with the help of policy instruments. The instruments that can be employed for the implementation of ICAM comprise the whole range of those that are used for environmental, natural resource, agriculture, tourism, transport nad energy management, as well as for land use and urban affairs. Two broad classes of voluntary agreements between various parties (e.g. industry, tourist enterprises, environmental groups and public authorities) to achieve environmental or conservation objectives.[1]

Regulatory Instruments

Regulatory instruments are most widely used in environmental management and in other fields of governmental activities where ht market mechanism is absent or ineffective. They reflect the "command and control"[2] philosophy of management and until recently were practically the sole instruments of environmental management. The range of issues covered by regulatory instruments includes land use planning, building regulations, construction guidelines for the coastline, conservation regulations, standards for anti-fouling paints for boats, fishing quotas, marine transport regulations, aquaculture requirements and licensing of various other activities.

Land use planning, zoning and building regulations, when properly implemented, define the shape and nature of coastal development. Pollution regulations help to maintain environmental quality; other regulations define activities in a way to preventing pollution or aesthetic damage and to manage and conserve resources.

Economic Instruments

Economic instruments are used in conjunction with regulations to supplement them in areas where economic efficiency is important, where regulations failed and/or where funds need to be raised to implement public policy e.g. for environmental infrastructure. The main classes of economic instruments for coastal management etc.[3]

- Charges can be used to supplement pollution control regulations: e.g. effluent charges; fees for non-compliance with regulations; administrative charges to cover expenses; user charges imposed on all publicly provided services such as water supply, sewerage, harbor use, etc. to make their use efficient and to cover expenses.
- Development taxes are mainly used in conjunction with land use management, and are generally imposed on highly profitable and environmentally sensitive developments such as coastal tourism. They also provide revenue.
- Subsidies can be granted under exceptional circumstances to finance control measures on pollution from public or private activities where such measures are urgently needed e.g. old industries. Unless subsidized, these industries would have to close. Other cases conservation measures need to be subsidized from public funds.
- Resource pricing is an important instrument in resource management of coastal land, coastal wetlands, forests and marine resources. This is now becoming politically more and more acceptable; it leads to better resource management and generates revenue e.g. for purchasing land for conservation.

Bargaining and Negotiation

Bargaining and negotiation with industry can be used in conjunction with either regulatory or economic instruments. This method is becoming ever more frequent in dealing with one particular industry group or with an industrial association on a regional basis.[4]

Specific agreements with industry or other groups, e.g. tourism associations, can be particularly useful instruments in coastal areas where more stringent pollution or conservation standards might be needed which can be imposed nationally but can be negotiated locally.

Zonation

In zonation, the coastal area is divide in to geographical zones for management purposes. On the land size, zones can be determined on the basis of distance inland from the water's edge, with the greatest restrictions placed on use in the zone closet to the water's edge and successively less restriction imposed in zones located farther inland.[5]

Zoning can also be based on elevation above sea level, with the greatest restrictions placed on the lowest zones.

Zoning of Coastal land in Australia

Australia's great barrier reef law defines three types of zones in order to protect the sea, lake, river shores, and shore strips and to utilize the shore for the benefit of society.[6]

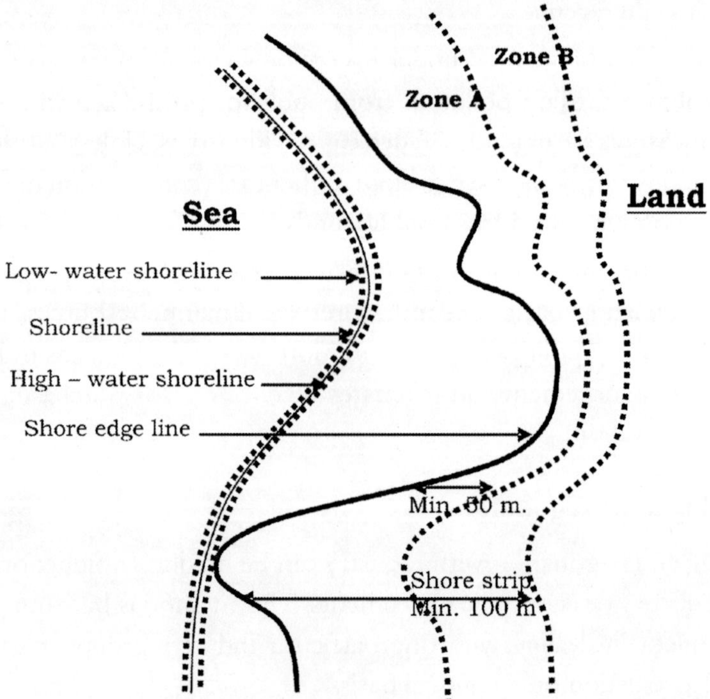

Shore

The shore is defined as the area between the shoreline and the shore edge line. It is illegal to excavate in this zone, and to mine sand, gravel, and the like at scales that might alter the shore.

The following area subject to land use permits:

1. Infrastructural and other facilities such as piers, ports, harbours, bridges, lighthouses, fisheries, installations or breakwaters that affect either shore protection or utilization of the shore for the public interest;
2. Facilities for shipyards, ship-dismantling plants, and acquaculture, which cannot be located inland because of the nature of the activity.

Zone - A

Zone A is defined as the first 50 meters (164 feet) width of the shore strip. Apart from structures that ca be built on coastal shore as described above, no building of any kind is allowed in this zone; it is used only for pedestrian aces for sightseeing and recreational purpose.

Zone - B

Zone B encompasses the remainder of the shore strip; it is at least 50 meters wide. It can contain roads and recreational and tourism facilities open to public use; public waste treatment plants can be built there, subject to land use permits.

Conflict Resolution or Techniques for Consensus Building and Integration

The high social value associated with coastal areas and the rich private returns provide by past development are likely to generate numerous and severe conflicts in the future. Some of the conflicts are of a "vertical" nature, i.e. they occur between the authorities and interests at various levels (international, national, regional and local), while others are "horizontal": conflicts between the users and activities at one nad the same site or at adjacent sites.[7] Especially important are the conflicts between the interest of individual users of coastal resources and the coastal population at large. A reasonable and just solution to such conflicts is one of the most important objectives of any coastal area management.

In practice, the conflicts are resolved every day within the administrative, legal and social framework of a coastal area. However, the resolution of more important conflicts requires special techniques and it is the task of the government and coastal managers to create the framework, assure access and make use of these techniques, which are basically of two types: arbitration and legal procedures.

Within the arbitration system there are procedures for working through administrative and independent arbitrators:[8]

(a) Formation of an ad hoc task force (commissions, scientific bodies) for resolving a particular problem: this can be implemented at all levels and its efficiency depends on factors such as members selected, set of objectives, level of authority, and funds available. In most cases such bodies propose solutions, while decisions are left to other authorities.

(b) Formation of long term or permanent bodies to monitor a particular process, orient it and even resolve the conflicts: inter-ministerial councils, interagency councils, local authorities' councils. Such bodies are often entitled to take decisions and they also carry the public responsibility for those decisions.

(c) Generation of a policy dialogue through discussion among interested parties in potential conflict is often used by moderators or facilitators. The special value of this technique is that it can provide a relatively objective insight into the various interest of the different information and find the basis for compromise solutions.

(d) Nomination by the authorities of qualified intermediaries when a dialogue is impossible or has been interrupted. their role is much more active and responsible than that of facilitators as, in many cases, they propose their own solutions after they have heard all parties and studied all individual interests.

(e) Creation of an arbitration procedure is used for cases where it is a impossible to find a solution through negotiations (environmental mediation). Legal authority or the consent of the interested parties is an essential prerequisite for its application. Decisions of the arbitrators bind all parties and therefore their impartiality and their ability to understand the issues are basic to the arbitration process.

Solution though legal procedure is used in cases when all other techniques have failed and one of the parties requests legal protection or claims rights he believes he is entitled to. The principal shortcoming of the legal procedure is that is usually long and expensive and that sometimes it is not capable of using highly complex technical information in an appropriate manner.

In certain cases involving international issues international arbitration is required which might be pursued wit the help of a mutually accepted arbitrator or through the courts.

IMPLEMENTATION OF THE STATE COASTAL PLAN

The outcomes, principles or policies are not intended to be read in isolation, but as an integrated package in the context of the Coastal Act. Schedule 4 to the plane identifies where there is a legislative responsibility by local and state agencies to consider the contents of the State Coastal Plan. The Coastal management outcomes, principles and policies are to be considered pursuant to legislative responsibilities identified in Schedule 4. The state Coastal Plan has the effect of a State Planning policy under the Integrated Planning act 1997 and there fore a matter of State interest. The Plan will be one of the matters that are coordinated and integrated into new planning schemes during their preparation, had regard to for impact assessment applications if it has not been appropriately reflected in the planning scheme, and considered in Ministerial community infrastructure designations.

Schedule 4 also identifies legislative responsibilities which may be of relevance to coastal management where there is no specific statutory requirement for local and sate agencies to consider the State Coastal Plan. As part of the on-going vision of achieving integrated coastal management, the Environment Protection Agency will work in partnership with these agencies to establish agreements and protocols which outline implementation of the State Plan by these agencies. In addition, there are numerous other actions and activities undertaken by coastal management outcomes and that are outside of legislation and statutory processes. In the interests of integrated coastal management, it is encouraged that such groups and bodies also reflect the outcomes, principles and policies of the State Coastal Plan.

Australian Coastal Management Philosophy

Development of soundly – based coastal management arrangements is a complex task which must provide for resolution of conflicting demands put on the broad communities of Queensland .The Queensland Government's preference is for coastal management which is focused on ecologically sustainable development and which recognizes community needs and values . The benefits of coastal management plans would be substantial in environmental and economic terms. Such benefits would come through careful husbandry of resources, provision of clear direction to coastal developers, users and administrators, and improved quality of life for users.

The philosophy behind the proposed Queensland Conservation Strategy is based on the concept of 'ecologically sustainable development'. To achieve this end, policies and decisions relating to management of the coast should be guided by four principles:

- Intergenerational equity
- To be consistent with this principle, the current generation's decisions should not leave an impoverished coast for the next

- Natural resources valued appropriately. The use of many environmental assets such as clean water, productive mangrove forests and the aesthetic qualities of coral reefs and beaches is assumed to be free. Others such as fish stocks, minerals and extractive materials may be undervalued. Under pricing of resources contributes significantly to inefficient resource use and environmental degradation. To ensure that balanced decisions can be made on the use of coastal natural resources, the pricing of these resources should reflect their real value to society. Account should also be taken of the extent of and natural resource values of all areas currently afforded 'protected' status in Queensland's coastal zone.
- Dealing cautiously with uncertainly
- The complexity of natural ecosystems means the environmental impact of our actions is seldom predictable. In some instances, adverse effects may take years to appear and the link between cause and effect may be unclear. By dealing cautiously with uncertainty, the risk to the

environment and the potential for adverse effects on present and future generations can be minimized.

- Taking a global perspective
- The principle of taking a global perspective recognizes that human actions in one region may affect human welfare adversely in another. The global perspective also acknowledges that because many of the world's resources are finite, degradation or loss of such resources affects all people.

Figure 1: State Coastal Management Plan Consultation Components

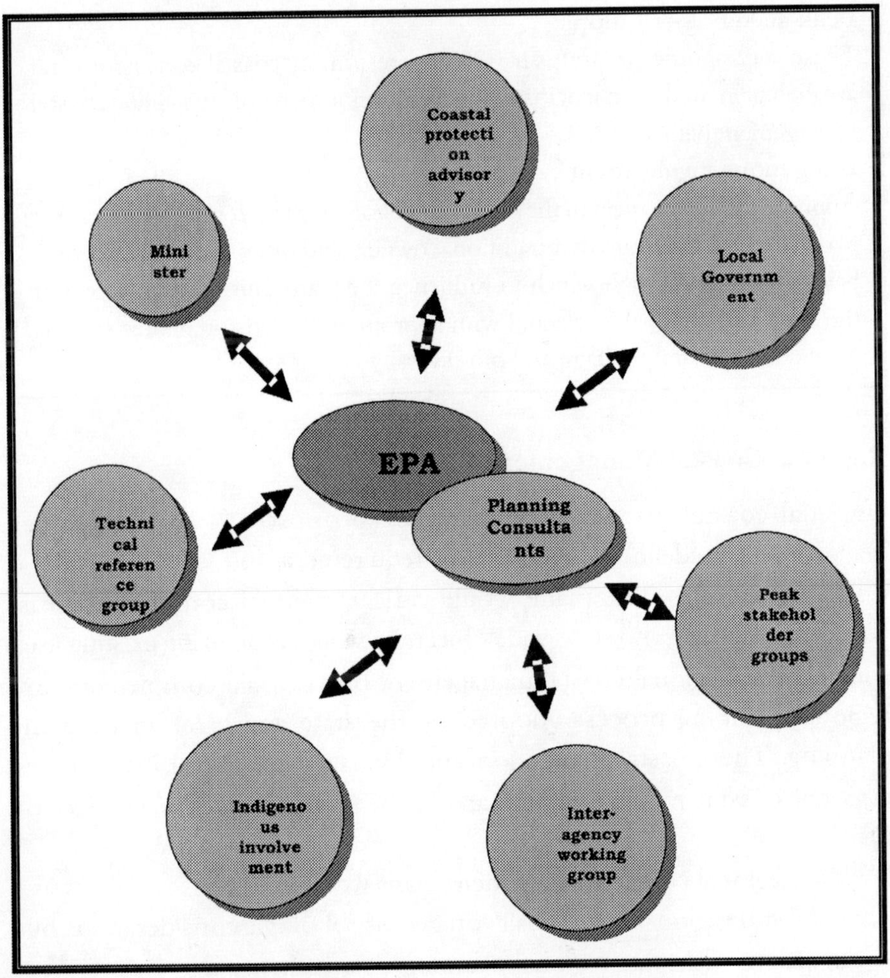

Coastal Protection Advisory Council (CPAC)

CPAC, in accordance with the Coastal Protection and Management Act 1995, provides advice to the Minister regarding coastal management.

Technical reference group

This group comprises representatives with a high level of expertise in the various sectors relevant to coastal zone management. It will review and evaluate material proposed for inclusion in the plan.

Inter agency working group

This group comprises representatives from State government departments and agencies which have jurisdiction over aspects of coastal management in Queensland. This group will operate as a review and negotiation forum for issues related to essential technical consideration.

Peak stakeholder groups

These very significant groups have an interest in key coastal zone issues and are being invited to participate in the development of the State coastal management plan.

Indigenous involvement

Appropriate involvement in the development of the State coastal management plan is critical to ensure that traditional owners and other indigenous people have a channel through which to influence the plan. This needs to occur at the State and regional levels and with appropriate groups on mattes such as native title, cultural heritage and bio-diversity.

Regional Coastal Management Plans

Regional coastal management plans are proposed to bring together management guidelines, conservation requirement and legislation into a workable package. The plane would reflect regional community ideas, government policy, and state-wide objectives while recognizing existing uses and tenures. Regional coastal management plans would complement any regional planning process adopted by the state and local government planning. The Coastal Protection and Management Act 1995 requires regional coastal management plans to be produced for each part of Queensland's coast.[9]

The regional coastal management plans would:

- Establish regions based ideally on geomorphologic considerations but in accord with state regional planning arrangements;

- Be prepared using adequate data coupled with local knowledge and input;
- Establish formally community consultation processes;
- Establish detailed policy and management guidelines including coastal buffer zone widths allow delegation of control over many aspects to local government;
- Use existing land use planning processes supplemented by special purpose strategic plans for complex areas with competing uses;
- Use the proposed Coastal Protection Act and revised Marine Parks Act to provide zonings over water areas and other specific controls;
- Be subject to regular review; and
- Incorporate the state-wide Coastal Protection Plan.

The Queensland coastline has been divided into eleven regions with a regional coastal management plan to be prepared for each region:

- Gulf of Carpentaria
- Cape York Peninsula Coast
- Torres Strait
- Wet Tropical Coast
- Cardwell-Hinchinbrook Coast
- Dry Tropical Coast
- Whitsunday Coast
- Capricorn Coast
- Curtis Coast
- Wide Bay Coast
- South-east Queensland Coast

Draft regional coastal management plans were released for public comment for at least 40 days before final regional coastal management plans produced. Till now, the Cardwell-Hinchinbrook Regional Coastal Management Plan is well advanced. Substantial work has also occurred on coastal management plans for the following regions:

- Wet Tropical coast;
- Curtis Coast;

- Wide Bay Coast; and
- South-east Queensland Coast.

Cardwell-Hinchinbrook Regional Coastal Management Plan

The Cardwell-Hinchinbrook regional coastal management plan is currently being prepared for a 15400sq km planning area. This distinctive section of Queensland's coast contains terrestrial and marine environments, including the Wet Tropics of Queensland World Heritage Area and the great Barrier Reef World heritage Area. The area also includes;[10]

- Coastal settlements such as Cardwell, South Mission beach and Lucinda;
- Significant primary industry activity, mainly sugar cane, concentrated on the coastal plain; and
- Cultural resources connected with human occupation of the area for thousands of years.

The outstanding natural and cultural features of the planning area are a draw card for tourists and recreational enterprises, contributing significantly to the economy of the coastal region. The development of the regional coastal plan to date has involved an intensive series of meetings of the regional consultative Group, a representative advisory group formally appointed by the Minister. This group has been supported by:

- Terrestrial and marine issues working groups;
- A whole of government working group;
- An Aboriginal issues working group; and
- A scientific reference group.

In addition, a draft control district has been proposed and key coastal sites have been chosen. Large scale maps featuring this information will be available at the Environment Protection Agency offices at Cardwell, Ingham, Townsville and Brisbane. The objectives of the Coastal Act for Cardwell-Hinchinbrook coastal zone strategies broadly relate to:

- ❖ coastal resources;
- ❖ uses and activities;
- ❖ management and administration; and
- ❖ Information and consultation.

Responsibilities under the State Plan

The coastal Act binds all persons, including the state and, as far the legislative power of the parliament permits, the Commonwealth and other States. As the State plan will have statutory effect under the Coastal Act, all persons with responsibilities in the coastal zone will need to have regard to the provisions of the State plan.

State Government (including government owned corporations)

All state Government agencies and corporations will have a responsibility to take into account the goals, principles and policies of the State pan when making planning and management decisions relating to development or resource allocation in the coastal zone. These include but will not be limited to:

- Environment Protection Agency(EPA) in carrying out its statutory and decision-making functions under various legislation including , for example:
  - ❖ acting as a referral agency or assessment manager roles under the Integrated Development Assessment System under the IPA;
  - ❖ acting as an administering authority under the Environment Protection Act 1994;
  - ❖ Authority under the Canal Act 1958, Beach Protection Act 1968 and Harbour Act 1955;
  - ❖ carrying out responsibilities under the Cultural Record (Landscapes Queensland and Queensland Estate) Act 1987;
  - ❖ preparing regional coastal plans under the Coastal Protection and Management Act 1955; and
  - ❖ assessing loan subsidies for local government annual capital works programs and applications for funding assistance under natural disaster relief arrangements.
- Queensland Parks and Wildlife Service (QPWS) in carrying out its statutory and other decision-making functions under various legislation, including but not limited to the Marine Parks Act 1982 and the Nature Conservation Act 1992 , for example:
  - ❖ the taking of plants or animals (e.g. dugong, turtles etc.);

- removal of material from a marine park;
- discharging of wastes into a marine park;
- preparation of management plans for protected areas;
- permits for tourist and other commercial activities;
- motorized water sports; and
- taking of marine products.

- Department of Natural Resources (DNR) in carrying out its statutory and other decision-making functions under the Land Act 1994 relating to , for example:
  - managing State coastal land on the coast;
  - issuing of leases and permits to occupy;
  - vegetation management,
  - converting and renewing tenure and granting easements (sections 122, 167, 177-180, 262 and 362); and decisions under the Forestry Act 1959 relating to:
  - regulation of forest operations such as timber harvesting;
  - permits to extract water;
  - removal of vegetation or fill from watercourse; and
  - removal of quarry material from a water course (sections 38, 57,58, and 70-71); and planning activities relating to water allocating planning.
- Department of Primary Industries (DPI) in carrying out statutory and other decision-making functions under the Fisheries Act1994 relating to , for example:
  - permit to remove marine plants;
  - approvals aquaculture licenses; and
  - approval for certain activities in a fish habitat area.
- Queensland Fisheries management Authority (QFMA) in carrying out its statutory and other decision-making functions under the Fisheries Act1994 relating to for example :
  - exercising responsibilities for regulations in relation to taking of fish;

- ❖ preparation of fisheries management plans.
- Department of Communication and Information, Local Government and planning (DCILGP) in carrying out its statutory and other decision-making functions relating to , for example:
  - ❖ reviewing planning schemes under the IPA; and
  - ❖ coordinating the preparation of regional planning strategies (e.g. wide Bay 2020);
  - ❖ Department of Transport in carrying out its statutory and other decision-making functions under the Transport Infrastructure Act 1994 relating to, for example :
  - ❖ waterways transport management planning;
  - ❖ provision of public marine infrastructure;
  - ❖ marine safety;
  - ❖ pollution responses in coastal water;
- State Government in designating land for community infrastructure under the IPA.

Local Governments

Local governments within the coastal zone will have a responsibility to take into account the State plan when carrying out their statutory and decision-making functions relating to , for example:

- Preparing planning schemes for their local government authority under the IPA , as it is intended that the state plan will be an issue of State interst under that Act;
- Assessing development applications under the Integrated Government Act 1993;
- Designating land for community infrastructure under the IPA.

Commonwealth Government

The Commonwealth Government will be encouraged to have regard to the state plan when making planning and management decisions. This will be achieved through involvement in Commonwealth management and planning processes in the coastal zone memorandums of understanding and other management arrangements.

Community

All other stakeholders involved in the management of the coastal zone will be also having a responsibility to have regard to the state plan. These include but are not limited to:

- Non-government organizations, community groups and individuals seeking funding for environment and land management initiatives(e.g. Coast care, Land care, Natural Heritage Trust);
- Industry groups preparing strategic industry programs and codes of practice; and
- Integrated catchment management groups, in the preparation of their plans and strategies.

Figure 2: Source of the Nine Coastal Issues of State Significance

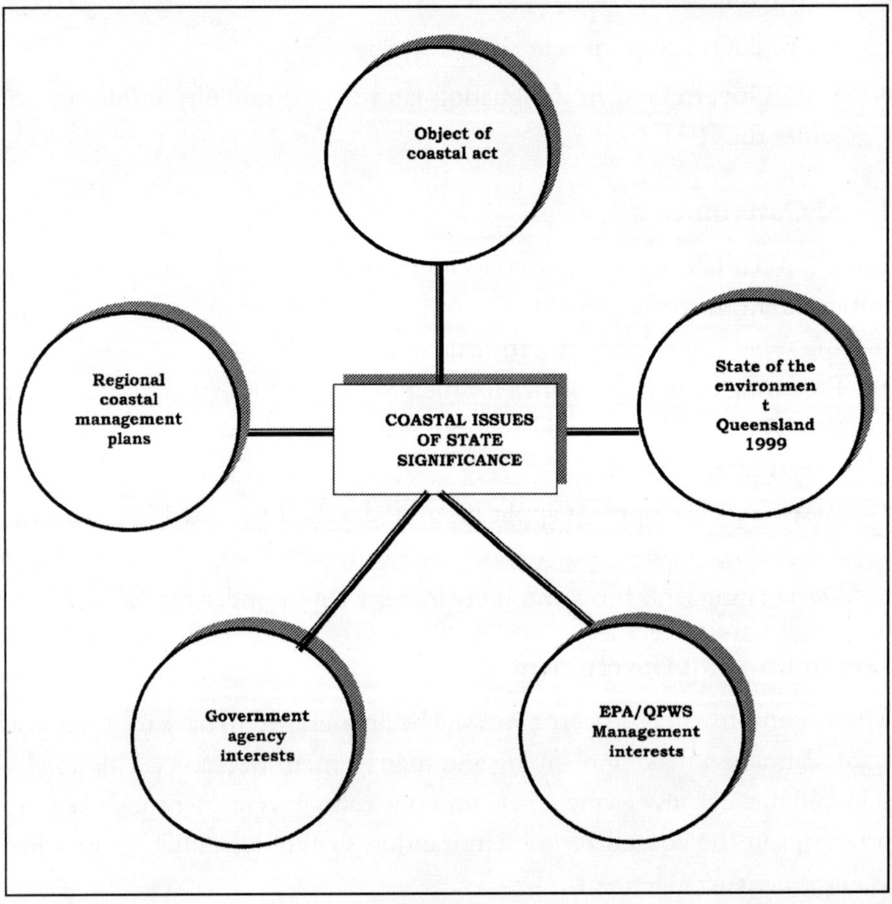

Figure 3: Relationship Between State Plan and other Planning, Management and Assessment Functions

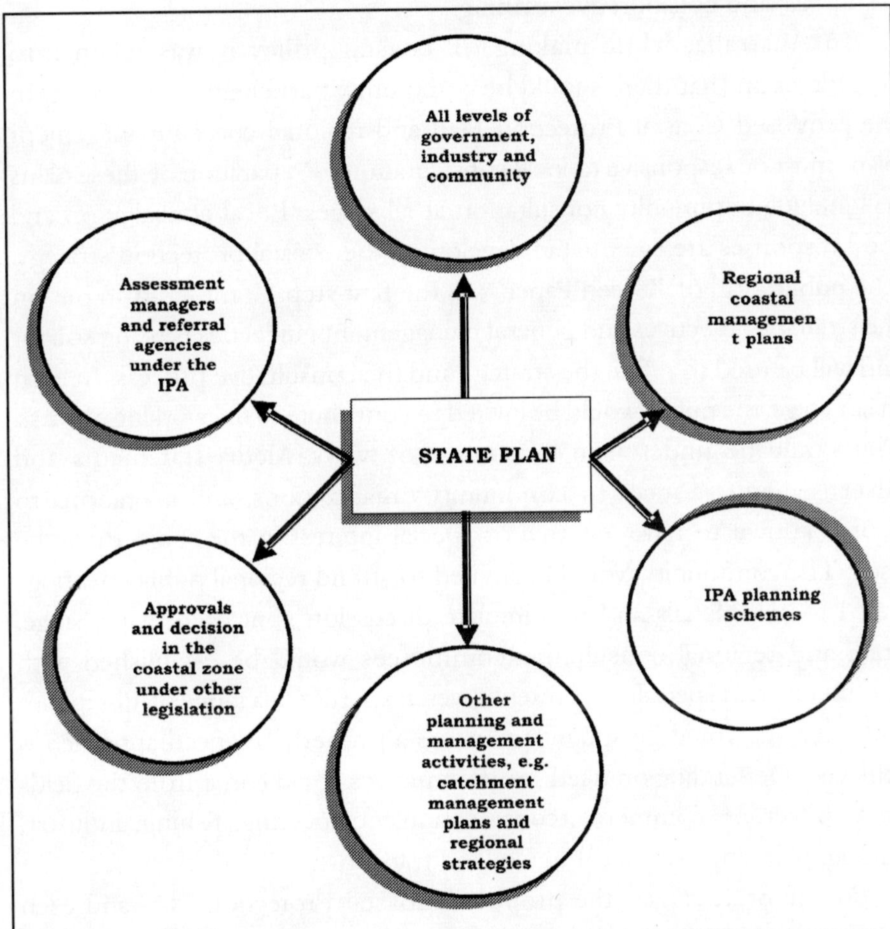

Community Involvement in Coastal Policy in Australia

The "community" is really many communities and includes indigenous peoples commercial and recreational fishers , residential developers, government agencies(including port authorities and nature conservation departments) , tourism, industries locating on the coast, nature-lovers, and the general coast-using and dwelling public.

Community involvement not only improves the quality and relevance of policy stewardship, it also helps build skills or "capacity" with in the community so they can do it more and better each time. Community can be involved and capacity built through a range of processes including: collaboration in policy making; valuing local knowledge; building relational resources; and collaborative learning.

In Australia, while making of coastal policy it was taken into consideration that there should be community participation at all level. In the proposed Coastal Protection Plan and regional coastal management plans must be responsive to local considerations. Preparation of these plans will include community consultation at all stages. Local consultation and local responses are essential in developing the coastal protection strategy. The publication of 'Green Paper' was the first step. Community in put on the strategy, objectives and general management guidelines is being sought and will be used to refine the strategy and the consultative process. At each major stage, the public would be invited to contribute to the working process. This could be undertaken in a range of ways. Media statements and advertisements, notices to community organizations, and invitations to people known to have a gernal or special interest in the subject may be used. The community would be invited to attend regional public meetings called to give details and to stimulate discussion abut each major stage. State and regional consultative committees would be established with community and specialist representatives. Expertise in a range of disciplines and interests would be sought to ensure a properly balanced approach is achieved .Depending on need , representatives could come from the fields of architecture, commerce, conservation, engineering, fishing, industry, mining, planning , science, tourism and transport.

At the draft stages, the proposed Coastal Protection Plan and each proposed regional coastal management plan had gone on public display and public comment sought.

According to the "Green Paper: A discussion paper":[11]

> "….. Proposed legislative changes would be expected to provide a coordinated legislative framework for coastal management, including establishment of advisory committees to manage and focus local inputs. Local authorities could be expected to be heavily involved in the planning and decision making, especially about local matters and community sensitivities…."

Thus, in Queensland, the State government has stressed upon in the community involvement in coastal management at every stage so that the

Figure 4: State Coastal Management Plan Consultation Process

Proposed timelines for plan development and consultation

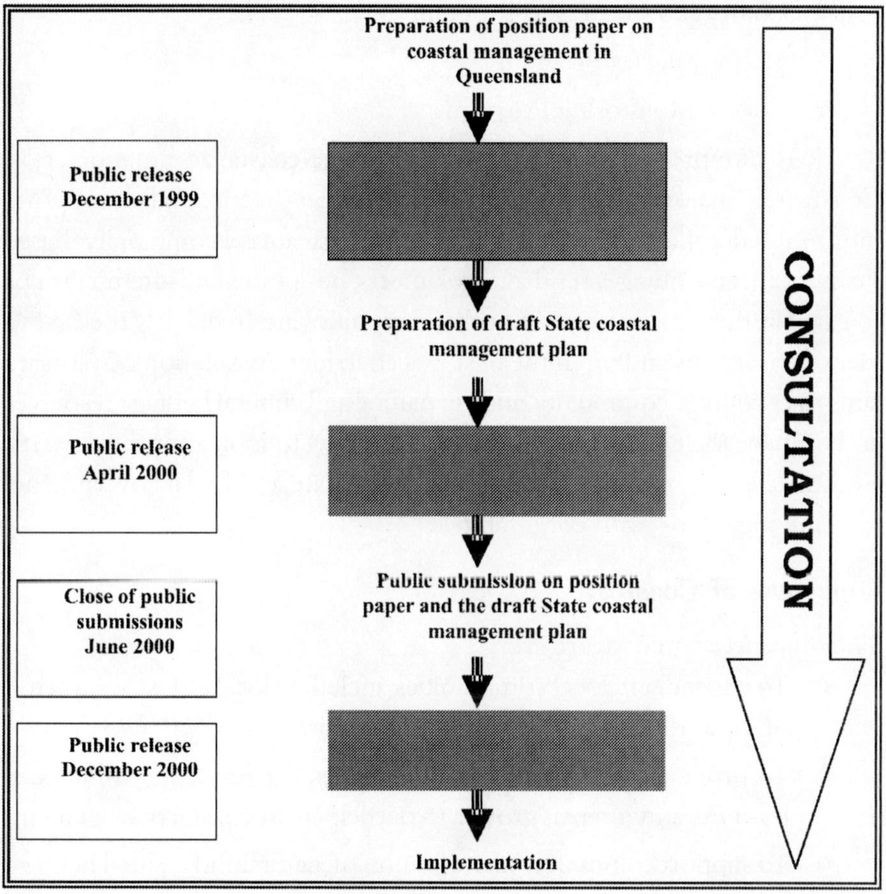

policies should be 'pro- development' and people should participate in development process.

Grants to help Coastal Management

Under the umbrella of the Commonwealth's Natural Heritage Trust, it is delivered cooperatively by all three spheres of government—Commonwealth, and State Territory and Local Government. The Commonwealth, and state and Territory Governments provide matching funding for Coastcare community grant while Local Government provides financial and in kind support for coastcare projects. Coastcare and Coasts & Clean Seas and Environmental Protection Agency in Queensland manage both programs with the Queensland Government contributing to grant funds for the following programs :

- Coasts and Clean Seas Program
- Marine Species Program
- Coastal Monitoring Program

Coastcare provides funding to help manage coastal and marine areas. Coastcare's major focus is on-ground activities but it is also supports motoring, education and planning activities. Coastcare is a community- based program that encourages residents, volunteers, businesses and interest groups to care for their coastal areas. Local communities are frequently the first to identify problems and often the best-placed to identify solutions. Coastcare aims to encourage community pride in natural and cultural heritage resources and to make the community more aware of how to look after these assets. Coastcare is an excellent example of federal, State and Local governments working together – with communities.

Objectives of Coastcare

The objectives of coastcare are:

- To engender in local communities, including local industries, a sense of stewardship for coastal and marine areas;
- To provide opportunities and resources for residents, volunteers, business and interest groups to participate in coastal management;
- To support community identification of natural and cultural heritage resources;
- To facilitate interaction between the community and bodies with responsibility for managing coastal areas.

The Coastcare Network

Coastcare provides support to the community, industry groups and government agencies through the Coastcare Network. The coastcare Network is made up of the National Office in Environment Australia, Canberra, State and Territory Coordinators and 30 Regional Facilitators around the country. In some states, Coastcare is referred to under a different name, for example:

- ❖ In western Australia the program is called – Coast west/ Coastcare;
- ❖ In Victoria the program is called – Coast action/ Coastcare; and
- ❖ In some areas of New South Wales and Queensland, Dunecare is funded by Coastcare.

Coastcare Projects 2000 -2001

Federal Environment Minister Robert hill and Queensland Environment Minister Dean Wells announced funding of $523,231 for 38 Coastcare projects in Marsh 2001. Coastcare will be involved in activities such as:

- ❖ Monitoring flat back and green turtle nesting sites in the Townsville region;
- ❖ Stabilizing the Tannum Sands Northern foreshore;
- ❖ Continuing to monitor seagrass in Harvey Bay;
- ❖ Rehabilitation Cairns Central Swamp;
- ❖ Constructing an interpretative platform and nature trail along Eprapah Creek (Redlands);
- ❖ Undertaking ecological assessment of Point Looking (North Stradbroke Island) marine environment;
- ❖ Rehabilitating headlands and foreshore s in Maroochy shire;
- ❖ Stabilising and rehabilitating Rolling stone Creeks (Townsville region) and
- ❖ Constructing environmental education panels on Noosa Spit.

Coasts & Clean Seas projects 2000-2001

Coasts &Clean Seas projects address a wide range of coastal management issues. Councils have trialed methods of reducing storm water pollution in marine and estuarine areas, Department of primary Industry (DPI) and the aquaculture industry have trailed methods to improve the quality of discharge from acquaculture, and community groups have monitored estuarine and marine water quality. In February and March 2001, Federal Environment Minister Robert Hill announced grants for eight projects, which will receive funding of more than $1.2 million. Brisbane City Council received $250,000 to reduce urban stromwater pollution of Morton Bay. The fund will be used to construct a wetland; gross pollutant traps, a sediment basin and stromwater reuse facility at Bridgewater Creek.

Table 1
A Comparative Analysis of Iczm Approach in Both Countries

	India	*Australia*
Background variables and socio-economic text		
Total population	936 million	
Percentage of population on the coast	25%	75%
Per capita GNP	$320	$18.000
Major ethnic groups and religions	72% Indo-Aryan. 25% Dravidian; 80% Hindu, 14% Mulsim	93% Caucasian 7% Asian and other 75% Christian
Political system characteristics		
Type of Government	Federal Republic	Federal Parliamentary Democracy
Colonial heritage	British	British
Concentration of power among national level institutions	Pluralistic	Some pluralism
Autonomy of sub-national levels of government	Some autonomy	Substantial autonomy
Maritime jurisdictions	12-NM territorial sea (1967) 200 – NM EEZ (1976)	12-NM territorial sea, 200 NM EEZ
Major coastal and ocean issues	Environmental degradation due to coastal urbanization and accelerated industrial development; pollution coastal hazards and disasters; uncontrollable exploitation of mangrove forests and coral reefs	Habitat destruction, resource depletion, use conflicts, government fragmentation, offshore oil development marine protected areas, coastal fisheries.
Primary level of government concerned with ICM	National	Provincial (State); also national and local
Nature and timing of ICM efforts	1974, Water Prevention and Control of Pollution Act (Central and State Water Boards); 1981. Department of Ocean Development: 1982. Ocean Policy; 1991. Coastal Zoning Law. National program on	State: 1994-95, Western Australia State Coastal Review; 1995 Queensland Coastal Management Bill.Ongoing, Victoria coastal and Bay Management Act; 1995

	marine sensing information service; 1996. Beginning of ICM activated at state level.	– 1996, New South Wales Revised Coastal Policy: 1996. Tasmanian Draft State Coastal Policy
Overall approach to ICM	Top down	Bottom up with top down assistance
Type of approach to ICM	Regulatory	Regulatory on ocean uses, studies, consensus building intergovernmental incentives
Extent of implementation of ICM	Partial implementation	Implementation just beginning
Importance of external assistance	Off little importance	Not relevant
Importance of UNCED influence	Off little importance	Somewhat
Effectiveness of ICM	No data	Too early to tell
Movement toward policy integration	Little	Some: Commonwealth inter departmental coastal committee, intergovernmental coastal reference group (federal and state governments), national coastal advisory committee (including community and industry), state nad federal memoranda of understanding (MOUs).

IMPLICATION OF COASTAL ZONE MANAGEMENT IN INDIA.

The policies mentioned in chapter 3 are at the national level and hence are applicable to all the coastal states of India. The Ministry of Environment, Forest and Wildlife, with the following institutions monitors' implementation of these policies: (1) Central Pollution Board (CPCB) and state pollution control board; (2) coast guard, other similar government organization, nongovernmental organizations, and vigilance agencies.

Other ministries and institutions which are linked with the Coastal Zone Management Plan are the Ministry of surface Transport: Ministry of Tourism Development; Department of Ocean Development; Department of Science and Technology; Forest Survey of India; Botanical Survey of India; Zoological Survey of India; and Central Marine of Fisheries Research Institute, Center for Environment Education, and many other research institutions and universities.

Though these policies have been formulated and implemented, the benefits realized are only partial for the following reasons:

1. the population , both in rural and urban areas , has increased in the past few decades;
2. lack of man power and funds;
3. lack of awareness of the importance of coastal zone management among the population, especially those living along the coast ; and
4. Unchecked human activities.

Figure 5: Organizational Setup for Coastal Zone Management Implementation in India

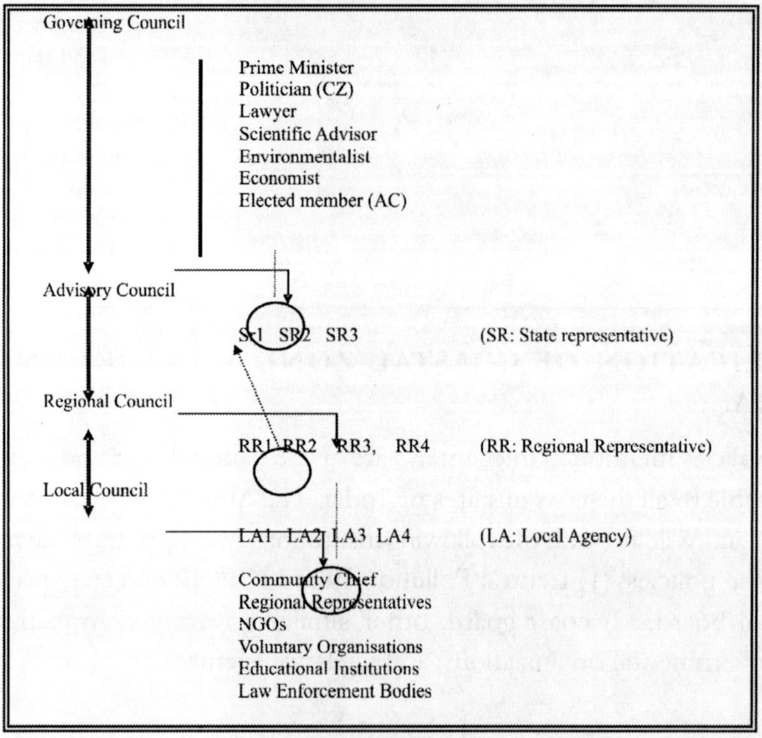

For the past few years the government of India has taken considerable effort to implement these policies through imposing strict standards and monitoring by government agencies (such as the CPCB; Ministry of Environment, Forests and Wildlife; environment; consultants, and so forth) .A recent article (India Today, 1996) highlighted the actions taken by the CPCB regarding the industries not complying with the pollution standards. In respect, CPCB has approached the Ministry of Environment, Forests and Wildlife to increase the power to deal with the erring industries. This is example of ho the system is becoming tuned for upkeep of the living standards and to protect the environment.

Growing concern among the population about the living standards and the status of coastal inland waterways has led to the creation of various nongovernmental and agencies for sensitizing the public on the various issues and creating an awareness through the media. As a part of the exercise, these agencies have educated the public on the importance of a healthy environment and involved them in social activities (WAMP News, 1995). These agencies also have studies the action plans drawn by government, debated on the issues, and come forward with suitable suggestions.

The implementation of CRZ raises interalia the following questions:

- Which is the line to be considered for the purpose of "NOTE" to clause (1), i.e. is it the same HTL spoken of in the main clause(1) or some other line and in particular, the line of normal level of water on banks of rivers, creeks and backwaters?
- Whether the application of clause (1) in relation to the creeks, rivers and back waters is confined to a belt of 500 metres from the HL (Landward side) or it goes even beyond 500 metres (Landward side)?
- The words "which are influenced by tidal action"(in the landward side) qualify the words "backwaters" alone or words preceding "backwaters" like "rivers", "creeks"?
- Since the clause as well as "NOTE" refer to the HTL , is it possible to conceive HL, on each bank of the river so as to carve a "No development zone "(NDZ) (minimum 100 meters) along side the banks of the river.
- Would it be right to say that the purpose of CRZ is to protect the coastal belt of 500 meters and that the area beyond that (landwards)

was not in contemplation of the CRZ and what distance to be left alongside the riverbank was left to the CRZ and what distance to be left alongside the river bank was left to the concerned authorities granting the permission for construction to decide. As a matter 5 of fact, the concerned authorities had marked as "No Development Zone" ranging between 15-20 meters depending upon the site.

First of all, it is of utmost importance for defining to what extent CRZ regulations apply. Clause 1 with the note reads:

"Now, therefore in exercise of the powers conferred by Clause (d) of sub- rule 5 of the Environment Protection) Rules, 1986, and all other power vesting in its behalf, the Central Government hereby declares the coastal stretches of seas, bays estuaries, creeks, rivers and backwaters which are influenced by tidal action (in the landward side) up to 500 meters from the High Tide Line (HTL) and the land between the Low Tide Line (LTL) and the (HTL) as Coastal Regulation Zone and imposes with effect from the date of this Notification, the following restrictions on the setting up and expansion of industries operations or processes etc. in the said Coastal Regulation zone (CRZ) . For purposes of this Notification, the High Tide Line (HTL) will be defined as the line up to which the highest high tide reaches at spring tides."

"Note: The distance from the High Tide Line (HTL) to which the proposed regulations will apply in the case of rivers, creeks and backwaters may be modified on a case by case basis for reasons to be recorded while preparing the Coastal Zone Management Plans (referred to below); how ever, this distance shall not be less than 100 meters or the width of the creek, river or backwater whichever is less."

The words "in the landward side up to 500 meters from the High Tide Line" are decisive. They don't permit any expensive interpretation even in respect of the tidal action. Even the tidal action spoken in the clause 1 must be necessarily confined to the belt of 500 meters cannot go beyond 500 meters landwards side. These are regulations imposing restrictions. By their nature itself, the interpretation has to be restricted and not expansive. A plain reading of the same indicates that the Note does not apply to estuaries and bays but it applies only the rivers, creeks and backwaters.

A simple question therefore, arises whether the note in its applications to the rivers, creeks and backwaters can go beyond the 500 meters stretch (landward side) or is confined with in it. A plain reading shows that in respect of coastal stretch of seas, bays, estuaries, necessarily the zone extends up to 500 mts., but as far as rivers creeks and backwaters it is reduced up to 100mts.

However, one thing is clear that the distance to be counted is from the High Tide Line (HTL). This High Tide Lines (HTL) referred to in the main clause is admitted, parallel to the coast. The last part of the note reads thus:

> "However, this distance shall not be less than 100m or the with of the creek, river or backwater whichever is less."

The words 'this distance' are significant. The starting point is the distance from High Tide Line (HTL). Consequently, the minimum 100m distance within the river, creek & backwater must necessary be parallel to the banks of the river. It for instance, the backwaters are not at all influenced by tidal action there will be no need even to keep 100m distance and same principle applies for creeks and rivers. The logical conclusion is that the restriction will not apply if the rivers, creeks and backwaters are not subject to tidal action and even they are subject to tidal actions the application of the regulation will not go beyond a belt parallel to coastal High Tide Line (HTL) with in rivers, creeks and backwaters. This is due to three reasons:

- Exclusion of estuaries and bays.
- 'Note' cannot go beyond the main clause. This was one of the crucial points in the interpretation of the clause 1 of CRZ regulations.
- In the main clause or the 'Note', nowhere there is reference to the normal level of the waters within the river or maximum level of the waters in the creek of the river for the purposes of counting distance of 100m.

The same answer can be given in a different manner. Let us visualize that 'estuary' or 'bay' has a breadth wider than 500 mts and portion thereof goes landward side beyond 500mts. As per clause (1) it will not apply at all to the portion which is out side 500mts.The attempt now made by the draft notification to change the wording of the clause is with out any legal foundation. The attempt now made by the draft notification to fix 100mts line on the both sides of the river is meaningless. There is no High Tide Line (HTL) at all at the banks of the river. High Tide Line exists only on the coast of the sea within the precise meaning of clause 1. At the mouth of the river there are two forces which operate. One is unidirectional steam current originated from the upper stream course which comes up to lower stream course where the sea and river meet, and the second is where there is a fusion of oscillating tidal currents against the stream currents producing different and variable effects.

Reading the notification, appointing the Goa Coastal Management Authority, would it be possible to arrive at a conclusion that the Goa Coastal Management Authority has the power to clear the Coastal projects?

Can there be a justification to the mark the coastal belt of 500mts in a continuous line regardless the coast is fragile or not?

The perusal of the notification and different powers conferred upon the Goa State Coastal Management authority, will show that it will not be possible to spell there form that Goa State Coastal Management Authority has been conferred powers to clear the coastal projects even though in the fitness of the things such powers ought to have been conferred upon them. If the purpose of the CRZ Notification is to protect fragile coasts, the restriction should no apply to the cases where there is no fragile coast, but there is a cliff more than 10mts above Mean Sea Level (MSL) and plateau above. Then the restriction should apply in such a case is evident from the draft notification dated August 5, 1999, in particular, proposed amendment clause (5) (e) which reads;

> "It is an area with an elevation of more than 10 mts from the Mean Sea Level at any point within 100 mts from inland tidal water body."

The other question which causes problems in implementations of CRZ can be if there any conflict between category (2) (CRZ-2) and category (3) (CRZ-3) of clause (6) because the category (2)(CRZ-2) covers municipal areas, where the municipal areas wrongly stand included in category (3) CRZ- 3 of the same clause 6(1)?

For the purpose of CRZ-2, one of the criteria followed is that developed area stands in the category of (2)-CRZ-2 and in terms of the precise definition of developed are is that 'area within the municipal limits' fall with in CRZ. Such area having been included in category 2 it could not find place in category 3. The wrong inclusion in clause 3 is therefore required to be deleted.

Notes

1. Tortlage, C.A.(1990). Environmental Assessment. A Practical Gude, Gower Publishing Company, Aldershot, UK.
2. *Ibid.*, 1, pp. 25.
3. *Ibid.*, n.1, pp. 27.
4. OECD: (1991., Environment Policy. How to Apply Economic Instruments, Organisation for Economic Cooperation and Development, Paris.
5. *Ibid.*, n.4, pp. 35.
6. Australia RAC (Resource Assessment Commission)(1993). Resource Assessment Commission Coastal Zone Inquiry –Final Report: Canberra: Australia Government Printing Office.
7. Fisher, R. and W. Ury" (1991). Getting to Years. Negotiating Agreement Without Giving In, Houghton Mifflin Co., Boston, MA.
8. *Ibid.*, n.7, pp. 125.
9. Draft State coastal Management Plan (October 2002). Environmental Protection Agency , Queensland Government, Brisbane.
10. *Ibid.*, n.9, pp. 11.
11. Green paper: coastal protection strategy (1991). Proposal for managing Queensland's coast Department of Environment and Heritage, Queensland Govt., Brisbane.

CHAPTER 6

CONCLUSION

"THE KEY TO MINIMIZING CONLFICTS IN THE COASTAL ZONE IS POPULATION MANAGEMENT."[1]

Integrative coastal zone management (ICZM) is a process that recognizes the distinctive character of the coastal area – itself a valuable resource for current and future generations. ICZM is multipurpose oriented; it analyzes implications of development, conflicting use, and interrelationships among physical processes and human activities, and it promotes linkages and harmonization between sectoral coastal and ocean activities. The goals of integrated coastal management are to obtain sustainable development of coastal and marine areas, to reduce vulnerability of coastal areas and their inhabitants to natural hazards such as storms and accelerating sea level rise, nad to maintain essential ecological processes, life support systems, and biological diversity in coastal nad marine areas. It is possible to pinpoint four key features which are central to the ICZM approach. These are:-

1. The use of a set of principles based on the special character of the coasts and oceans to guide ICZM decision making.
2. The need to ultimately work at ICZM from both directions – bottom up (involving the local community level) and top down (involving the national government).
3. The need to have a coordinating mechanism or mechanisms to bring together coastal and ocean sectors, different levels of government, users, and the public in the ICZM process.

4. The need to have good (relevant) science available on a timely basis to inform the ICZM decision making process.

Another point in ICZM approach is to stress on to need to tailor the ICZM approach to fit the unique circumstances of each country that undertakes such a program. Countries differ a great deal; in their resource bases, levels of economic development, systems of government, cultures and traditions, needs and expectations, and approaches to government regulation and resource management. A successful ICZM program will incorporate these distinctions into its structure and, to the maximum extent possible, will build on existing organisations and arrangements adding new institutions or procedures only to the extent necessary to fill gaps or meet new requirements – for example, to coordinate nad harmonize coastal activities.

MAJOR FINDINGS

Although both countries have pursued a the ICZM approach, major findings are :-

1. Problems faced by coastal and marine managers exhibit similar patterns in both study areas. On the whole, environmental degradation, marine pollution, fishery depletion, and loss of marine habitat are problems faced by both areas. India experiences conflicts among uses and among agencies administering coastal and marine programs, as seen in court cases reviews (chapter – 1). In India and Australia have a commonly seen "bundle" of problems involves environmental degradation and pollution due to urbanization, fishery depletion through overfishing and improper fishing methods (such as the use of dynamites) coral reef depletion and degradation, and loss of mangrove forests and wetlands through competing activities such as acquaculture, tourism, and expansion of human settlements.
2. The evolution of each ICZM program differs due to each countries unique combination of geography, development issues, and political system; some of the common patterns include the creation of environmentally oriented institutions (Ministry of Environment and forest, Department of Ocean Development (DOD) in India) and in Australia (Environmental Protection Agency etc.) in 1970s and 80s. partially in response to the United Nations Conference on the

Human Environment; the creation of secotral coastal and ocean programs in the 1980s or earlier to deal with problems such as shoreline erosion, coastal pollution, and the need for marine protected areas; and growing concerns with integrated management in the 1990s.

3. It is difficult to access the extent of implementation of ICZM. Although both countries are in the ICZM implementation phase, it is difficult to determine what exactly face they are. The evaluating data need to make these assessments are notably lacking. It is possible too, that in many cases on the ground changes are not yet taking place.
4. A similar bundle of ICZM tools and approaches is seen both case study areas. The specific ICZM programs in both areas often combine regulatory approaches (e.g., prohibiting development in hazardous areas to control coastal erosion or regulating particular activities in marine protected areas); coastal and marine policy development (development of general goals, guidelines, and standards, typically at the national level, to guide the ICZM management process); planning processes (examining conditions in a particular coastal area or for the nation's entire coast, envisioning future desirable states, and studies to diagnose natural system and socio economic system issues and government capacity for ICZM; consensus – building and participatory approaches to address particular coastal and marine use conflicts and other problems.
5. The importance of external assistance for ICZM for India.
6. A movement towards greater integration (intersectoral, integovernemtal, spatial and interdisciplinary) is evident in recent years in both countries. The past several years have been seen an increase in the number of mechanisms for coordination and consensus building – for example, new national level institutions, state federal coordination mechanism (Australia).

The coastal zone is characterized by dynamic and interactive physical, ecological, social and economic components and activities. In both areas i.e. Goa and Queensland, half of all population growth in past 20 years has occurred in the non-metropolitan coastal zone. Associated with this population growth has been a change in activities, whereby traditional land uses have been replaced capital- and development- intensive uses. Public access to coastal resources has increased in some places and declined in others. There has also been significant move away from concentrated, intermittent use of coastal resources for recreation to permanent, widespread uses of those resources, particularly for residential purposes. The uses and values of the coastal zone resources are determined by their location relative to other areas or resources. This relativity exerts a strong influence on the patterns of human use ad activity, and this in turn, engenders conflict about and competition for alternative uses. In past decade the increase in building development in the non- metropolitan coastal zone has been mostly in the form of new residential dwellings, which have been responsible for a high proportion of capital investment in the zone. Domestic tourism is the significant contributor to the overall tourism industry and to associated developments in the coastal zone; international tourism has grown rapidly than domestic tourism in the past decade is an important component of tourism in particular parts of the zone. Many uses of coastal zone resources have significant direct, indirect and cumulative impacts on the environment. At present there is little scientific understanding of the long term consequences of these impacts. The present study observes the effects on coastal zone resources of these changes have been widely noted, in present study's view the following are the most prominent effects:

- Urbanization;
- Habitat depletion;
- Pollution;
- Competition for and conflict about resources.

Underlying Changes

Changes in the coastal zone resources uses are most evident in the dramatic increase in the number of people living, working and recreating in the zone. Population growth in the non-metropolitan coastal zone has increased dramatically in the past 20 yrs, and much of this growth has occurred in a belt from south-eastern Queensland to the south coast of New South Wales. Before 970 the non – metropolitan coastal zone was used primarily for agriculture, resources extraction (for example, sand mining), tourism, holiday homes and associated recreation, and commercial and recreational fishing. Traditional small urban settlements along the coast are now the focus of accelerated population growth and urbanization. Same is the case of Goa (in North District).

These changes have produced the following outcomes;

- Land previously used foe rural purposes has been subdivided and converted to urban and semi-urban purposes.
- Many new developments are concentrated along a narrow belt of coastline and inshore marine areas.
- Increased reservation of coastal lands and for preservation and recreation purposes.
- Access to coastal zone resources has both increased (for example, through provision of more roads and other infrastructure and decreased (for example, through the conversion of publicly accessible lad to private development).
- There has been much greater use of the non-metropolitan coastal zone for long term occupancy (residence) that has increased demands on resource managers, particularly state and; local governments.
- The intensity of resources use has increased.

Economic Consequences

Changing patterns of land use and population growth in the non-metropolitan coastal zone have had a number of important economic effects:

- The traditional economic bases (farming, mining, and fishing) of many parts of the accessible coastal zone are progressively changing o urban-oriented economies. Many development pressures have arisen through the process of urbanization.
- Some economic development opportunities have been forgone ; but new economic opportunities have been created; for example, some areas with economic potential have been set the coastal zone are being realized, and other are being investigated .
- Under pricing in the use of important resources, for example, water for consumption and disposal, and land for development.

- The costs of coastal management and development have increased, including the costs of providing for infrastructure, services and management by all spheres of government. As a consequence:
  - State and local authorities have had to increase their borrowing to meet infrastructure and management costs;
  - most decisions relating to lad development have not been taken in the context of meeting the full costs of development;
  - increased demands have been made on developers to meet the costs of managing impacts.

Social Consequences

There have been dramatic consequences of rapid urbanization and the changing patterns of land uses in the coastal zone some places. Evidence presented to the study has identified a number of these consequences[2], including:

- Growth in demand for social services and infrastructure in dispersed locations.
- Reduced quality of experience in some uses of coastal zone resources.
- Increased access to coastal zone resources for recreational use in some area,
- Loss of the aesthetic quality of some natural environments.
  - Replacement of traditional activities, with consequent of job changes and losses.
  - Changing demographic structures, in particular the specific age groups in specific localities (for example, retirement centers and new growth centers.
  - Demands by particular groups for exclusive use rights over coastal zone resources (for example, for mariculture development in some estuaries and for tourist developments in some areas.

Ecological Consequences

The study has received evidence of wide spread and growing community concern about the ecological effects coastal development and ecological impacts associated with population growth in the zone.[1] Among the impacts are the following:

- Loss of coastal habitats, especially wetlands, through development and associated infrastructure provision, as well as from agriculture and fishing.
- Degradation of many coastal habitats, including dunes and beaches, wetlands, coral reefs, and estuaries, due to increased pressure from human activities.
- Introduction of exotic plants and animals.
- Increase in soil erosion and associated soil loss.
- Increased risk to some endangered and commercial species.
- Significant direct, indirect and cumulative effects that are poorly understood.
- Decline water quality of rivers, inshore waters and the ocean as a result of urban, industrial, marine- based and agricultural pollution. Integrative coastal zone management

REQUIREMENTS IN INDIA

As in most of the developing nations, the coastal environmental problems and issues in India are also concerned with the following three main conditions; environmental degradation, resources reduction and user conflicts. The integrated coastal zone management plan has been recognized as a tool for addressing these ensure livelihood security and environmental stability in coastal zones. India is still lacking a comprehensive ICZM plan. In developing an ICZM plan, many approaches are possible, depending on the status of coastal resource use and areas to be covered. Where the conflicts have already surfaced it is most pragmatic to use a "problem oriented" approach. In case where coastal resources are not under threat, the more classical system of a resource base approach is possible.

The primary focus of the planning effort should be identifying the problems and the issues to be addressed, deciding upon the type of management mechanism to be used, and determining the points at which such management interventions will be integrated with the existing framework. It is necessary that consultative processes are built into the planning effort. Coastal zone management planning requires the cooperative effort of the State and Central Governments. If adequate consultations are not carried out from the commencement of making the plan unimplementable[2].The institutional methodologies for development of ICZM will depend upon a variety of factors. If the problems are limited, one or two experts can be assigned to study the problems and prepare a report. However, if the problems are manifold and complex , a number of sectors such as socio-economic and resource profile geomorphology and coastal process, fishery and aqua cultural forest and wild life management, agriculture, water resources, energy, industrial development, tourism, port and shipping, water supply, sanitation and environmental management etc. may have to be studied and synthesized into one report. This cannot be completed by one or two experts. Therefore, necessary that once the sectors have been identified for study, it may be appropriate to also identify the most appropriate experts who could understand the study in respect of specific sectors. Before sectoral studies are commissioned to the experts, detailed instructions, including terms of reference and general guidelines for experts, may have to be worked out.[3]

In any case, it would be appropriate to establish and inter- agency\inter-ministerial\ inter-departmental steering committee vested with authority for coordinating the planning effort and promoting inter-ministerial operation. It should have the responsibility for overseeing and supporting the development of the plan and its subsequent implementation. One of the important tasks of the steering committee would be to consolidate the study prepared by different sectoral experts with a view to reducing overlap and evolving a coordinate approach. It would also be necessary for the committee to review the draft report, and ensure overall consistency and uniform style in the presentation, approach, data and conclusions. It should Clearly lay down policy directions, advice and recommendation on the various aspects regarding the plan. The inter-ministerial steering committee should hold periodic meeting of the outline and the terms of reference provided for the study. As in case of Goa , an agency for ICZM should not be merely an authority for regulatory measures , but also should work as an agency should promote at all levels.

ICZM combines development management and resources management. It considers, coordinates and integrates the interests of all appropriate economic sectors. It is accomplished by managing the coastal area as a single unit. To accomplish its purposes, ICZM in India requires several national actions including the following:

- An imperative to tailor ICZM to fit the physical socio economic and political context in India.
- A study of physical and socio economic variables establishes which problems and opportunities are present in a coastal or ocean area (specifically) why ICZM is needed, and what its goals and objectives should be. An understanding of the country's political system is crucial to determining how best ICZM can proceeded and by whom it should be carried out, and answers such questions as, who needs to be convinced to establish ICZM:, and Whose behaviour needs to change to make ICZM effective?
- In understanding a political system for ICZM purpose, two questions are central: (1) What is the degree of concentration of power and authority among national, level institutions? (2) What is the division of authority between national and subnational (provincial, local) levels of governments?
- Political will at the national local levels is essential to establishing ICZM. Recognition of the need for an ICZM program can develop in many different places the national government the local community, the NGO community, a donor agency - but wherever it first emerges, it must find its way to and ultimately be accepted by both the national and local or community levels of government since both generally play important roles in ICZM implementation.
- Support of coastal users, NGOs, and the public is crucial to ICZM initiation. In this regard, it is useful to create a coastal users group (users is broadly defined) that (1) includes representatives from all groups likely to be affected by ICZM, (2) fully informs members about the ICZM process, (3) is structured so members perceive that their suggestions nad input are fully considered (i.e., are not a "rubber stamp" for already agreed to government actions) and can actually affect the way the ICZM program is defined and ultimately implemented.
- ICZM need not be implemented all at once and for a country's entire coastal zone. In many cases a phased approach may be more

appropriate –for example, if urgent problems exist more in one part of the nation's coastal zone and less so in others; if one coastal area is institutionally, technologically, or politically read for ICZM and others are not; if funding and staff limitations dictate an incremental approach; or if it is desirable to conduct an ICZM or pilot approach in a specific coastal area before applying it generally.

- Fruitful inter-governmental partnership (National and Local Level) may be built through the following means (1) identification and pursuit of common interest, such as reducing loss of life and property due to coastal hazards, rather than focusing on questions of owernship and control; (2) identification and use of unique expertise, talent, and data that exist at the two levels; (3) deferral of difficult issues, such as those involving jurisdiction and division of management responsibilities and revenues, until a history of working together has been established, and (4) use of respected outside expertise for difficult issues.
- Achieving an understanding on resources and environmental objectives among the various coastal stakeholders;
- Establishment of agencies for coordination of coastal affairs;
- Initiation of a system for review of development projects, including environmental assessment;
- Accumulation of technical information;
- Design and development of effective planning and management programs.

I will conclude my research by saying that, one of the most important thing in coastal management is population management. A rising population in this part of our geography threaten the continued development of resources. The world coastal zones are exists and edits for a obliged population. The resources of coastal zone provides a better life for most of its inhabitants zone provides a better life for most of its inhabitants and are a lots stone to others. But for an upwardly mobile group the ocean is not a necessary accompaniment to achieve a better life style. For a more effective development of the coastal zone, the most important problem is population management.

Notes

1. Golbere Adard D.(1994). Coastal Zone Space : Prelude to Conflict? UNSCO Publication.
2. Australian Institute of landscape architects, Submission 6; The Australian Surf rider Association, submission 74; G Westcott,Submission76; Cape York Land Council,Submission292; North Land Council, Submission 211.
3. Reports on Australian Heritage Commission 340; Australian National parks and Wildlife Service, Submission 304; Ballina Environment Society, Submission 393.
4. DOD(Department of Ocean Development) 1996. Report of the Expert Committee on Ocean part of the coastal zone. Government of India, New Delhi.
5. *ibid* 1.

APPENDIX - 1

Some definitions of the coastal zone for planning and management.

The following are definitions of the coastal zone used to defined areas within which coastal management policies apply. Chapter 1 describes the advantages and disadvantages of each type of definition.

Table
Fixed Distance Definitions

Country	*Inland Boundary*	*Ocean Boundary*
Australia (State of New South Wales)	1 Km from LMW	3 n mile from coastal baseline
Brazil	2 Km from MHW	12 km from MHW
Coastal Rica	200 m from MHW	MLW
China	10 km from MHW	15 m islbath (depth)
Spain	500 m from highest storm or tide line	12 n mile (limit of territorial sea)
Sri Lanka	300 m from MHW	2 Km from MLW

Sri Lanka Coast Conservation Act (1990)

The area lying within a limit of three hundred metres landward of the Mean High Water Lane and a limit of two kilometers seaward of the Mean Low Water Line and in the case of rivers, streams, lagoons, or any other body of water connected tot he sea either permanently or periodically, the landward boundary shall extend to a limit of two kilometers measured perpendicular to the straight line base line drawn between the natural entrance points (defined by the Mean Low Water Line) hereof and shall include waters of such rivers, streams and lagoons or any other body of water so connected to the sea.

Variable Distance Definitions

The South Pacific Regional Environment Programme (1993)

The coastal zone is a region of indeterminate and variable width. It extends from and includes, the wholly marine (i.e. the seabed, the overlying waters and their resources) to the wholly terrestrial (i.e. beyond the limits of marine incursion and the reach of salt spray). Linking these two environments is the tidal area that forms a transition between land and the sea.

Definition According to Use

United States Federal Coastal Zone Management Act (1990) Section 304.

(Note that each coastal state must interpret the Federal definition though the production of maps and charts).

The term 'coastal zone' means the coastal waters (including the lands therein and thereunder) and the adjacent shorelands (including the lands therein and thereunder), strongly influenced by each other and proximity to the shorelines of the several coastal states, and includes islands, transitional and intertidal areas, salt marhes, wetlands and beaches. The zone extends, in Great Lakes waters, to the international boundary between the United States and Canada and, in other areas seaward to the outer limit of State title and ownership ... (continues with list of Act) .... The zone extends inland from the shorelines only to the extent necessary to control shorelands, the uses of which have a direct and significant impact on the coastal waters.

Australian Commonwealth Coastal Policy (1995)

For the purpose and actions of Commonwealth, the boundaries of the coastal zone are considered to extend as far inland and as far seaward as necessary to achieve the coastal Policy objectives, with a primary focus on the land sea interface.

United Kingdom Government Committee Report on Coastal Zone Protection and Planning (1992)

We conclude that definitions of the coastal zone may vary from area to area and from issue to issue, and that a pragmatic approach must therefore be taken at the appropriate national, regional or local level.

World Bank Environment Department (1993)

For practical planning purposes, the coastal zone is the special area (original bolding), endowed with special characteristics, of which the boundaries are often determined by the special problems to be tackled.

OECD Environment Directorate (1991, 1993)

What constitutes the coastal zone depends on the purpose at hand. From both the administrative and scientific viewpoints, the extend of the zone will vary depending on the nature of the problem. Accordingly, the boundaries of the coastal zone should extend as far inland and as far seaward as necessary to achieve the objectives of management.

Australian Commonwealth House of Representatives Inquiry (1980)

Any definition of the coastal zone should be flexible, and should depend on the issue being confronted.

New South Wales Government Draft Revised Coastal Policy (1994) – Option 5

An issues based definition where the boundaries of the coastal zone extend as far inland and as far seaward as necessary to achieve the policy's objectives, with a focus on the land sea interface.

BIBLIOGRAPHY

REPORTS/PRIMARY SOURCES

1. A Preliminary Report on the Western port Bay Environmental Study: Report for the Period 1973 1974 (Abridged Version). 1974/5. Mel-bourne, Victoria: Ministry for Conservation.
2. Annual Report (1995 96) : Department of Ocean Development, Gov-ernment of India, New Delhi, India.
3. Annual Report (1995 96): Ministry of Environment and Forests, Gov-ernment of India, New Delhi, India.
4. Annual Reports From 1991 to 1997 National Institute of Oceanography, Goa.
5. Coastal Committee of New South Wales (1974) Draft Revised Coastal Policy for New South Wales, (1997) Government of New South Wales Sydney.
6. Commonwealth House of Representatives Standing Committee on Environment and Conservation (1980) Australian Coastal Zone Management, Australian Government Publishing Service, Canberra.
7. Commonwealth of Australia (1995) Living on the Coast: The Commonwealth Coastal Policy, Australian Government Printing Service, Canberra.
8. CPCBC Central Pollution Control Board (1980). The management of Coastal Sand Dunes in South Australia., Adelaide: Coast Protection.
9. CSIRO (1996) Australia: State of the Environment 1996, Commonwealth Scientific and Industrial Research Organization, Melbourne.
10. District Census Handbook of Goa., 1991.
11. DOD (Department of Ocean Development (1997) – Annual Report.

12. DOD (Department of Ocean Development) (1996) Report of the Expert Committee on Ocean part of the Coastal Zone. Government of India, New Delhi.

13. Donalds, B., Eliot, I. and Kay, R.C. (1995) Final Report of the Review of Coastal Management in Western Australia: A Report to the Minister for Planning, Coastal Management Review Committee, Perth.

14. Evans, H.G., K. F. Parr, and R. J. Eagle, (1983). Coastal erosion report, Tweed Shire. Sydney NSW: Public Works Department NSW, Coastal Branch.

15. Goa: Sub regional Plan Town and Country Planning Organisation, Ministry of Works and Housing, 901, New Delhi.

16. Government of Australia (1975) Great Barrier Reef Marine Park Act 1975, Government of Australia, Canberra, Australia.

17. Joshi AB (1995) Coastal Erosion – An overview. In: Course manual on coastal erosion, protection and Coastal Zone Management Vol. II. Beach Erosion Board, Ministry of Water Resources, Government of India, New Delhi, pp. 1-26.

18. Master Plan for Pollution Control in Mandovi Zuari Rives in Goa Tech-nical Report No. 79, N. 10, Goa, 1980.

19. Master Plan for Tourism Development in Goa. Town and Country Planning Development, Goa, July, 1984.

20. Ministry of Agriculture Government of India, Fisheries Division (1995) Fisheries Statistics, New Delhi.

21. Ministry of Environment and Forest (1987) Annual Report.

22. New South Wales Government (1990), Coastal protection policy, Sydney.

23. Prescott, J.R.V. (1985), Australia's Maritime Boundaries, Canberra Studies in World Affairs, no. 16, Canberra: Department of International Relations, Australian National University.

24. Queensland Department of Environment and Heritage, Moreton Bay strategic plan, Queensland Government, September 1991, Coastal protec-tion strategy green paper 3.

25. Ramachandran S. (1997) Report on Case Studies on Coastal Fragile Areas, vol. I. West Coast Submitted Central Pollution Control Board, Government of India, New Delhi.

26. Regional Development Plan for Goa 1986 2001 A.D. Town and Country Planning Department, Goa, 1987.

27. Report of the task Force on Eco Development Plan for Goa, Government of India, Planning Commission, New Delhi, 1992.

28. Sorensen, J., 1993, A Conceptual framework for integrated coastal zone management, OECD, World Coast Conference 1993.

29. UNCED (1992) Agenda 21- United Nations Conference on Environment and Development: Outcomes of the Conference Rio de Janeiro, Brazil 3-14 June.

30. UNEP (1982): Achievements and Planned Developments of UNEP's Regional Seas Programme and Comparable Programs sponsored by other bodies.

31. UNEP (1985): Environmental Problems of the Marine and Coastal Areas of India National Report.

32. UNEP (1986): Environmental Problems of the Marine and Coastal Areas of Bangladesh, National Report, UNEP Regional Seas Reports and Studies No. 75, 47 pp.

33. UNEP (1986): Environmental Problems of the Marine and Coastal Areas of Pakistan National Report, UNEP Regional Seas Reports and Studies No. 77; 55 pp.

34. UNEP, (1986): Environmental Problems of the marine and coastal are of Maldives, National Report, UNEP Regional Seas Reports and Studies No. 76, 31 pp.

35. UNESCO. (1987): Development of marine areas under national jurisdic-tion: problems and approaches in policy making, planning, and manage-ment, United Nations Economic and Social Council, New York, 22 pp.

36. UNESO 1984: Comparing Coral Reef Survey Methods, Report of a regional UNESCO/UNEP Workshop. Phuket Marine Biological Centre. Thailand, 13 17 December 1982. UNESCO Reports in Marine Science, U.N. Educational Scientific and Cultural Organisation, Paris, 170 pp.

37. United Nation (1992): "Agenda 21", In : The Outcomes of the United Nations Conference on environment and Development Rio de Janeiro, Brazil, 3 14 June, 1992.

38. Zigterman, R. and De Campo, J. (1993) Green Island and Reef Management Plan, Queensland Department of Environment and Heritage, Great Barrier Reef Marine Park Authority, Cairns City Council, Cairns Port Authority and Department of Lands, Cairns, Australia.

SECONDARY SOURCES

Books

1. Agarwal, A. and S. Narain eds. (1985); The State of India's environ-mental 1984 85, Centre for Science and Environment, New Delhi, 398 pp.

2. Ahmad, Y.J. and G.R. Sammy (1985), Guide lines to Environmental Impact Assessment in Developing Countries, Hodder and Stoughton, London, 52 pp.
3. Anutha, K. and O'Sullivan, D. (1994) Aquaculture and Coastal Zone Management in Australia and New Zealand, Turtle Press, Hobart, Tasmania.
4. Armstrong, M. (1986) A Handbook of Management Techniques, Kogan Page, London.
5. Asian Development Bank (1991) Environmental Evaluation of Coastal Zone Projects: Methods and Approaches, Asian Development Bank, Manila, Philippines.
6. Bandopadhya, J. (1985), ed. India's Environment Crisis and Response, Natraj Publishers, New Delhi.
7. Beatley, T., Brower, D.J. and Schwab, A.K. (1993) An Introduction to Coastal Zone Management, Island Press, Washington DC.
8. Bird, E., and Paul Culen (1990), Recreational uses and problems of Port Philip Bay, Australia, In Recreational uses of coastal areas, ed. P. Fabbri, 39 51, Hingham, M.A.: Kluwer Academic Publishers.
9. Brahtz, J.F.P. (1972), ed. Coastal Zone Management Multiple use with conservation, John Wiley and Sons, New York.
10. Brown, V.A. (1995) Turning the Tide: Integrated Local Area Management for Australia's Coastal Zone, Commonwealth Department of the Environment, Sports and Territories, Camberra.
11. Bryne, G.A.A. Wynne, and R.I. Thomas (1983), Adelaide Coast protec-tions strategy review, Paper presented at Sixth Australian Conference on Coastal and Ocean Engineering.
12. Burbridge, P.R. and Koesoebiona (1981), Coastal zone management in Southeast Asia. In: Southeast Asia Seas: Frontiers for Development, McGraw Hill. Pp. 110 135.
13. CCD. (1990): Coastal Zone Management Plan, Sri Lanka Coast Conser-vation Department, Colombo, Sri Lanka, 100 pp.
14. Chapman, C. (1983), Freshwater discharge, In: Coastal Ecosystems Management: A Technical Manual for the Conservation of Coastal Zone Resources, J.R. Clark (Ed.), Robt. E. Krieger Publishing Co., Mel-bourne, FL. Pp. 634 639.
15. Clark, J.R. (1977) Coastal Ecosystem Management: A technical Manual for the Conservation of Coastal Zone Resources, John Wiley, New York.
16. Classen, D. B. Van R. and P.A. Pirazzoli (1988), Remote Sensing: A Tool for Management, In: Coral Reef Management Handbook, Kenchington, R.A.

and B.E.T. Hudson (Eds.), United Nations, UNESCO Regional Office for Science and Technology for South East Asia, Jakarta, pp. 69 88.

17. Considine, M. (1994) Public Policy: A Critical Approach, Macmillan Education Australia, South Melbourne.

18. Desai, S.S. (1976) Goa, Daman, Diu and Dadra Nagar Haveli, Publica-tion Division, New Delhi.

19. Dixon, J.A. (1989), Coastal Resources: Assessing Alternatives, In: Coastal Area Management in Southeast Asia: Policies, Management Strategies and Case Studies, Chua, T.E. and D. Pauly (Eds.), ICLARM Conference Proceedings 19, International Centre for Living Aquatic Resources Management, Manila, Pp. 153 162.

20. Goldberg, E.B. (1994) coastal Zone Space – Prelude to Conflict?, UNESCO, Paris.

21. Goodhead, T. and Johnson, D. (eds) (1996) Coastal Recreation Management: The Sustainable Development of Maritime Leisure, E. and F.N. Spoon, London.

22. Haward, M., and A. Bergin (1991), Australian Intergovernmental Rela-tions and Coastal Zone Policy, In Coastal Zone '91 : Proceedings of the Seventh Symposium on Coastal and Ocean Management, 737 751, New York: American Society of Civil Engineer.

23. Jhingran, A.G. and P.K. Chakrabarti (1990), An Approach to Coastal Zone Management and Planning in West Bengal, Inland Fisheries Socie-ty of India, Cochin India, 53 pp.

24. Kausher, A., Kay, R.C. Asaduzzaman, M. and Paul, S. (1994) Climate Change and Seal Level Rise: The Case of the Bangladesh Coast, Bangladesh Unnayan Parishad, Dhaka, Centre for Environmental and Resource Studies, New Zealand; Climatic Research Unit, England; Dhaka, Bangladesh.

25. Kelleher, G. (1993) Progress towards as global system of Marine Protected Areas. In Proceedings of the Fourth Fenner Conference on the Environment, Sydney, Australia, pp. 36-38, IUCN.

26. Lawrence D., and D.M. Dight (1991), The Torres Strait Baseline Study: Environmental protection of a Tropical Marine Environment in Northern Australia, In Coastal Zone '91: Proceedings of the seventh Symposium on Coastal and Ocean Management, 1125 1139, New York : American Society of Civil Engineers.

27. Mukhi, S., Hampton, D. and Barnwell, N. (1988) Australian Management, McGraw Hill, Sydney, Australia.

28. Premchand, K. and C.M. Harish (1990 91): Rising Sea level Concern along south west coast of India in J.D. Millman (eds.), Sea Level rise and Coastal subsidence: Problems and strategies, John Wiley & sons, New York.

29. Radok, R., (1976) Australia's coast. Rigby, Adelaide, 100 pp.

30. Rajagopalan R. (1986) Coastal Zone Management in : Rajagopalan R (ed) Voice for the Oceans, The International Ocean Institute (India), Madras, pp. 36-38.

31. Richards, J.M. (1982) Goa, Vikash Publications, New Delhi.

32. Thom B.G. (1984). Coastal Geomorphology in Australia Academic Press, Sydney.

33. Thomas, I., (1996) Environmental Impact Assessment in Australia, Federation Press, Sydney.

34. Thorman, R. (1995) Suggested Framework for Preparing Regional Environmental Strategies (Draft Guidelines), Australian Local Government Association, Canberra, Australia.

35. World Commission on environment and Development (ed.) (1987) Our Common future, Oxford University Press, Oxford.

36. World Resources Institute (1992) World Resources 1996-97, Oxford University Press, New York.

37. World Travel and Tourism Council (1995) Travel and Tourism's Economic Perspective. Special Report of the World Travel and Tourism Council, Brussels, Belgium.

38. World Wide Fund for Nature (1996) Fisheries crisis overshadows World Oceans Day, World Wide Fund for Nature News Release.

39. Zann, L.P. (1995) Our Sea, Our future: Major Finginds of the State of the Marine Environment Report for Australia, Ocean Rescue 2000 Program. Department of the Arts, Sports and Territories, Canberra.

Journals / Periodicals

1. A lock, D. (1991) Education and Extension: Management's best strategy. *Australian Parks and Recreation*, 27(1), 15-17.

2. Alder, J. (1993) Permits, an evolving tool ion the day to day management of the Cairns section of the Great Barrier Reef Marine Park, *Coastal Management,* 21(1), 25-36.

3. Alder, J. (1996) Education of enforcement – the better deal? In *Great Barrier Reef Science, Use and Management*, Vol. II, p. 221, James Cook University, Townsville.

4. Amarasinghe, S.R. and H.J.M. Wickremeratne (1983), The evolution and implementation of legislation for Coastal Zone Management in a developing country The Sri Lankan experience, In: *Coastal Zone '83*, Vol.III, American Society of Civil Engineers, New York, Pp. 2822 2841.

5. Amaratunga Carol (1984): Coastal Zone Management in Sri Lanka A case study, Second International Conference on Science and the Man-agement of Protected Area (SAMPAA), *Coastal Conservation Advisory Council of Sri Lanka* 23 25th April.

6. Ansari, Z.A. *et. al.* (1984) Effects of Domestic Sewage on Sandy Beach Microfauna in Goa, India, *Hydrobiologia*, 111 (3), pp. 229 33.

7. Ansari, Z.A. *et. al.* (1986), Spatial and Temporal Changes in Benthic Macrofauna from Mandori and Zuari Estuaries of Goa, West Coast of India, *Indian Journal of Marine Science*, Vol. 15, Pp. 223 229.

8. Bird, E.C.F. (1990), Artificial beach nourishment on the shores of Port Phillip Bay, Australia, *Journal of Coastal Research S.I.* 6:55 68.

9. Biswas, A.K. (1987), Environmental concerns in Pakistan, with special reference to water and forests, *Environmental Conservation* 14(4): 319 328.

10. Born, S.M. and Miller, A.H. (1998) Assessing networked coastal zone management programs. *Coastal Management*, 16 229-243.

11. Champen, D.M. (1981) Coastal Erosion and the Sediments budgets, with special reference to the Gold Coast, Australia, *Coastal Engineering*, 4: 207-227.

12. Chapman, D., and R. Hildreth (1985), Coastal erosion management in Australia and the U.S. In *Coastal Zone* '85: Proceedings of the Fourth Symposium on Coastal and Ocean management 91 106, New York : American Society of Civil Engineers.

13. Chapman, D.M. (1981). Coastal Erosion and the sediments budgets, with special reference to the gold coast, Australia, *Coastal Engineering*, 4: 207-227.

14. Choudhury, A.K. (1987), Climatology of the estuarine region of West Bengal, *U.N. Educational, Scientific and Cultural Organization Training Course (Calcutta),* Wildlife Institute of India, Dehradun, Pp. 63 73.

15. Clark, J.R. (1992), Integrated Management of Coastal Zones, FAO *Fisheries Technical Paper No. 327,* United Nation/FAO, Rome, 167 pp.

16. Cocks, K.D. (1984), A Systematic Method of Public Use Zoning of the Great Barrier Reef Marine Park, Australia, *Coastal Zone Management Journal*, 12:359 383.

17. Crawford, D. (1992), The Injured Coastline: A Parliamentary report on Coastal Protection in Australia, *Coastal Management* 20, 189 198.

18. Cullen, P., and E. Bird (1980), The Management of Coastal Sand Dunes in South Australia, Victoria: *Geostudies.*

19. Cullen, P.W., and Bird, E.C.F. (1980). The Management of Coastal and Dunes in South Australia. Adelaide: Coast Protection.

20. Cullen. P (1982) : Coastal Zone Management in Australia" *Coastal Zone Management Journal,* Vol. 10, 3, pp. 183 21.

21. Freestone, D. (1991), ICZM: The Problem of boundaries, In: The Status of Integrated Coastal Zone Management: A Global Assessment, J.R. Clark (Ed.), *CAMPNET,* University of Miami/RSMAS, Miami, Fla, Pp. 75 77.

22. French, G. (1991), Protecting the Great Barrier Reef, Maritime Studies, No. 59, pp. 9 13, July/August.

23. FRRL (1994), Tree and Palm Plantation Project in Cyclone prone Areas of Bangladesh (The Coastal Greenbelt Proposal). Main Report, ADB TA No. 1816 BAN, Fountain Renewable Resources Ltd., Brackley, Northamptonshire, U.K., for Asian Development Bank, 109 pp.

24. Gardner, A. (1990), Legislative implementation of integrated catchment management in Western Australia, *Environmental and Planning Law Journal* 7:199 208.

25. Hayes, M.O. (1985), Beach erosion, Coastal Resources Manage-ment: Development Case Studies, J.R. Clark (Ed.), *Coastal Publication* No. 3, Research Planning Institute, Columbia, S.C. Pp. 67 200.

26. Hensen, J., R. Ruedy, M. Sato and K.Lo (2010). Global surface temperature change. *Reviews of Geophysics,* Vol. 48 (4).

27. Hinrichsen, D. (1994) Coasts under pressure, *People and the Planet,* 3(I), 6-9.

28. Hinrichsen, D. (1996) Coasts Under Pressure, *http://wwwenews.com/magazines/issues/current/960601-001.html.*

29. Jevrejeva, S., Grinsted, A., Moore, J. and S. Holgate (2006). Nonlinear trends and multiyear cycles in sea level records. *J. Geophysics Res.,* 111, C09012,

30. Jha, A.K. (1989), Green House Effect, Sea Level Raise and Indian Coastal Zone", *Third Concept,* Vol. 3, No. 26, pp. 55 59, New Delhi.

31. Joliffe, I.P. and C.R. Patman (1985), The Coastal Zone: The Challenge, *Journal of Shoreline Management,* Vol. 1, No. 1, Pp. 263 293.

32. Jones, P.D. and Moberg, A. (2003). Hemispheric and large-scale surface air temperature variations: An extensive revision and an update to 2001. *Journal of Climate* **16**: 206-223.

33. Kay, R. C., Panizza, V., Eliot, I.E. and Donaldson, B. (1997) Reforming Coastal Management in Western Australia. *Ocean and Coastal Management,* 35(1), 1-29.

34. Kay, R.C. and Lester, C. (1997) Benchmarking Australian Coastal Management. *Coastal Management*, 25(3), 265-292.

35. Kay, R.C., Kirkland, A. and Stewart, I. (1996) Planning for future climate change and seal level rise and induced coastal change in Australian and New Zealand. In *Greenhouse: Coping with Climate Change* (eds. W.J. Bouma, G.I. Pearman and M.M. Managing), pp. 377-398,m CSIRO Publishing, Wellington, New Zealand.

36. Kenchington, R.A. and Crawford, D. (1993) On the meaning of integration of coastal zone management. *Ocean and Coastal Management*, 21, 109-127.

37. Lowry, K. and Sadacharan, D. (1993) Coastal Management in Sri Lanka. *Coastal Management in Tropical Asia,* 1 (September), 1-7.

38. Mcyill, J.T. (1958). Map of Coastal landforms of the world. *Geographical Review* 48, 402, 405.

39. Mcyill, J.T. (1958). Map of Coastal Landforms of the world. Geographical Review 48, 402, 405.

40. Murty, C.S. et.al. (1980) : "Beach Morphological Variation over Micro time Scales, Goa, : *Indian Journal of Marine Sciences*, Vol. 9, pp. 35 44.

41. Nair, M.M. (1987): Coastal Geomorphology of Kerala, *Journal Geolog-ical Society of India,* 29: 450 458.

42. O'Brien, R.J. (1988), Western Australia's non Statutory Approach to Coastal Zone Management: An Evaluation, *Coastal Management*, 16: 201 214.

43. O'Brien, R.J. (1988), Western Australia's non statutory approach to coastal zone management: an evaluation, *Coastal Zone Management,* Vol. 16, No. 3, pp. 201 214.

44. Olsen, S. (1987), Sri Lanka completes its Coastal Zone Management Plan, *CAMP Newsletter*, August 1987, p.7.

45. Samsuddin, M. and G.K. Suchindan (1987): Beach Erosion and Auction in Relation to Seasonal Long Shore Current Variation in the Northern Kerala coast, India, *Journal of Coastal Research* 3(1): 55 62.

46. Sengupta, R. and *et al.* (1984), Present Status of Environment Pollution in and around Goa." *Sovenior of Indian Heritage Society,* Goa Chapter.

47. Thom, B.G. (1978). Future trends in Coastal Geomorphology. *Australian Geographer* 14, p. 64-67.

Important Web Sites

1. *http://www/iucn.org*
2. *http://www.bcic.com/english/opportunity/listof.htm.*

3. *http://www.acri.fr/CEO/index.html.*
4. *http://ebenhopson.com/*
5. *http://www/igbp.kva.se/loicz.html*
6. *http://www.insula.org/magas.htm*
7. *http://environment.miningco.com/msubcei.htm.*
8. *http://infinitefaculty.com/cz97/*
9. *http://bigfoot.wes.army.mil/c820.html.*
10. *http://192.107.66.21/www/ceo/index/html*
11. *http://www.coastalmanagement.com/newlinks/html*
12. *http://www.jsdnp.org.jm/envir3.htm*
13. *http://athene.hbz-nrw.de/elsevier/0964569/sz976239/*
14. *http://www.eeeee.net/fi01031.html.*
15. *http://www.ce[.umep.org/*
16. *http://crc.gso.uri.edu/linx.html.*
17. *http://www.coastalliance.org/pppress.htm*
18. *http://wave.nos.noaa.gov/OCRM/czm/czmsitelist.htm,*
19. *http://www/walis.wa.gov.au/marine/terrestrial_atlas/available_maps/coastal.html.*
20. *http://www/lic/wisc.edu/coastgis/cgispubs.htm.*
21. *http://www.ios.bc.ca/ios/mehsd/coast/*
22. *http://www.nos.noaa.gov/cz97/*
23. *http://data.ecology.su.se/*
24. *http://www/hydroconsult.se/iczm.html*
25. *http:/www.minvenw.nl/projects/netcoast*
26. *http:www.psu.ac.th/corin/import-t.htm.*
27. *http://www.nric.gov.au.amsat.czerm.old/facts/coastalz.html*
28. *http://buchholdt.com/EbenHopson/archives/ArchivesIndex .html.*
29. *http://www.start.or.th/mirrors/loicz/cstdata.htm.*
30. *http://gfc.dfo.ca/habitat.aifcon.htm.*
31. *http://www.oceansconservation.com/iczm/iczmhome2.htm*
32. *http://www.anr.ces.purdue.edu/anr/anr/swine/pptregs/tsldo14.htm*
33. *http://www.dmu.dk/CoastalZoneEcology/Descriptdb.htm.*
34. *http://habitat.pac.dfo.ca/mpa/iczm/need2.htm.*

35. *http://www.maritimes.dfo.ca/science/mesd/he/events/meetings/msg00026.html.*

36. *http://www.comp.glam.ac.uk/pages/reseach/graphics-ip/gis-coast.html.*

37. *http://www.oceansconservation.com/iczm/community/pacif ic/marlifes.htm.*

38. *http://kellia.nioz.nl/loicz/newslett/number1/newslet1.htm*

39. *http://www.gnofn.org/endrdminerals/mrscoast.htm.*

40. *http://florence97.ers-synposium.org/participants/data/lodge/*

41. *http://www.nric.gov.au/amsat/czerm/concepts/whatczm.ht ml.*

42. *http://www.americanoceans.org.*

43. *http://www.ca.seafood.org*

44. *http://www.cmc.ocean.org*

45. *http://core.cast.msstate.edu*

46. *http://www.cglg.org*

47. *http://www.coustea.org*

48. *http://www/glc.org*

49. *http://www.fw/vt.edu/fisheries*

50. *http://www.cousteau.org.*

51. *http://www.earthisland.org/ei*

52. *http://www.rsmas.miami.edu.edu/iof*

53. *http.//www.nfi.org*

54. *http://www.seaweb.org*

55. *http://www.wcspa.com*

56. *http://www.fw.vt.edu/fisheries*

57. *http://estd.wvu.edu*

58. *http://www.irf.org.*

59. *http://www.millersv.edu/~ccs/contents.html*

60. *http://www.uwimona.edu.jm/usd/*

61. *http://www.unesco.org/csi/*

62. *http://www.nos.nogga.gov/ocrm/czm/welcome/html*

63. *http://www.fao.org*

64. *http://www.pamda.org*

65. *http://www.unep.ch/*

66. *http://www.ciesin.org/IC/iucn/IUCN/IUCN.html*

67. *http://www.gbrmpa.goc.au*
68. *http://www.ncl.ac.uk*
69. *http://www.wantree.com.au/*
70. *http://www.netpar.com.br/*
71. *http://www.ecouncil.ac.cr*
72. *http://www.ust.hk/~webrc/reef.html*
73. *http://nic.in*